Grow Rich in the New Africa

*Navigating Business Opportunities
on the Continent*

Lauri E. Elliott
Hartmut Sieper
Nissi Ekpott
Nwakego Eyisi

Published by Conceptualee, Inc.

Published by Conceptualee, Inc.:

PO Box 96503 #36250
Washington, DC 20090
United States

ISBN-13 9780983301523 Print Book
ISBN-13 9780983301554 Electronic Book
LCCN 2011914090
The New Africa Series, Volume 2
08012012

Other Contributor: Sam Mokorosi
Book Cover Design by Vin Furlong
Cover Photo Background by Makio Kusahara
Foreword by Sven Boermeester

Business & Economics / International / General

However long the night,
the dawn will break.

(African Proverb)

Welcome to the new dawn in Africa –
a new paradigm for a new day!

Other titles and content on insights, resources, and strategy for business and investment in Africa can be explored at:

http://www.afribiz.info

http://www.afribiz.net

http://www.neuafrika.com

http://www.trans-africa-invest.com

Table of Contents

Preface

Lauri Elliott

A lot has happened in Africa in just this last year since we released our first book, *Redefining Business in the New Africa*. First and foremost, Africa has sustained solid economic growth while threats of another global economic crisis loom – the U.S. recovery remains slow, the Eurozone continues to remain on the brink of another recession, and growth in China and India has slowed.

Africa's political climate has remained relatively stable with peaceful elections in 2011-2012 in Nigeria, Zambia, Senegal, Democratic Republic of Congo (although considered to be a flawed election by both internal constituents and international observers), and others. However, there remains significant unrest in Libya and Egypt after the Arab Spring of 2011 and there was a coup in Mali in the spring of 2012.

On the social side, Africa still has many challenges related to health, education, and poverty. One of the major issues looming is the growing youth population and unemployment across the continent as this was one of the social issues that fueled the Arab Spring in the background in 2011. North Africa can see a repeat of this if the new administrations do not solve the problem, and the unrest will spread to Sub-Saharan Africa if things do not change in the next few years in that region.

There are, however, many great developments on the continent like the major drop in infant mortality on the continent as told by a story in the Economist[1] – the speed of the drop is moving at twice the pace it was in the 1990s. Also, South Africa was chosen with Australia and New Zealand to host the Square Kilometer Array of telescopes.

While many have said that the 21st century is Africa's century, I sense that as the global economy rebalances Africa will see a decade of unprecedented growth and development beyond what we have seen in the modern era – even surpassing China. (In the first chapter, I discuss some of the shifts I believe will contribute to this.) This will launch Africa in such a way that the 21st century will truly be Africa's century.

Finally, as Africa has demonstrated things change quickly there, we would like to announce that our "New Africa" books are now an annual series. *Grow Rich in the New Africa* is being released as the second book in the series.

---

[1] May 19, 2012. African Child Mortality: The Best Story in Development. *The Economist.* http://www.economist.com/node/21555571. (Accessed online on May 23, 2012.)

Foreword

Sven Boermeester

World Trade Centers Africa Initiative

With its dynamic, large growing middle class, natural resources, and domestic demand, Africa will see phenomenal progress in the next decade. At World Trade Centers Africa Initiative[2] (WTC), we know that Africa is the last, great trade and investment region and, like the authors, we are dedicated to catalyzing the growth of this region so that Africa serves a major global role – bringing prosperity to its people and others around the world.

Being situated in over 10 African countries and having more than a dozen international commercial exchanges with organizations allows us to spread the facts about Africa to the far reaches of the globe. We consider Conceptualee, and Afribiz, as a partner in this effort through their media channels and publications like *Grow Rich in the New Africa*.

The World Trade Centers Africa Initiative (WTC) is ecstatic to work with the authors – Lauri, Hartmut, and Nissi. They possess a vision and passion for Africa's economic development on par with ours. We hope that you will also join us in spreading the positive story of Africa, as well as in taking advantage of the tremendous opportunities on the continent.

---

[2] World Trade Centers Africa Initiative website - http://www.wtc.co.za

The Context

1

Introduction:
Emerging Shifts in Africa
Lauri Elliott

While it is always good to reflect and learn from the past, the New Africa cannot be looked upon through lenses of the past, but must be looked at through a new set of lenses that are shaping not only the continent but the globe. Economic, social, and political shifts abound not just due to injustices done, but expectations of a new generation. We are in a new era and Africa is positioned to be significant in it.

Africa is being seen in a much more positive light, even though good news about it is still miniscule compared to negative or troublesome news. And, like most countries in the world, African countries will see tremendous shifts (e.g., Arab Spring and other social shifts, political shifts where governments are not aligned with their people, economic shifts in structures that control markets) over the next decade which will impact how business and investment opportunities shape the continent.

In *Redefining Business in the New Africa*, we spoke about trends in Africa around geopolitics, economics, business, and the future of Africa from a broad perspective. One trend was the economic stability and strength that many African countries had achieved in the last 10 to 15 years through economic reforms and prudent financial management, which is helping them ride the global economic slowdown. Another trend was the positive turn in the demographic burden to a demographic divide as

Africa's youth mature. Still yet another trend is the increasing geopolitical influence of Africa as seen through South Africa's admission into the unofficial BRIC economic bloc.

Here, in *Grow Rich in the New Africa*, I want to share emerging shifts that will collectively change the dynamics of business in Africa over the course of the next 10 to 20 years. First, I need to make a distinction between a trend and a shift. A trend is something demonstrating a pattern heading in a certain direction. A shift is something that takes you from one state into an entirely new state. In this case, it is into the New Africa in a globalized world.

We want you to think beyond what you can see, so that you can be more successful in Africa.

Governance and Democracy

BRIC, and now BRICS, has become a very popular term signifying key emerging markets, yet very few people understand the actual importance. For all intents and purposes, BRICS is an economic trade bloc in which its members – Brazil, Russia, India, China, and South Africa – can leverage their assets for economic advantage and geopolitical influence.

It is not a formal government network structure, but an informal one which wields an increasingly larger amount of influence due to its members' economic power. It is not alone though. Informal government networks are a significant paradigm shift that will continue to play a key role into the future, affecting all regions and countries. It is important for citizens of countries, including businesses, to understand why these structures exist, who is involved, how they operate, and what impact they have on each one of us.

These informal government networks do not fit into the traditional mold of governing. Merriam-Webster defines governing as "to exercise continuous sovereign authority over; especially, to control and direct the making and administration of policy...."[3] Formal government structures fit this definition, carrying the requisite authority. However, they can be slow to respond.

According to Dr. Anne-Marie Slaughter, former Director of Policy Planning for the U.S. State Department under Hilary Clinton, "If you have global problems you can't solve them by individual nations acting alone. You have to have some ability for the most important nations in a particular issue area to come together to solve those problems."[4] Informal, global governance networks allow for this, but they do not have the authority to carry out their decisions.

Let's look at the G7, or Group of Seven. It was formed in 1976 with the intention of stabilizing the international economy in a timely manner. It was comprised of financial ministers from the U.S., Canada, France, Germany, Italy, Japan, and the United Kingdom. The group was not a formal government structure and therefore only possessed "soft power." Its decisions could only be carried out to the extent that the financial ministers carried them out within their own countries in each one's official capacity, as well as influencing the larger government and political machines within their countries to go along.

---

[3] Merriam-Webster. *Governing.* http://www.merriam-webster.com/dictionary/governing. (Accessed online on January 14, 2012.)
[4] Slaughter, A. (2011). "Interview with Anne-Marie Slaughter." Interview by Lauri Elliott.

The G7, which was created to address global economic issues by the major economies at the time, was replaced by the G8. And, the G8 has now been replaced by the G20. The G20 was formed in the 1990s to address the Asian economic crisis, but also includes Turkey, South Africa, and other emerging countries.

Slaughter notes that informal, global government networks are not just focused on economics. Today, there are networks of judges, health ministers, environmental ministers, and others formed to address global issues. And to add to the mix, networks of this sort are not just in the government realm. These types of networks are forming in all spheres of society from advocacy to business.

The mix of these informal and formal structures has great impact on our everyday lives. For example, while making a decision related to climate change, decisions made by global bodies can impact how much local communities in developing nations will benefit from the carbon economy.

The rise of informal, global governance networks can prove positive for developing nations in increasing influence when they have limited say in formal institutions like the International Monetary Fund (IMF) in the short term. Slaughter indicates that the IMF has been pressed to increase the voting power of developing nations, but to do so that means European countries will have to give up voting power. This will not be an easy transition and will ultimately have to be resolved for the IMF to maintain its relevance in a global world.

Slaughter also shares that while informal global governance networks can work fast, they only really work when everyone carries out what was agreed to as there is no legal, or formal, recourse. In the height of the global economic crisis, the G8 agreed to bring down their debts and to not manipulate their currencies. The U.S. has not lived up to either commitment, and there is no formal document, like a treaty, to bind it to those commitments.

So what is there to look forward to in the future? Slaughter believes that eventually we need to find a way to link some of the most effective informal networks to the more formal institutions, like the African Union. Before this can happen the informal networks will need to prove that they are effective, diverse, and comprised of key stakeholders.

An Emerging Shift in Leveraging Natural Resources

With the growing global population, and consumption by that population of food, water, and other resources, money will flow to the regions that have those resources and Africa happens to be a prime location.

Let me first state that in no way should Africa solely, or largely, rely on natural resource wealth for development or prosperity, but as most economists agree, the next 10 to 20 years will bring strong increased demand for commodities until other solutions, such as solar power and food technology, become more mainstream to handle the increasing demand. Therefore, African countries need to leverage every option to spread development and growth inclusively during this period based on the strengths they have.

Every African needs to understand the strategic shift this creates for the continent. If governments and communities play the hand they have been dealt wisely, they will erase much of the poverty in communities surrounding these natural resources. First, there are very few places on the earth that have the variety and abundance of natural resources that Africa has, which means developed and emerging nations will be clamoring for them. Second, demand for the resources will grow on the continent itself as people move up the socioeconomic scale and consume more. While other nations are panting after resources, e.g., China, to help support their growth, Sub-Saharan Africa will have the majority of what it needs in terms of raw resources and basic labor.

The result of the climax of this eventuality is that Africa will have significant geopolitical clout, which needs to be used in balance so that the global economy is not shut out because today's economic growth involves a combination of local, regional, and global markets. While it will be evident that Africa and the world still need each other, the value Africa brings will be clearly articulated and demonstrated. Because Africa possesses an abundance of natural resources, and other strengths, you will see the world converging on Africa like it has with China (and even more so). Once this reaches critical mass, African countries will have the geopolitical clout they have been seeking.

Let me demonstrate how some of aspects of this strategic shift are occurring. One of the key world systems in place is commodities brokering, which disrupts the natural supply and demand cycle for commodities. They can push up prices and hold onto supply to make "profit." This system doesn't add much value to the value chain, but it ends up taking wealth from the value chain of which it is not a part. The volatility we see in prices for commodities has a lot to do with this system. They bet to win on shortages in agriculture, oil, and minerals, exacerbating an already fragile position. Only a small percentage of people and organizations benefit from this system as it stands. But one of the losers of Africa's strategic shift will be this way of doing business. Its current form will evolve into something different as it doesn't add much, if any, value.

As an example, the Ethiopian Commodities Exchange (ECX) was developed several years ago so that Ethiopia would see more benefit from the crops that it produces. ECX has developed a value chain that ties commodities, like coffee and beans, produced in rural areas to the global markets. Agricultural commodities are sold directly to the world at market prices.

Another simple example is DR Congo's mining code change which will no longer allow foreign businesses to extract minerals without creating a local presence and adding value. Other countries are tightening the grip as well, e.g., the export of scrap aluminum is prohibited in South Africa, Nigeria, East Africa (soon), etc. One reason is that local demand for metals for manufacturing is growing and exports cause short supplies in African countries. Another reason is that foreign firms buy the resources cheap and then ship to facilities overseas to process, making big money on them but not bringing much inclusive benefit in African countries.

Because the demand for commodities will remain strong for a long time and the dynamics of getting access to these natural resources are changing, this will force foreign interests to re-think their business models because the demand for the resources does not go away. You will see more private investment directly into mining and processing facilities on the continent as the Chinese have been doing.

I get a lot of inquiries about commodities and I tell everyone the same thing. Business has changed. You either invest in operations in the country, do it right, and bring value, or you will find yourself locked out of opportunities on the continent within the next five to ten years.

Another interesting example is for minerals required in technology like coltan. The story of how militias have been selling coltan from the DR Congo on the black market while exploiting and placing local Congolese in bondage is well reported. A consequence was that industries and even governments instituted conflict-free mineral regulations to prevent companies from promoting this problem. Conflict-free minerals legislation passed in 2010 in the United States, as part of a financial reform bill.

Way before then, I shared how simple (not necessarily easy) it would be to build legitimate supply chains in the DR Congo to bring inclusive benefit to the country, eliminate a lot of the black market, and improve the supply to world markets. To me it was an obvious solution, but one thing about big industries and systems is that they do not change, for the most part, until something disrupts their business models.

Now that conflict-free laws are creating a real problem for major technology companies like HP and Sony from getting an adequate supply of coltan and other minerals, 21 global electronics companies, NGOs, and the U.S. government formed the Public-Private Alliance for Responsible Minerals Trade in 2011. This alliance wants to build a legitimate supply chain for minerals from the DR Congo through certified mines. While I won't negate that corporations can have a conscience, because I believe business done right brings benefit for everyone and I think the private sector is the main tool for driving economic growth, they often don't change until they see significant threats to their bottom lines.

Also, I want to note that, on the whole, Africa's natural resources are seen as commodities, which while necessary, do not give the perception of having high value except when they are in short supply. What consumers see being of value is the end product, e.g., mobile phones and clothing. Therefore, much of the potential in creating wealth is passed onto others instead of Africa because it is not producing the intermediary, or end, products.

The concept of what is of value and who holds that value, however, will change in the next decade. In an interview I conducted with Denis Slieker of Face the Future, he said that a new value has been placed on African resources because of climate change. The mere fact that communities who plant trees, which helps mitigate climate change, and make money from their efforts by selling their carbon credits on different carbon exchanges means that Africans are creating a service out of the stewardship of the land in their control – and the world finds value in that. I believe this is the beginning of many shifts in the concept of value, which will be favorable to Africa more than any other region. When more of this happens, markets will shift overnight.

The Rise of the Global-African Youth Consumer

What do the global consumer and African youth (age 15-24) markets have in common? Everything, the African youth market is increasingly representative of the new global consumer class.

Demographically, Africa as a region has the fastest growing population in the world. This population will surpass India's, as well as China's, population as soon as 2025.

Currently, a large percentage of Africa's population is under the age of 15. Even though the Global African consumer group is still emerging, this youth "bulge" is getting ready to mature. Soon these youth will be full-fledged citizens and challengers. We have seen evidence of their emergence as citizens and challengers of the status quo with the political upheavals in North Africa. There are even minor movements in Senegal, Uganda, and other countries in Sub Saharan Africa. Many see these upheavals as being rooted in politics, but in actuality, this is a shift in societies caused by a younger generation rising up – politically, socially, and economically.

While African youth have unique identities attributed to the continent's history, heritage, culture, identity, and social structures, there is little indication that, at a basic level, they are inherently different from other youth globally. How could this be?

The African youth of today are exposed to new and different experiences. Technology is one medium through which youth become exposed. As more and more youth are able to connect with anyone anywhere through the web and phones, they begin to have new experiences which can change how they think of themselves and others, as well as their expectations and behaviors.

Another avenue for exposure for African youth is through migration to other countries for school, work, etc. While some may remain in foreign countries for most of their adult lives, today's youth (turned adult) often retain strong connections with their home countries, which may indirectly influence culture in their homelands. Some of these youth become young adults who are transmigrants – people who have become part of at least two national cultures and regularly cross-migrate between the countries. They serve as bridges between the cultures and develop social and business ties that bring the two worlds together.

As youth become citizens with rights, privileges, and responsibilities, as well as challengers to the status quo, they also become increasingly important consumers. Many of the influences affecting them socially and politically will also affect how they consume. In a paper by Richard Kahn and Douglas Keller titled, *Global Youth Culture*[5], these influences are described as, "global and local, as well as homogenizing and diversifying, influences (which) continuously merge in the lifestyles, performances, and sociopolitical practices of contemporary youth." So, today's youth will develop unique identities that will reflect local and global, as well as diverse and homogenous influences to which they are exposed. This also means that the individual identities of youth are as complex as the societies around them.

---

[5] Kahn, R., & Keller, D. *Global Youth Culture*. http://pages.gseis.ucla.edu/faculty/kellner/essays/globyouthcult.pdf. (Accessed online on January 9, 2012.)

This presents quite a conundrum for businesses. How in the world do you drive your business model around individual identity versus mass consumption?

The first step is to understand what this new age of identity means. In the article, *The Facebook Generation*[6], I described the Age of Identity as:

> *This is a new consumer paradigm. We are seeing the beginning of the Age of Identity. Consumers better understand their unique identities and what they value these days. They prioritize based on what allows them to live out their unique identities.*
>
> *The principle drivers of identity-focused consumers can still be understood in the context of Maslow's Hierarchy of Needs. Maslow says that needs drive individual motivation. Needs start with survival issues around food, water, and shelter. As people develop and move up the socioeconomic scale, their needs change from needs to connect with family and friends to self-esteem found through education and career. The final levels of actualization and transcendence speak to people achieving mental and spiritual acuity. In other words, people become attuned to their unique identities and personalities.*
>
> *The difference in the consumer markets moving forward is that an increasingly larger number of consumers will not prioritize based on needs indicating lack, e.g., self-esteem, safety, relationships. They will focus on needs that allow them to fully live out their identities. As the old saying goes: "To thine own self be true."*

---

[6] Elliott, L. (2010). The Facebook Generation. *Brainstorm Magazine*. http://www.afribiz.net/?p=5494.

For African youth, this identity process does not mean a subjugation, or elimination, of their family and local culture. It means a new identity, which is unique to the individual but synergizing many different influences.

I was recently asked if local brands would push out global brands in Africa as the natural inclination is to identify with something that is African. While this can be a factor, the dominate driver will still be, "Does the brand help me live my life as I choose? Does it resonate with who I perceive myself to be or want to be?" Where African brands have competitive advantage is that they should initially understand their African markets and in being African they help build the image and identity of Africa on the continent and around the globe. They can maintain this momentum by delivering on the mandate presented to them by African youth consumers.

For youth, having a voice as individuals and in groups is very important. So, the second step is to listen to and act on the voices of youth, or the voice of the customer. This means market research, as well as communicating and engaging with African youth.

Until now, this was a difficult feat for businesses that did not have on-the-ground representatives, which is still one of the best approaches to reaching customers. With technology, however, businesses can get input and feedback from youth almost in real time in Africa, particularly in urban areas.

Companies like EXP Digi in South Africa and Bongo Live[7] in Tanzania are using mobile and Internet technologies to develop fast, reliable, more affordable market research solutions focused on youth and young adults. As examples, EXP Digi was able to identify which brands (e.g., Nike) youth in South Africa most recognized from an SMS survey. And, Bongo Live can

---

[7] Bongo Live website – http://www.bongolive.co.tz

tell you that about 57% of young adults (21-30) in Tanzania are interested in promotions about electronics, computers, and mobiles while only about 22% are interested in promotions about hardware and equipment. In both instances, data can be available within days instead of weeks or months.

Companies also need to be adept at finding trends from distributed "voices" on the Internet. Being able to collect and analyze data from the web and social networks is key.

The third step is being able to identify and act upon emerging patterns you find as you listen to the youth. This is a whole new paradigm for business intelligence. We are no longer responding to, but anticipating the next evolution in our consumer markets.

As a final note, this new Global African youth consumer market will require new business models. Businesses can no longer focus on developing a product to meet requirements of the masses. One thing they need to figure out is how to deliver configurations that fit the individual, but at a price point that fits the African market.

The Rise of African Indigenous Nations

When Europe scrambled for Africa in the 19th century, it broke up the continent geographically and administratively in structures opposed to the long-held structures of indigenous nations. Along with African indigenous nations, Native Americans, and other indigenous people, have experienced similar horrors around the world.

In some cases, whole populations were wiped out. In Africa, there was a period where so many people were dying or being transported elsewhere that the continent's population size was negatively affected.

But the 21st century presents a different proposition for indigenous nations around the world. For example, Africa's population is one of the largest in the world with the fastest growth rate. In 2100, one in three people in the world are expected to be of African descent. This suggests a rise in both formal and informal power as people move up the socioeconomic scale, however, this is not guaranteed as several challenges in health, education, poverty, etc. remain significant.

Many African indigenous nations face these challenges because they remain at the periphery of the modern society, located in rural regions. Most African countries are faced with how to dramatically improve even basic services in rural communities. In some countries like Ethiopia, the challenge can be more significant where the majority of people still live in rural communities.

When you hear this, you may wonder what different proposition is presented to African indigenous nations. The proposition that is presented to a significant number of these nations is the undeveloped land on which they sit contains hidden wealth.

Before getting to the opportunity for African indigenous nations, let's look at the story of Native American nations. Native Americans were forced from their traditional lands and placed on reservations in the 19th century in the United States. Since then, most of these nations have been in decline on the periphery of U.S. society. But something changed the landscape for a number of these nations because they were given self-autonomy long ago. In essence, they are nations within a nation and rule their lands separate from, but still within the bounds of, the U.S. government.

This one concession made by the U.S. has created new cash revenue streams into Native American communities in the form of casinos. Many U.S. municipalities traditionally prohibited gambling, so as large casino operators were looking for places to expand, they found partners in Native American communities. While there are arguments about the social consequences of casinos in Native American communities, a number of these nations were awash in cash when the global economic crisis hit in 2008.

The Native American nations' experience with casino businesses demonstrates the possibility of non-traditional business opportunities for both indigenous communities and business industries. African indigenous nations with control over land, say those in Zambia, may present a unique business case for businesses and investors.

With the increase in global demand for commodities in the next twenty years, African indigenous nations with these undeveloped assets are inherently wealthy.

The Royal Bafokeng nation in South Africa is an excellent example of how an African indigenous nation is developing its natural wealth and its people. In fact, Royal Bafokeng, with a population of approximately 300,000, sits on one of the largest sources of platinum in the world. The nation is still led by its traditional royal family. King Kgosi Leruo Molotlegi is the current monarch. However, the assets of the nation are organized as a community-based investment enterprise called Royal Bafokeng Holdings (RBH). The asset portfolio is becoming more diversified with mining (69%), telecommunications (10%), cash (10%), services (7%), infrastructure (2%), financial services (1%), and manufacturing (1%). RBH has invested in companies like Vodacom South Africa, DHL Express South Africa, Zurich Insurance Company South Africa, and Astrapak South Africa. The portfolio was worth approximately USD$5 billion in 2010.[8] Royal Bafokeng citizens are the major shareholders in RBH through a trust.

---

[8] Royal Bafokeng Nation. *Annual Review 2010*. http://www.bafokengholdings.com /a/files/RBH_annual_review_2010.pdf. (Accessed online on November 4, 2011.)

On the social development side, Royal Bafokeng has a vision and social development plan. Some of the major components are a college and the Royal Bafokeng Stadium, which was one of the stadiums used for the FIFA World Cup in South Africa in 2010. The nation also invests in enterprise development, education, and arts and culture.

The nation is a part of South Africa but operates under a combination of indigenous laws and South African national laws. While not elected, King Molotlegi operates under Bafokeng laws which incorporate mechanisms to ensure that his majesty, or any other monarch, carry out the will of the people. There are also multiple levels of local government, e.g., elected village representatives which represent their communities in the King's Consultative Council. While not a democracy as Western people understand it, these mechanisms help ensure that the will of the people is heard and carried out. The corporate structure of RBH, however, reflects typical forms of corporate governance, including a board of directors, shareholders, and executives.

Royal Bafokeng is not an isolated nation and embraces both its traditions and what the world can bring to them. RBH has external business investments and partnerships to leverage the asset portfolio. On the social side, King Molotlegi reaches out to others to enrich the lives of Bafokeng citizens. His majesty visited New Zealand in 2011 to seek out partnerships in education and culture with the Maori, an indigenous people.

Royal Bafokeng is the architect and administrator of its future, as well as being a steward of inherited resources that can benefit both the nation and the world. It has been able to hold on to its traditional identity and customs while still embracing the modern world.

Other indigenous nations need to recognize and operate in this position even when struggling with major challenges like poverty. As more African indigenous nations understand this position and focus on community wealth building along with personal wealth, they will be able to tap into the wealth their assets hold. While Royal Bafokeng is a model, each African indigenous nation will create its own unique space.

For businesses and investors venturing into Africa and looking for land and resources, they may have to get away from the concept of private ownership. Indigenous land is, by and large, community property under the administration of traditional leaders. Leasing land will be a more likely model to gain access to land. In a country like Zambia, which has a lot of arable land and abundant water resources suitable for large scale farming, over 90% of the land is owned by indigenous nations. Even in countries like the DR Congo, where the government owns the mining rights on local lands, indigenous nations still reside on the land and agreements must often be reached with them about business plans.

Most importantly, businesses and investors will need to seek strategic partnerships with indigenous nations instead of "takeover" models of business. First, African governments are increasingly limiting predatory business models. In Zambia, indigenous nations cannot just sell a large chunk of land to foreigners. In the DR Congo, foreign investors need to establish local facilities to bolster local economies instead of just extracting minerals. From a competitive perspective, indigenous nations will be able to pick and choose with whom they work as demand increases, leaving those with the wrong business models out in the cold.

Also, as the citizens of the indigenous nations benefit from the increased value in their assets, they become desirable consumer markets. Royal Bafokeng, with a population of 300,000, is essentially a medium-size city consumer market.

The rise of African indigenous nations is an emerging shift that will rapidly advance in the next twenty years. It won't become readily apparent in the next five years, but as global demand for resources increase and the nations position themselves, we should see indigenous nations taking new positions in economic, political, and social spheres in Africa and the globe.

The Rise of New Wealth

The Economist published an article[9] in 2011, which retracted its "hopeless" tag on Africa and said it is the "hopeful" continent. The article also shared that Oprah Winfrey (worth $3 billion) is no longer the richest person of African descent, but Aliko Dangote (worth $13.8 billion) of Nigeria is. How things have changed.

In 2011, ten of the richest Africans had a combined worth of approximately $47 billion. While this represents stores of wealth and not annual income, it is still staggering that only a few people have wealth greater than the annual revenue generated in many countries of the world. The fact that these individuals have accumulated such wealth isn't a problem. In fact, it's a good sign that Africa is on the rise.

It is not only a few Africans on the continent who are becoming wealthier. The African middle class (including lower middle and high middle) numbered about 313 million, or 34.3% of Africa's population, in 2010, according to the African Development Bank (AfDB).[10] This represents almost three times the number of people that were considered middle class in 1980.

---

[9] (December 3, 2011). Africa's Hopeful Economies: The Sun Shines Bright. *The Economist.* http://www.economist.com/node/21541008. (Accessed online on December 5, 2011.)

[10] African Development Bank. (April 20, 2011). *The Middle of the Pyramid: Dynamics of the Middle Class in Africa.* http://www.afdb.org/fileadmin/uploads/afdb/Documents/Publications/The%20Middle%20of%20the%20Pyramid_The%20Middle%20of%20the%20Pyramid.pdf/. (Accessed online on October 2, 2011.)

The challenge still remains that the economic growth that fueled economies globally in the last decade was by and large unequal – the rich getting richer and the poor getting poorer (or going nowhere). This unfortunately is also the case in many parts of Africa.

While there are many reasons for this, some are rooted in the weaknesses in the current free market/capitalist economic models. I have suggested before that free market/capitalist economic models need to evolve to provide economic opportunity for all. Current models still too often allow a few to control markets and opportunities. However, redistribution of, or state-dominated, wealth is not the answer, creation of new wealth is.

So, where does all this new wealth come from? First, I want to return to points I made in other sections of this chapter. The increased world population and increased consumption will make commodities – mineral, metal, and agriculture – extremely valuable. Because Africa has an abundance of natural resources, proper strategy and implementation should make sure that Africa develops much more of this wealth. While Africa, because of both internal and external influences, has not lived up to its potential, better overall governance, more savvy leadership, more vocal and active citizens, etc. are increasingly directing Africa along the right course. However, the next ten years will be volatile. This will not be unique to Africa as world structures will transform, but not easily.

Next we can look to two key population segments in Africa that have heretofore been marginalized – youth and indigenous nations. African youth are one of the fastest growing population segments and represent a huge consumer market. Second, indigenous nations sit on a lot of the arable land for agriculture and from which minerals are extracted (this varies from country to country). Businesses will eventually seek out the opportunities represented by these groups, and like natural resources, if the human capital is developed, the wealth will follow.

Also, technology and innovation will have a lot to do with it. As ICT infrastructure continues to grow on the continent, people will be able to tap into more knowledge, connections, and resources to improve their livelihoods. To catalyze this potential, researchers, like Lucienne Abrahams and Mark Burke of the University of Witwatersrand in South Africa, are informing government policy by urging government to support the potential in "home" economies.

The ICT sector will bring new wealth to more people in the industry as we have seen in Western markets, but more importantly ICT is one of the enablers for creating and collaborating on new innovations. It still sticks out in my mind how through crowdsourcing with the public, Goldcorp discovered mineral deposits not identified before on land they owned.

Then, there are intangible assets, including intellectual property. Intangible assets are the fastest growing asset class. Companies actually account for intangible assets in their book value. In the report, *The Power of Intangible Assets*[11], it says that the intangible value of companies as a percentage of market capitalization has doubled every ten years while tangible book value decreased (based on 2005 data) on the S&P 500.

---

[11] Cordoza, K., Basara, J., Cooper, L., & Conroy, R. (April/May 2006). The Power of Intangible Assets. *Intellectual Asset Management.* http://www.ipxi.com/system/files/ThePowerofIntangibleAssets.pdf. (Accessed online on October 3, 2011.)

Africa has not been as sufficiently represented in building wealth from intangible assets as Western markets have. Unfortunately, most countries are not well-diversified within primary sectors like mining and agriculture, much less secondary (e.g., manufacturing), tertiary (e.g., services), and quaternary (e.g., intellectual) sectors.

South Africa is the leading country on the continent for diversified secondary, tertiary, and quaternary sectors. Recent examples include a new affordable and modularized defense airplane called the AHRLAC; solar-powered, containerized, connected school by Samsung and a portable waste plant.

More broadly, Africans are excellent at what is called "work-around" innovations. They solve problems with what they have access to and what they can afford. For example, a Kenyan farmer developed an affordable, small incubator for the small-scale farmer market. This innovation will help small-scale farmers increase the production of eggs and chickens to serve local markets, which have sufficient demand, and thereby increasing their incomes. As more of these "work-around" innovations become commercialized, there will be an increase in wealth as well.

Africans already hold a lot of intangible assets, even intellectual property, in their indigenous knowledge and heritage. What has been difficult is protecting it and understanding the value that it brings to others outside of African communities, so as not to be exploited and be able to develop the value into a commercialized product.

The sources of new wealth already mentioned are logical observations, leading to a new future in Africa if the continent stays on track. But there are other sources of new wealth – a change in what is considered most valuable and the ability to trade in concepts – that will re-map the entire globe. They will shape the "New Africa" more than any other source of wealth.

An example of a change in what is considered valuable is the carbon market. The issues of climate change are dominating global discussions and governance, resulting in the development of the concept of carbon offsets – those who create too many carbons pay those who offset the carbon gases.

Africans manage a good portion of the natural resources that support the environment in which all people live. As we speak, projects involving African communities in sustainable development, like re-forestation, bring new revenue into those communities. People who have been pitied and recipients of aid now have the power to create a foundation for a sustainable future and become architects of their own destinies.

There are also traces of trading in concepts. The world is in a transitional state from transacting in physical assets to intangible assets – social capital, concepts, knowledge, and others. We see platforms like Innovation Exchange on which people get paid by major companies for the best innovative idea and social currency, but it is a very fragmented landscape. In order for this to explode, the value in ideas must be as easy to quantify and exchange as cash.

Imagine anyone in Africa, or anywhere, who has an innovative idea that someone finds of value can get paid in a transactional currency. This is a transformation of the principle of bartering, which is only a shadow of what this could be.

I have been pondering this problem for a long time. As an entrepreneur myself, there is always the continual struggle to get sufficient capital to establish and grow a new venture, which is our core business. Having gone through the creation of several brands, we have developed a process for transforming ideas into tangible, profitable ventures. Yet, we have hundreds of ideas that are useful solutions for different markets that we cannot develop because of capacity tied to the amount of resources we have available. In this new paradigm, we would be paid for these ideas, increasing our wealth and providing additional capital to the ventures we want to develop.

Some consider this a little far-fetched, so I haven't written about it until this time. Everything changed when I read, *Opportunism: How to Change the World – One Idea at a Time*, by Shraga Biran. For the first time, I see a framework that can be executed from a policy and structural level, which means that implementation can follow. He says of this emerging economic paradigm, "value of an opportunity is so great that it must be understood as a positive asset – not a means to create wealth but a form of wealth in itself."[12]

When we are speaking of an economy based on ideas, however, it is not about vague or broad ideas for the most part. It is focused around an opportunity. Opportunity is something that someone sees that others have overlooked and make it something of value. In business and to me, this represents a sustainable business model which provides value to a market and for which they are willing to pay. It is putting pieces together so that the sum of the pieces is greater than the individual pieces (and something that can be leveraged to do more).

To a great degree, this type of economy cannot exist until many people in a society see themselves as creators instead of just workers. According to Biran, "...a creator uses his human capital: the accumulation of individual intelligence, education, expertise, and imagination to discover or create wealth. This person cannot be replaced, but can be assisted by new knowledge industries."[13]

---

[12] Biran, S. F. (2011). *Opportunism: How to Change the World – One Idea at a Time*. New York: Farris, Strauss and Giroux.
[13] Ibid.

While not at full thrust, the shift is beginning to occur with African youth. In a small study of African international students in the United States, many whose parents became successful professionals but still with moderate means, express their desire to become entrepreneurs and go back to Africa to make a difference. They want to develop wealth for themselves and for others.

And finally, if this is the seed of the African youth generation, this means they will be able to multiply the wealth on the continent in infinite ways that could never have been conceived before this generation. Biran summarizes how this can be done very well, "The shift from physical to intellectual property as a growing component in the economy also creates an almost infinite source of dynamism, because – unlike natural resources such as fossil fuels, newly opened prairie, or even the grains of sand that are processed into silicon chips – the human intellect never runs out."[14]

What does all of this have to do with business in Africa? If firms do not capture these waves of change, they will find themselves left behind on the continent.

Conclusion

There are indeed several major trends at work, pushing Africa to a positive future – economic reforms and prudent financial management, natural resources, technology, demographics, democracy and transparency. However, there are shifts that will unseat the current state of Africa and the world that are not as easy to see. Some might call them undercurrents.

The shifts in governance, youth maturing into citizens and consumers with unique "identity" imprints, natural resource demand leading to geopolitical and economic clout, position of indigenous nations on the

---

[14] Ibid.

continent, and new paradigms for wealth creation will not keep Africa and its global position in a natural, evolutionary direction going forward, but will entirely disrupt the status quo and replace it with something wholly new and different. This is a repeat phenomenon that we continually see in industries when a new innovation hits it unexpectedly, as in the case of Apple's introductions of the iPod and iPhone.

These shifts can only be anticipated through the process of identifying and capturing emerging patterns. This requires firms to be adaptable, nimble, and fluid. They need to be able to re-configure business models and operations at will to stay ahead of the curve. It's no longer about building massive infrastructure, but building intelligent and nimble infrastructure models. This process reminds me of Lego creations, in which 1,000s of basic pieces serve as building blocks for any design that you can imagine.

Because Africa is underdeveloped, many see it through old lenses in which it will take decades to build it sufficiently using traditional models. However, this underdevelopment also serves as a lever for rapid advancement, or leapfrogging. Africa does not have the time to respond to its potential and issues as other regions had to stay ahead of the changes occurring globally. It can only make adequate progress if it stays one step ahead of these global changes. And those who intend to be a part of Africa's future must do the same.

2

Economic Landscape in Africa
Nwakego Eyisi

The African continent has 54 sovereign nations, of which the majority is found in Sub-Saharan Africa (SSA). The World Economic Outlook for April 2012[15] projects the growth of North Africa countries[16] to range from -7.3% in Sudan to 76.3% in Libya in 2012. The projections for Sub-Sahara African countries range from -2.7% in Swaziland to 35.9% in Sierra Leone.

The economies of the African continent are diverse, from oil producers to those driven by services. Seventeen of the SSA economies have reached emerging economy status, according to Steve Radelet, author of *Emerging Africa: How 17 Countries are Leading the Way.*[17]

It is impossible to summarize the economic outlook of the continent by looking at it as a whole. This chapter, therefore, provides an economic outlook for the five major African sub-regions – north, south, west, central, and east.

---

[15] International Monetary Fund. April 2012. *World Economic Outlook: Growth Resuming, Dangers Remain.* http://www.imf.org/external/pubs/ft/weo/2012/01/pdf/text.pdf. (Accessed online on May 23, 2012.)

[16] The World Economic Outlook reports North African countries as Algeria, Djibouti, Egypt, Libya, Mauritania, Morocco, Sudan, and Tunisia. You will not find this among other data sources.

[17] Radelet, S. (2010). *Emerging Africa: How 17 Countries are Leading the Way.* Washington: Center for Global Development.

North Africa after the Turmoil

The North Africa region consists of Algeria, Egypt, Libya, Mauritania, Morocco, and Tunisia. Growth rates in North Africa are generally lower than SSA.[18] However, infrastructure deficits that plague Africa are less pronounced in North Africa and the GDP per capita for North Africa on average easily doubles that of West, East, or Central Africa.[19]

Political Outlook

The Arab Spring started in late 2010 with Algeria and continued into 2011. It is expected to die down in 2012.[20] Governments in Egypt, Libya, and Tunisia were overturned while the government in Algeria was able to quell the uprising there. Morocco and Mauritania did not experience uprisings although Morocco was pushed to move up a constitutional referendum relaxing power of the monarchy.

Tunisia and Egypt had fairly peaceful changes in leadership compared to Libya's uprising. Moammar Gadhafi was overthrown and killed violently. Libya is probably the most vulnerable of all the North African countries. Gadhafi's leadership style left a large vacuum in Libyan politics and the

---

[18] Data accessed on January 19, 2012 at
http://www.africaneconomicoutlook.org/en/data-statistics/table-2-real-gdp-growth-rates-2001-2011/. Libya's high GDP is as a result of the restart of the economy after the overthrow of the Gaddafi regime in 2011.
[19] Data accessed on January 19, 2012 at
http://www.imf.org/external/pubs/ft/weo/2011/02/weodata
[20] Libya and Egypt are still experiencing significant unrest with frequent protests in Egypt and cities like Benghazi and Misrata in Libya operating autonomously from the national government as of June 2012.

international community is concerned that groups like Al Qaeda could exploit that vacuum and destabilize the region. In other words, Libya could be the new Somalia, according to Bill Clinton.[21]

Although the uprising was started by secular groups, regional experts expect Islamist parties to eventually gain the upper hand politically.[22] This is because Islamists are much more experienced and organized than emerging secular groups and ready to fill the power vacuum.

Former leaders Hosni Mubarak (Egypt), Moammar Gadhafi, and Ben Ali (Tunisia) banned and/or exiled Islamist groups to Europe and North America to maintain power and this has worked in favor of the Islamist parties in that it has properly positioned them (in these times) to take power.[23] Recent elections in Tunisia and Egypt have demonstrated this.

Keep in mind that although Islamists have won elections that the issue in the Arab Spring was freedom, so Islamists will also be under pressure to address the issues of the people and freedom. They will be as challenged as the former regimes, if not more so, by young Arabs with greater expectations and aspirations.

---

[21] Bingham, A. (March 2, 2011). Clinton's Biggest Fear: Libya As a Big Somalia, Says Al Qaeda Affiliates Are Biggest Threat. *Political Punch.* http://abcnews.go.com/blogs/politics/2011/03/clintons-biggest-fear-libya-as-a-big-somalia-says-al-qaeda-affiliates-are-biggest-threat/. (Accessed online on January 19, 2012.)

[22] Fam, M., & Laghmari, J. (October 27, 2011). Tunisia Islamist Party Takes Lead of 40% in Early Results of Balloting. *Bloomberg.* http://www.bloomberg.com/news/2011-10-25/tunisia-islamic-party-calls-for-coalition-after-taking-lead-in-elections.html (Accessed online on January 19, 2012.)

[23] Hope, B. (July 14, 2011). Back Again, Egypt's Exiled Islamists No Longer Have to Lie Low. http://www.thenational.ae/news/world/middle-east/back-again-egypts-exiled-islamists-no-longer-have-to-lie-low. (Accessed online on January 13, 2012.)

Economic Outlook

Morocco (4.3%) and Mauritania (3.6%) maintained solid growth in 2011 as they did not experience political turmoil. [24] After the civil unrest of 2011, economic growth in the entire region is expected to rebound this year.

Before the region's political turmoil, most of the countries had been introducing market reforms. These reforms have been ongoing since the early nineties and have yielded some good results. For example, GDP per capita for the region doubled between 1999 and 2012.[25] Central banks have also reformed and are much more efficient as evidenced by lower inflation rates for countries in the region.[26] The region has also attracted significant foreign direct investment from 1999 until now.[27]

Tunisia, Morocco, Mauritania, and Algeria are projected to have budget deficits of less than 6% this year. [28] Libya is projected to have a surplus of at least 6.8% while Egypt will have the highest deficit at 9.8%. The deficit accumulation is largely due to food price shocks and subsidies needed to supply food cheaply to the general population. Food subsidies are needed to help prevent further civil unrest in the region.

---

[24] International Monetary Fund. April 2012. *World Economic Outlook: Growth Resuming, Dangers Remain.* http://www.imf.org/external/pubs/ft/weo/2012/01/pdf/text.pdf. (Accessed online on May 23, 2012.)

[25] Data accessed at http://www.imf.org/external/pubs/ft/weo/2011/02/weodata. (Accessed online on January 22, 2012.)

[26] Ibid.

[27] Data accessed at http://www.africaneconomicoutlook.org/en/data-statistics/table-10-foreign-direct-investment-2003-2008-usd-million/. (Accessed online on January 22, 2012.)

[28] Data accessed at http://www.africaneconomicoutlook.org. (Accessed online on January 21, 2012.)

Apart from Egypt where inflation is expected to reach 12.2% this year, other countries inflation numbers are below 5%.[29] This is as a result of subdued economic activity following the global recession and effective monetary policy.

Foreign debt-to-GDP ratios are currently below 13% for Egypt (12%), Algeria (1.7%) and Libya (7.3%), while Mauritania, Tunisia and Morocco's foreign-debt-to-GDP ratios are 63%, 41%, and 23% respectively. Although Mauritania's debt is high by African standards, it is much lower than it was in 2009, when public indebtedness reached an all-time high of 92% of GDP. Mauritania is currently rescheduling its debt agreement with some of its creditors (Kuwait, Libya, and the Abu Dhabi Fund for Development). Public indebtedness is expected to fall to 50% of GDP in the future due to increased earnings from commodity exports and prudent fiscal management. On the whole, the fiscal picture for the region is stable.

Building Success in the South

The Southern Africa Development Community (SADC) is a trade and development bloc, whose aim is economic integration following the independence of Southern Africa states. SADC is made up of fifteen countries – Tanzania, Seychelles, Madagascar, Namibia, Zambia, Zimbabwe, South Africa, Mozambique, Angola, Botswana, Lesotho, Swaziland, Democratic Republic of Congo (DR Congo), Malawi, and Mauritius.

---

[29] Ibid.

Movement towards greater integration in the past has been hampered by a lack of political independence, civil wars, and a lack of political will. Today, the end of civil wars in Angola and the DR Congo, plus the realization that greater economic integration will expand the economy of this region is at the forefront of a renewed push towards integration.

Political Outlook

The political outlook for the region is fairly stable. Madagascar is the only country that is experiencing political uncertainty due to a military coup in 2009. The country is looking to new elections in 2013.

The mining rich, eastern DR Congo[30] is also unstable due to pockets of rebels still active. This could undermine the peace agreement signed by the DR Congo, Uganda, and Rwanda in 2010. After what many considered to be flawed presidential and parliamentary elections in the fall of 2011, the country remains at peace but problems in the Northeast region of the country remain in the news.

The Africa National Congress (ANC) will hold internal elections in 2012. It is expected that moderate forces will prevail. This development should allay investor fears that South Africa will move left as evidenced by threats by the ANC to nationalize mines.[31] Although President Zuma[32] is

---

[30] Q&A: DR Congo Conflict. *BBC News.* http://www.bbc.co.uk/news/world-africa-11108589. (Accessed online on January 19, 2012.)

[31] (December 3, 2011). Nationalisation in South Africa: A Debate that Will Persist. The Economist. http://www.economist.com/node/21541040. (Accessed online on January 19, 2012.)

[32] Bremmer, I. (August 25, 2011). South Africa's Political Elite Mines Nationalization Debate for Advantage. *Foreign Policy.*

generally a non-interventionist in his running of the economy and moderate on the issue of nationalization of mines, sentiment may change as politics can be unpredictable.[33]

Angola will hold presidential and parliamentary elections this year. President Dos Santos has been in power for over 30 years. Although he is yet to announce his candidacy, he may run again. If Dos Santos runs, it is very likely he will win. This will make him the longest serving president in Africa, and Angola could also be vulnerable to civil unrest as a result.

Today, Zimbabwe has a government of national unity, and its economy was one of the fastest growing in the world last year.[34] This growth follows almost a decade of economic contraction due to political uncertainty around Robert Mugabe's government. Although Mugabe is still part of the government of national unity, the political situation is expected to improve as elections will occur soon. Lesotho and Seychelles will also hold parliamentary elections this year.

Zambia, Botswana, Malawi, Seychelles, Mauritius, South Africa, and Namibia have consistently had free and fair elections. The most transparent, politically advanced, and richest countries in Africa are in this region – Seychelles, Mauritius, South Africa, Botswana, and Namibia.

---

[33] Julius Malema, the ANC Youth League leader, is a major proponent of nationalizing mines. However, he was expelled from the ANC in 2012.

[34] Data accessed at http://www.africaneconomicoutlook.org/en/countries/southern-africa/zimbabwe/. (Accessed online on January 19, 2012.)

Gross Domestic Product (GDP)

The combined GDP (real exchange rate) for this region is $471 billion.[35] This is larger than the GDPs for the major Eastern and Central Africa regional trading blocs.

South Africa, with a GDP (real exchange rate) of $357 billion[36], is by far the largest economy in the region and responsible for at least 60% of economic activity. South Africa powers the economy of this region. Countries like Namibia, Lesotho, Swaziland, and Zimbabwe are heavily dependent on South Africa. The Namibian, Lesotho, and Swaziland currencies are pegged to the South African Rand.

Even though the South African economy powers the region, economic growth in Angola, Zambia, DR Congo, Tanzania, Zimbabwe, and Malawi is higher than South Africa.[37] Greater economic integration will allow South African multinationals, and foreign multinationals located in South Africa, to tap into neighboring countries' growing consumer markets. This will expose investors to a market of 257 million people and a combined GDP of over $400 billion.[38]

---

[35] Data accessed at http://www.sadc.int/english/about-sadc/. (Accessed online on January 19, 2012.)

[36] Data accessed at http://www.imf.org/external/pubs/ft/weo/2011/01/weodata/. (Accessed online on January 19, 2012.)

[37] Data accessed online at https://www.cia.gov/library/publications/the-world-factbook/rankorder/2003rank.html. (Accessed online on January 20, 2012.)

[38] http://www.sadc.int/english/about-sadc/

Growth Rate

The average growth rate for this region is 3.8% in 2011.[39] Tanzania (6.7%), Zambia (6.6%), DR Congo (6.9%), and Zimbabwe (9.3 had growth rates of at least 6.6% in 2011.[40] Economic growth in Tanzania, Zimbabwe, DR Congo, and Zambia was primarily driven by high commodity prices and expansion in mining as the global economy rebounded.

Market reforms in telecommunications are also responsible for high growth rates. Countries in the region are also reforming agriculture for trade and food security reasons, which is also enhancing growth.

Mauritius, Seychelles, and South Africa had growth rates below the regional average because their markets are more mature. For these countries, mining, manufacturing, retail trade, and tourism are major growth drivers. Madagascar grew by only 0.5% in 2011 because political uncertainty following the coup of 2009 has discouraged investment.[41]

Another major driver of growth is private consumption. As countries open up their economies, it creates jobs and grows the middle class so that they have money to spend. Consumers are buying cars, homes, and other durables.

---

[39] International Monetary Fund. (April 2012). *Sub-Saharan Africa: Sustaining Growth Amid Global Uncertainty.*
http://www.imf.org/external/pubs/ft/reo/2012/afr/eng/sreo0412.pdf. (Accessed online on May 24, 2012.)
[40] Ibid.
[41] African Development Bank. (2011). *Madagascar Country Profile.*
http://www.africaneconomicoutlook.org/en/countries/east-africa/madagascar/. (Accessed online on January 19, 2012.)

Inflation

The inflation average for this region was 8.3% in 2011.[42] DR Congo (15.5%), Angola (13.5%), Madagascar (10.6%), and Mozambique (10.6%) all experienced double-digit inflation in 2011. Zimbabwe (3.5%) and Seychelles (2.6%) inflation rates were lower than 4%. Inflation is expected to remain about the same for the region in 2012.

The majority of countries (apart from Mauritius and Seychelles) still grapple with inflation due to power shortages and poor transportation infrastructure, like railroads. This has also hurt the manufacturing sector.

South Africa, Swaziland, Mauritius, Lesotho, and Swaziland are oil importers and countries like Angola, which sells crude oil, may still have to import refined crude due to inadequate, or non-existent, refining capacity. This increases costs for households and business, as well as increases inflation.[43]

Overall, inflation numbers have significantly improved in the last decade due to effective central banks and better budgetary coordination.[44]

---

[42] Southern Africa Development Community. (2012). *Regional Economic Performance in 2011 and Medium-Term Prospects.* http://www.sadc.int/files/1613/3044/5755/Economic_Performance_2011_and_Medium_Term_Prospects.pdf. (Accessed online on May 31, 2012.)

[43] African Development Bank. (2011). *African Economic Outlook.* http://www.africaneconomicoutlook.org/en/outlook/macroeconomic-prospects/fiscal-and-external-positions-are-affected-by-commodity-prices/. (Accessed online on January 19, 2012.)

[44] African Development Bank. (2011). *African Economic Outlook.* http://www.africaneconomicoutlook.org/en/outlook/macroeconomic-prospects/monetary-policy-moving-towards-moderate-tightening/. (Accessed online on January 19, 2012.)

Foreign Debt-to-GDP Ratio

The average foreign debt-to-GDP ratio for the region in 2011 was 38.2%.[45] Zimbabwe's (142.2%) and DR Congo's (74%) external debt positions were extremely high compared to the rest of the region. Overall, the region has low external debt compared to countries in western developed nations.[46]

Debt ratios in the region are expected to go up in the future due to the need to finance infrastructure and current commodity shocks in the global markets. Taking on more debt will not necessarily negatively affect investment in southern Africa because most of the countries are moving from a low-debt position.

Economies across this region will continue to experience robust growth. They will likely borrow to pay for infrastructure, which can also have a positive effect on any economy. This is in stark contrast to western developed countries where debt has been accumulated for consumption purposes.

Rebuilding in the West

The West Africa region, as represented by the Economic Community of West African States (ECOWAS), is a political and economic trade bloc made up of fifteen countries – Benin, Burkina Faso, Cape Verde, Côte d'Ivoire, Gambia, Ghana, Guinea, Guinea-Bissau, Liberia, Mali, Niger, Nigeria, Senegal, Sierra Leone, and Togo. All countries have undergone political and economic reforms in the last decade and are undergoing

---

[45] African Development Bank. (2012). *African Statistical Yearbook 2012.* http://www.afdb.org/fileadmin/uploads/afdb/Documents/Publications/Yearbook_2 012_web.pdf. (Accessed online on June 4, 2012.)

[46] Data accessed at http://stats.oecd.org/Index.aspx?DataSetCode=GOV_DEBT. (Accessed online on January 19, 2012.)

economic expansion. Efforts to implement a functioning common market are well underway, if reforms stay on track this region of Africa could rival emerging markets elsewhere.

Political Outlook

Apart from Côte d'Ivoire, Mali, and Guinea-Bissau, the other countries are fairly stable. Guinea, Benin, Senegal, and Niger recently underwent successful transitions while post-conflict but fragile states like Sierra Leone and Liberia have had free and transparent elections. Economic growth is crucial to sustaining stability in these nations.

Ghana will hold presidential elections in 2012. This will be Ghana's first elections as an oil producer. The stakes are higher and analysts are keen to see if oil will be the game changer, or if oil could make elections in Ghana violent. The last elections saw the present government win by a slim majority. The government will want an outright majority this time.

Nigeria held elections in April 2011 with an overall peaceful conclusion. This election was very crucial for stability and prosperity in West Africa.

Due to the opaque nature of past elections in Nigeria, observers and investors wondered if civil unrest like what was seen in North Africa would come to Nigeria.[47] With the rise in attacks against Christians in northern Nigeria by the radical Islam group, Boko Haram, and the recent fuel price hikes after the removal of government subsidies, there are those questioning whether these will instead create civil unrest.

---

[47] Dicolo, J. (April 4, 2011). Next Problem for Oil: Nigerian Elections. *The Wall Street Journal.* http://online.wsj.com/article/ SB10001424052748703806304576236762483979964.html. (Accessed online on January 19, 2012.)

Nigeria is at least 60% of the region's GDP and population. Civil unrest there would destabilize the region and hold wide ranging implications for Sub-Saharan Africa. There are no countries that could absorb refugees from Nigeria. The Nigerian economy powers the region and countries like Benin, Niger, and others at this stage in their development would not have much of an economy without their neighbor.

Gross Domestic Product (GDP)

The combined GDP for the region for 2011 was $364.6 billion.[48] A decade (1999-2010) of steady economic and political reform has improved the livelihoods of West Africans. This is no small feat.

When the common market is fully implemented, a businessman in Ghana will not be restricted to a market of just 24 million people and GDP of $37 billion, but instead will have access to a $364 billion economy and 289 million people.[49] This is the key to rapid growth for the region. For investors and businessmen, the West Africa region becomes more attractive because of its size.

Growth Rate

The average growth rate for the region in 2011 was 4.7%.[50] While not as buoyant as the large emerging markets in Asia, the region clearly out performs countries in the West and some markets in Latin America.

---

[48] International Monetary Fund. (April 2012). *World Economic Outlook Database.* (Accessed online June 18, 2012.)

[49] Data accessed at http://www.africaneconomicoutlook.org. (Accessed online on July 1, 2012).)

[50] International Monetary Fund. (April 2012). *Sub-Saharan Africa: Sustaining Growth Amid Global Uncertainty.*

Ghana (13.7%), Liberia (6.9%), Nigeria (6.7%), Sierra Leone (5.7%), Gambia (5.6%), Guinea-Bissau (5.1%), Burkina Faso (5.1%), and Cape Verde (5.0%) have growth rates exceeding the regional average. Only Côte d'Ivoire (-5.9%) had a negative growth rate in 2011 as a result of the political situation in the country.

Growth in this region is powered by the agricultural sector.[51] Countries across the region are major producers of cassava, rice, cocoa, cotton, timber, rubber, etc. Rising prices for agricultural commodities has increased investment in this sector.

Other sectors like mining, construction, and information communication technologies (ICT) have driven growth due to increasing domestic demand and appetite for metals like gold on the international markets.[52] Also, reforms around contract law and economic liberalization have led to greater investor participation.

Inflation

The inflation average for the region in 2011 is estimated at 6.9%.[53] Guinea (21.2%), Sierra Leone (18.1%), Nigeria (10.2%), Ghana (8.7%), and Liberia (8.5%) have inflation rates above the average. Inflation averages for countries have improved a great deal; averages for the nineties were at least

http://www.imf.org/external/pubs/ft/reo/2012/afr/eng/sreo0412.pdf. (Accessed online on May 24, 2012.)

[51] African Development Bank. (2011). *African Economic Outlook.* http://www.africaneconomicoutlook.org/en/outlook/macroeconomic-prospects/the-export-led-recovery-is-broadening/. (Accessed online on January 19, 2012.)

[52] Ibid.

[53] African Development Bank. (2012). *African Economic Outlook.* http://www.africaneconomicoutlook.org/en/data-statistics/table-5-monetary-indicators/. (Accessed online on July 1, 2012.)

20%[54] for countries like Ghana and Nigeria. Central banks across the region have undergone reform in the last decade and are more effective in targeting inflation.

A key driver of inflation in all of Sub-Saharan Africa is poor infrastructure. Food crops are usually produced in rural areas, but lack of transport infrastructure, like roads and bridges, limits supply to urban population centers and drives up food prices. Also, lack of storage facilities means that crops cannot be stored for off-season and drought periods. For example, according to the Food and Agricultural Organization (FAO), Nigeria has consistently produced excess food in the last three years, but lack of infrastructure and storage facilities still contributes to double-digit inflation.

Monetary policy has limited effect on inflation in Africa. But for inadequate infrastructure, countries in the region would not be adversely affected by food price inflation on the international market.

Apart from poor infrastructure, recent oil and food price shocks, loose monetary policy, and election spending have also fueled inflation across the region. [55] The downside of inflation to the economy is that it discourages savings since the local currency is worth less. Poor savings has a damaging effect on the economy because banks lend this money to businesses in the real sector, so they can expand and hire people. Countries (Nigeria and

---

[54]International Monetary Fund. (April 2012). *World Economic Outlook Database.*
[55] (March 31, 2011). Election Campaign Spending Boosts Nigeria Car Imports. *Reuters.* http://af.reuters.com/article/topNews /idAFJOE72U0YT20110331?pageNumber=2&virtualBrandChannel=0. (Accessed online on January 21, 2012).

Ghana) with developed banking sectors in the region have very high (20% at least[56]) lending rates and employ significant resources to attract deposits.

Major economies across the region do not have enough credit to support growth. This is not just due to a high number of unbanked people, but also due to inadequate infrastructure causing inflation.

Other structural deficiencies in the region, like poor power infrastructure and inadequate gasoline supply, cause inflation in the manufacturing sector and hurt existing companies. Nigeria is notorious for inadequate power, but countries like Ghana and Senegal also suffer power shortages.

Infrastructure will improve in the long run (five years). But, this means that the business environment will remain somewhat difficult in the short run.

For French-speaking West African countries, the inflation outlook could worsen in 2012. This is due to the pressure on the euro to devalue as the downturn in Europe continues. The CFA franc is pegged to the euro. French-speaking countries in central Africa also face the same pressure due to the same pegging arrangement. However, Central African countries are stronger commodity producers, which should make them less vulnerable than their counterparts in West Africa.

Foreign Debt-to-GDP Ratio

The average debt-to-GDP ratio for the region hovers around 29.5%.[57] Nigeria has the lowest debt ratio at 2.3% of GDP.

---

[56] Central Intelligence Agency. *World Factbook.* https://www.cia.gov/library/publications/the-world-factbook/index.html. (Accessed online on January 19, 2012.)

The debt profile for the region greatly improved in the last decade due to economic growth, debt forgiveness, and other factors. Debt ratios are much better today than in the 1990s when they were above 80%.[58] West Africa's average is much lower when compared to the U.S. and countries in the Euro zone where debt is at least 70%of GDP.[59]

What this means for business and economics in the region is that these countries are in a good fiscal position and governments need not raise taxes to pay off debt. It also bodes well for investor confidence because governments are lean and the economies are efficient.

In the last decade, countries have ploughed back monies that would have gone to debt servicing into the economy, where it is sorely needed. It also signifies prosperity because only well-managed economies can maintain a low-debt profile.

Debt accumulation in recent years is due to borrowing to pay for infrastructure projects, oil and food price shocks, and increased spending to keep up demand due to the crunch of 2008.[60] It is expected that countries

---

[57] African Development Bank. (2012). *African Statistical Yearbook 2012.* http://www.afdb.org/fileadmin/uploads/afdb/Documents/Publications/Yearbook_2012_web.pdf. (Accessed online June 15, 2012.)

[58] International Monetary Fund. (April 2012). *World Economic Outlook.* http://www.imf.org/external/pubs/ft/weo/2011/02/weodata/. (Accessed online on June 15, 2012.)

[59] Ibid.

[60] African Development Bank. (2011). *African Economic Outlook.* http://www.africaneconomicoutlook.org/en/outlook/macroeconomic-prospects/fiscal-and-external-positions-are-affected-by-commodity-prices/. (Accessed January 10, 2012.)

will take on more debt in the future to pay for infrastructure projects.[61] Currently, they have the capacity since debt is still very low. At the same time, the economies are undergoing rapid expansion, which means that average debt for the region could still remain low.

Building on a French Foundation in Central Africa

The Economic and Monetary Community of Central Africa (CEMAC) was set up to promote economic integration amongst members who share a common currency, the CFA Franc. Member states include Cameroon, Chad, Republic of Congo (Brazzaville), Central African Republic, Gabon and Equatorial Guinea.

CEMAC's objectives include the promotion of trade and the creation of a common market. CEMAC countries, like their counterparts in French West Africa, do not have a free floating currency. The CFA franc is pegged to the euro. Monetary policy is limited to the regional central bank flooding the market with euros, or the CFA franc, when the CFA franc appreciates and vice versa to manage inflation and flow of investment. Countries in this region do not have an independent monetary policy. In other words, the French treasury regulates the value of the CFA franc.

The downturn in the Euro zone and the devaluation of the euro means that the CFA franc must devalue. This will have consequences for import and export trade and worsen the inflation outlook for the region.

---

[61] Redifer, L. (July 21, 2010). New Financing for Africa's Infrastructure Deficit. *International Monetary Fund.* http://www.imf.org/external/pubs/ft/survey/so/2010/car072110b.htm. (Accessed online on January 21, 2012.)

The gross domestic product (GDP) and population for this region is $115 billion (2011)[62] and 149 million respectively.[63] Even though CEMAC is smaller than her counterparts to the South (SADC) and West (ECOWAS), it has the advantage of a common currency, which could guarantee a faster movement towards a common market.

Political Outlook

Chad and Central African Republic are post-conflict, fragile states. Continued reform and economic growth is crucial to maintain stability in both countries. After decades of war, Chad has been relatively peaceful since 2009. Chad also has an unfavorable climate, which can fuel poverty and conflict.[64] The country is prone to drought due to desertification and Lake Chad, a major source of livelihood, is drying up.

The Central African Republic had successful presidential and parliamentary elections earlier this year. This should help in consolidating the fragile peace. However, the threat of conflict is real as rebel forces were active in November 2010.

---

[62] International Monetary Fund. (April 2012). *World Economic Outlook Database*.
[63] African Development Bank. (2012). *African Economic Outlook 2012*.
http://www.africaneconomicoutlook.org. (Accessed online on June 23, 2012.)
[64] European Solidarity Towards Equal Participation of People. *UN: Without Concerted International Action, Climate Change Will Fuel Conflict*.
http://www.eurostep.org/wcm/eurostep-weekly/1685-un-without-concerted-international-action-climate-change-will-fuel-conflict.html. (Accessed online on January 14, 2012.)

Gabon, Republic of Congo, and Equatorial Guinea have also held elections in the last two years. It is also important to note that several of the longest serving presidents (Cameroon, Chad, and Equatorial Guinea) in Africa are also in this region. The presidents of Cameroon and Equatorial Guinea have been in power for over 30 years.

Growth Rate

Average real growth rate for the region is 4.7% (2011).[65] Equatorial Guinea (7.0%), Gabon (5.8%), and Republic of Congo (5.3%) growth rates were higher than the regional average in 2011. Growth in recent years is mainly due to high commodity prices in the international market, especially oil. Also, expansion in construction due to demand from businesses and individuals, as well as infrastructure, is also another major driver of growth.

The telecommunication sector, due to market liberalization and proliferation of mobile phones, is another growth driver. Retail trade, because of a growing middle class, is picking up steam as well.

Inflation

Inflation average for the region is 2.45%.[66] Every country has an inflation rate below 3% except Equatorial Guinea (7.2%). Low inflation rates are a result of subdued economic growth for this region more than it is a reflection of effective monetary policy. Inflation averages for Africa's other regions are higher when compared to rates for the Central Africa region.

---

[65] African Development Bank. (2012). *African Economic Outlook 2012.* http://www.africaneconomicoutlook.org. (Accessed online on June 23, 2012.)
[66] Ibid.

Foreign Debt-to-GDP

The average foreign debt-to-GDP ratio for this region is 14.5% (2011).[67] Every country has a debt ratio of less than 22%. This means prudent economic management and better budgetary coordination exist on the whole. Debt accumulation is due to infrastructure development and high food prices.

As with a low budget deficit, this is good news for investors because it leaves more than enough room for CEMAC countries to borrow for infrastructural development, which will fuel economic growth.

Economic Expansion in the East

The East Africa region, as represented by the East Africa Community (EAC), was originally a political and trade bloc made up of five countries – Kenya, Tanzania, Rwanda, Uganda, and Burundi. All countries have undergone political and economic reforms in the last decade and are growing economically. As of the end of 2011, South Sudan was added to the EAC.

In 2009, the presidents of Kenya, Tanzania, Rwanda, Uganda, and Burundi signed into effect a common market protocol which will see goods, services, and labor flow through the region unhampered.

The region is regularizing the customs union, which allows for a common external tariff for goods coming into the EAC, which was a necessary precursor to the common market.

---

[67] African Development Bank. (2012). *African Statistical Yearbook 2012.* http://www.afdb.org/fileadmin/uploads/afdb/Documents/Publications/Yearbook_2 012_web.pdf. (Accessed online June 15, 2012.)

It is hoped that the deal will lead to a greater economic clout for the region. The common market came into effect in July 2010. The EAC was launched ten years ago and has a population over 133 million.[68]

Political Outlook

Rwanda and Burundi are post-conflict, but fragile states, especially Burundi. Rwanda has had a better transition from the wars of the nineties than Burundi. Burundi concluded elections last year. Both countries are fairly stable and committed to market reforms as a way out of poverty and securing long-lasting peace.

Kenya will hold presidential and parliamentary elections this year. After post-election violence due to irregularities in the 2007 election, Kenya has emerged from that conflict rather well. In 2010, Kenyans voted on a referendum for a new constitution. Threats of post-election violence destabilizing the country in the future look increasingly remote.

Tanzania rates well in terms of political stability and civil rights. Peaceful elections conducted in 2010 saw the ruling party win by a comfortable, but slimmer majority. Uganda also successfully concluded her elections last year.

Other potential sources of instability include the conflicts in eastern DR Congo and Somalia. Bomb attacks in Uganda in 2011 are a constant reminder of the dangers of having a failed state (Somalia) as a neighbor. With increasing movement of Somalian rebels in Kenya, both Kenya and Ethiopia have sent troops to Somalia to combat al Shabaab, an al Qaeda-linked, Islamist group.

---

[68]Official website - http://www.eac.int/

Gross Domestic Product (GDP)

The combined GDP for the region for 2011 was $83.5 billion.[69] Economic reforms in the past decade and recent developments, like the common market protocol, will guarantee that the economy for this region continues to expand.

The EAC brings tremendous benefit to its member countries, particularly the smaller ones. A country like Burundi with a population of less than 10 million people and GDP of only $6 billion will not be able to attract significant capital needed for development. A Burundi that is part of an $83.5 billion economy within the common market framework has richer economic prospects and will attract investment.

The EAC is also in a tri-partite agreement with the Common Market of Eastern and Southern Africa (COMESA) and the Southern Africa Development Community (SADC) to establish a free trade area of 26 African countries in North, South, and East Africa. This gives the EAC exposure to a market of at least half a billion people and a combined GDP of about $700 billion.

Also, major oil discoveries in Uganda (and South Sudan) will spur infrastructure development in this region. This will positively impact the middle class and demand for retail goods.

The traditional growth sectors for East Africa are mainly agriculture, mining, and tourism. Recent developments like the ICT boom in Africa means that retail and telecommunications are sectors to watch in the near future.

---

[69] International Monetary Fund. (April 2012). *World Economic Outlook Database.*

Growth Rate

The average growth rate for the region in 2011 was 5.5%.[70] Tanzania and Rwanda lead in this area with growth figures (above 6%) higher than the regional average. Tanzania's growth is mainly due to doubling of output in mining, particularly gold. Rwanda's relatively transparent economy is a magnet for investment. Also, both countries are largely more stable when compared to Kenya and Burundi.

Rising prices for agricultural commodities and metals on the international market, as well a growing domestic demand for ICT products is responsible for growth in the region. As the middle class grows, it drives growth in retail, real estate and other consumer-oriented sectors.

Reforms around contract law and economic liberalization have led to greater investor participation. Also, the EAC is developing a common investment code so that investors will find it easier to engage with the entire region.

Inflation

Inflation average for the region (2011) is 11.9%.[71] Only Rwanda (5.6%) and Burundi (8.3%) have inflation rates below the double-digit average. In recent times, high food and energy prices following the global downturn of 2008, as well as loose money and increased government spending, has fueled inflation.

---

[70] African Development Bank. (2012). *African Economic Outlook 2012.* http://www.africaneconomicoutlook.org. (Accessed online on June 23, 2012.)
[71] Ibid.

Foreign Debt-to-GDP Ratio

Average debt-to-GDP ratio for the region is 26.5%.[72] All countries have a debt ratio of 30% or less. As with other regions in Sub-Saharan Africa, this will allow room for borrowing to finance infrastructure projects in the future.

Conclusion

As growth in Western developed economies will continue to stagnate over the next five years, investors will need to look beyond their traditional markets to find greater gains. Africa is positioned well against Western developed markets, as well as emerging regions like Latin America and Asia. In fact, it is emerging market leaders like China, India, and Brazil that are leading a new wave of investment into the continent. Ernst and Young project that foreign direct investment will top $150 billion in 2015, almost twice as much as it was in 2010.

Looking out to 2016, the International Monetary Fund projects that economic growth in the SSA region will still be more than 5%, as long as the decline in developed markets does not worsen greatly and there are no major shocks. During the next five years, Africa will remain a good market alternative. And between 2016 and 2020, if global growth is rebalanced, investors who took advantage of this window of opportunity will find themselves positioned for the long-term growth potential on the continent.

---

[72] African Development Bank. (2012). *African Statistical Yearbook 2012.* http://www.afdb.org/fileadmin/uploads/afdb/Documents/Publications/Yearbook_2012_web.pdf. (Accessed online June 15, 2012.)

3

Reframing Risk in Africa

Hartmut Sieper

In today's world, business and investment risk has to be reframed. This chapter outlines the old and new paradigms of risk and gives some practical insights how entrepreneurs and investors can evaluate risks and opportunities in Africa.

The key points are:

- Investment and business risk in Africa is overemphasized, while risk in many industrial nations is underestimated.

- There are increasing systemic risks in the current financial system which has become very weak and vulnerable.

- In Europe, the United States, and Japan, flat or even shrinking economies will lead to higher competition, decreasing margins, lower returns on investment, and increasing general business risk. Some economic sectors will even face existential risk.

- Emerging and frontier markets will continue to grow, allowing competitive market players to achieve high returns on investment.

- The recent economic and financial crisis, as well as the heterogeneous character of the world economic recovery led to an increase in volatility of price movements and business conditions while the global imbalances are still increasing.

These developments will inevitably lead to a changing risk perception. Prevailing paradigms of risk control and risk management will be questioned, and new paradigms will be introduced. In fact, this process has already begun.

We are living in a world that is changing very quickly. The breakdown of socialism and planned economies in Eastern Europe has dramatically transformed the economic landscape of the world and led into the process of globalization. The former systems of two superpowers, the United States of America and the Soviet Union, are no longer in place. What we have now is a multipolar world, which we shared about in *Redefining Business in the New Africa*. New dominant players are gaining momentum and influence, such as China, India, Brazil, Russia, and South Africa (also known as the BRICS countries). Rising commodity prices are benefiting resource-rich countries.

The most dramatic change can be observed in the world financial system. Since the subprime crisis and the default of Lehman Brothers, its stability is deteriorating quickly. Now, we are facing a sovereign debt crisis for most countries of the developed world. The crisis of the Euro zone, in particular, has the destructive power of derailing the whole financial system. The possibility I alluded to early in 2011 in *Redefining Business in the New Africa*, and for which many told me I was wrong, has become a likelihood with discussions among European nations to allow the existing union to break up and form another.

Investment and business risks are rising tremendously. It is increasingly hard to measure and value risk properly. So-called safe havens in the financial industry are vanishing as sovereign bonds and major currencies are at risk and legislative changes dry up some offshore financial centers.

Currencies that were considered as being stable are about to lose their reputation as anchors of stability. This is not only true for the euro, which is set to break up in 2012 as one or more countries might be forced to leave the Euro zone, but also for the Swiss franc that is now tied closely to the euro. The U.S. dollar, as the number one world currency, is increasingly vulnerable because sovereign debt has reached a level that is not sustainable. The same is true for Japan and the yen.

A growing number of renowned financial experts are heralding the end of the financial system as it is now in place. There are clear signs that support this gloomy view. Greece is about to collapse. Interest rates of Italian sovereign bonds have recently crossed the level of 7%[73], which is considered as a line that must not be crossed - otherwise the country would no longer be able to serve its huge debt.

Also, Portugal and Ireland are in dire crises. Spain is in acute danger as well and just received a bailout from the European Union. The national economy of the UK is heavily dependent on the financial industry, which makes it vulnerable in case of a financial collapse. The big banks in France and Germany are lacking equity; some of them might have to be nationalized in case of major problems with sovereign bonds of some southern European nations. For example, Deutsche Bank has equity of 2.7% of total assets.[74] Commerzbank which has equity of 3.9% has reduced its loan portfolio from €142bn to €126bn from Q2/2010 to Q2/2011.

This negative outlook is confirmed with Standard & Poor's downgrading the U.S. AAA crediting rating it has held for decades last year and downgrading nine Euro zone countries – Austria, Cyprus, France, Italy, Malta, Portugal, Slovakia, Slovenia, and Spain – in January 2012. Italy's credit rating is now at the same level as Kazakhstan's and Portugal's credit rating is considered junk status. Investment risk in developed nations has increased dramatically over the last five years.

---

[73] Right now bond yields are tumultuous. As of January 17, 2012, Italian bonds have recently come below the 7% mark, but still hover close.

[74] According to the semi-annual report of Deutsche Bank as of June 30, 2011.

If you take a look at the interest rates that are remaining at absurdly low levels and not reflecting the inherent risk adequately, you must come to the conclusion that the vast majority of market participants are not yet realizing how big the risk really is. Let me ask you a question, "Would you be ready to lend money for 10 or even 30 years to someone who will never be able to pay back his overall debt, whose income is consistently lower than his expenses, and whose currency will probably be devalued before the loan's redemption?" - Probably not. As an example, the European Union expected China to help them, but China has shown no inclination in this current environment to do so.

However, all owners of treasury bonds issued by the United States and Japan are doing exactly this. The current yield of 10-year U.S. treasury bonds is 2% while Japanese bonds are yielding 1%. This is considerably less than the inflation rate. So, the real yield is negative. If you invest capital in such financial instruments, you are losing wealth each year.

It is high time to set out for new frontiers. If the profitability of businesses and yields of the capital markets in your home country are too low, you have to look for higher returns elsewhere. In other words, you should diversify your assets and sources of income. Africa is an excellent region in which to do so.

In past years, I spoke to many people about the tremendous opportunities that Africa has to offer. A few of them where already invested in the capital markets or involved in doing business in African countries. Some of them were planning ahead for entering Africa markets. But most of them are still afraid of making a positive decision and taking action. When I asked these people their reasons, they answered that the risk was too high. In many cases, prejudices or bad experiences in the past played a major role.

However, this is about to change. More and more companies and investors are not only thinking about entering African markets, but are already putting together implementation teams, founding legal entities, opening liaison offices, and working with local representatives.

I think it is safe to say that more companies will follow those early adopters as soon as more convincing success stories are told. However, whether you choose to wait to hear more success stories or not, the international risk climate has changed in Africa's favor.

New Paradigms of Risk Perception

As the following tables illustrate, the paradigms of risk perception are shifting fast.

Macroeconomic Risk

The old paradigm	The new paradigm
European countries and the U.S. include low macroeconomic risk as debt levels seemed to be sustainable and the long-term economic uptrend was intact, only interrupted by some short-lived periods of cyclical recession.	The probability of a double-dip recession in the United States and troubled European countries has risen considerably. In an adverse financial environment, even a depression is possible that might last for several years. Balance sheet recessions are more difficult to manage and to overcome than cyclical recessions because debt reduction and deleveraging takes some time.

The old paradigm	The new paradigm
Commodity and energy prices go up and down in minor swings, yet remain predictable and controllable, thus offering a stable business environment.	Commodity and energy prices have entered a major secular bull market that will continue for a long time as populous emerging markets like China, India, Brazil, and many prospering frontier markets will heavily invest in infrastructure in order to narrow the huge gap with the developed countries.
Developed countries are more prosperous, more stable, and less indebted than developing nations.	Developing countries are growing faster than developed countries. Most of them are less indebted than developed countries. Many of them are becoming more stable in economic, financial, and political terms.

Valuable sources for measuring macroeconomic risk are:

- United Nations organizations, e.g., UNSTAT, UNDP, UNCTAD, UNIDO, and UN-HABITAT
- International Monetary Fund (IMF)
- Organization for Economic Cooperation and Development (OECD)
- World Trade Organization (WTO)
- World Bank
- Local and bilateral chambers of commerce
- National organizations

Financial Risk

The old paradigm	The new paradigm
Western European countries, most Eastern European countries, and the U.S. are safe.	The sovereign debt crisis and the banking crisis in the western world cannot be easily solved. Each possible way out is very painful. There is an imminent threat of imposing one-time wealth taxes (also known as confiscation), nationalization, solidarity payments (newspeak for transferring wealth from good performing countries to defaulting countries), and other draconian measures.
Developed countries are more prosperous, more stable, and less indebted than developing nations.	Developing countries are growing faster than industrialized nations. Most of them are less indebted than developed countries. Many of them are becoming more stable in economic, financial, and political terms.
Before the euro currency was introduced, European national economies were mostly stable. This was also true during the first decade after the euro was established as a common currency.	The European Stability Mechanism (ESM) that will be introduced into European and national laws in 2012/13 represents a shift toward an autocratic, centralized political system. Investors and business owners should be prepared for unconventional political decisions leading to unwelcomed results.

Political Risk

The old paradigm	The new paradigm
Africa is high risk. Africa is seen as a single, high-risk investment target rather than as a continent consisting of many different nations offering great varieties of risk exposure.	A better understanding of African markets leads to a more detailed approach of measuring and anticipating political risk. The trend towards more democracy and good governance in Africa is fully intact.
High predictability of political decisions and actions in Western, developed countries.	Low predictability of political decision and actions. This is not only true for many European countries, but also for the MENA region, including Egypt, Libya, and Tunisia.
European countries enjoy sophisticated democratic political systems and are considered as safe places for doing business and making investments. The level of economic and financial freedom is very high.	The European Union is increasing its political power by issuing thousands of new laws and regulations and imposing control mechanisms, although various bodies of the EU are lacking democratic legitimacy.

The old paradigm	The new paradigm
Middle East and North Africa (MENA region) are relatively stable. Although the Israeli-Palestinian conflict cannot be solved, and Iran is threatening the region, most players and decision-makers are known and somewhat predictable. Egypt was a stabilizing factor in that game.	Following sudden and unexpected revolutions in Tunisia, Egypt, and Libya, as well as dangerous situations in Syria, Iraq, and Iran, the whole region is destabilizing. The political shift in North African countries toward Islamism removes the stabilizing factor regarding Israel. The breakout of a regional armed conflict with Iran as a centerpiece is a likely scenario. Even a full-scale war in the Persian Gulf is a possibility.

So, it is obvious that risk is everywhere – U.S., Europe, and emerging markets. In today's environment, the risk profiles between developed and developing economies are evening out with some emerging markets looking better than developed markets.

But the issue is still, how do you minimize risk in these dynamic, and even turbulent, times? How can all these risks be dealt with? In order to reduce risks to a level that is acceptable to you, you can apply the following measures:

- Insurance against political risk
- Transfer risk to other parties
- Spreading the portfolio risk over several asset classes, countries, sectors, investment styles, and business lines[75]
- Select lower risk countries, which include several in Africa

When large capital expenditures are involved in your business project and you are operating in a country with high political risk, an insurance against political risk should be purchased. The Multilateral Investment Guarantee Agency (MIGA), a member of the World Bank Group, promotes foreign direct investment by providing political risk insurance to investors and lenders against losses caused by noncommercial risks. In Germany, Euler Hermes offers similar insurance.

If you transfer risk to other parties, you will have to give away a part of your profit, thus lowering your return on investment. Therefore, outsourcing parts of your value chain should be considered carefully. Very good advice for beginners is to avoid countries where political, business, economic, and financial risk are unacceptably high. Africa is a diverse continent, consisting of 54 countries. Most of them are considered as being very risky. However, there are also some medium risk countries and a few low risk countries that business people and investors can focus on. By doing so, you avoid the great amount of risk right from the beginning.

---

[75] Markowitz, H. Portfolio Selection. *The Journal of Finance, 7(1)*, 77-91.

Euler Hermes Credit Insurance, a subsidiary of the Germany-based Allianz Group, derives country risk from the following risk factors[76] :

- Political Risk
- Economic Risk, with two sub parameters: Macro-Economic Risk, and Structural Business Environment
- Country Grades

In order to deal with the decreasing stability of the world financial system and to take into account disruptive events that have occurred more frequently over the past years, Euler Hermes has introduced two new parameters:

- The Cyclical Risk Indicator measures the risk of worsening payments in relation to the interdependence of national economies in the globalization process, the scarcity of resources (commodities), and the growth in cross-border trading.
- The Financing Flows Indicator measures the country's vulnerability to exogenous shock and its capacity to resist or avoid systemic shock. It mirrors the persistence of financial instability by taking into account financial disequilibria, volume of liquidity and capital flows, sovereign debts, and the crisis of certain banking systems, resulting in more volatile risk aversion.

---

[76] Euler Herms. *Country Ratings*. http://www.eulerhermes-aktuell.de/en/country-ratings/country-ratings.html. (Accessed online on January 14, 2012.)

Risk of Doing Business in Africa

When Western companies start thinking about expanding their businesses into African markets, they usually first do a lot of research. They try to find out as much as possible about commercial and legal frameworks, the current political situation and future scenarios, general living and working conditions, and the business environment in their specific sector. One of the best sources of doing this basic research is the Doing Business database developed by the International Finance Corporation (IFC).[77]

The competitiveness of 183 countries of the world is measured in a very practical way. Nine parameters are examined, and the results are aggregated into a single score labeled "Ease of Doing Business."

As a general rule, doing business is easier in developed countries than in developing countries. While some West and North European countries, along with some Asian nations and the United States, are high-ranking in most parameters, most Sub-Saharan African countries are found in the lowest ranks. North African countries are ranked higher, but still considerably lower than the average of the OECD countries.

Doing business in African markets can be very challenging. Many bureaucratic steps have to be undertaken before one gets a license or a permit. It can be difficult and time-consuming to hire people and even more difficult and very costly to get rid of them if they do not perform.

Access to the local credit markets can be very limited and interest rates can be very high. Trading across borders can imply many more procedures than in the Western world, making import and export activities more complicated. Corruption can be involved in many areas, but this fact is not covered by the Doing Business report.

---

[77] International Finance Corporation. *Doing Business.* http://www.doingbusiness.org. (Accessed online on January 12, 2012.)

Paying taxes can be easy or very difficult, depending on the country. Ownership rights of investors are well protected in some countries, while in others it is almost impossible to get a righteous judgment in case of dispute.

It is worth noting that western countries do not rank higher than their African counterparts in all disciplines. For example, paying taxes in Germany is very difficult, as the German tax law is the most complicated in the world. Protection of investors in most English-speaking countries is far better than in Germany, Austria, and Switzerland.

It is not surprising that high-ranking countries are doing much better in the global market than those countries where entrepreneurs and companies are confronted with bureaucratic systems, high transaction costs, trading barriers, and immature legal systems.

The good news is that many African nations have realized the need to improve their competitiveness if they want to excel in the global context. The countries of Mauritius and Rwanda belong to the top reformers of the world. Mauritius is ranking 23 in the world, followed by South Africa (rank 35), Rwanda (rank 45), Tunisia (rank 46), Botswana (rank 54), and Ghana (rank 63). On the lowest end of the list, there are the countries of Eritrea, Republic of Congo, Central African Republic, and Chad.[78]

Foreign direct investments into Africa focus on a handful countries. Capital inflows into low-ranking countries are negligible. If there are too many obstacles, high risk, time-consuming procedures, and high transaction cost, investors will not come.

---

[78] The African countries of Libya and Somalia are not rated.

Although Africa as a whole is one of the most attractive regions in the world in terms of economic prospects, there are many countries from which investors and business people can choose. Obviously, they will enter in those markets that provide the highest returns and offer the lowest risk.

The graph on the next page displays the relative ease of doing business of Sub-Saharan African countries and North African nations in comparison with the OECD high-income countries. One can see at first sight that Sub-Saharan African countries do not look attractive from this point of view. In all parameters they are considerably less competitive than the Western markets.

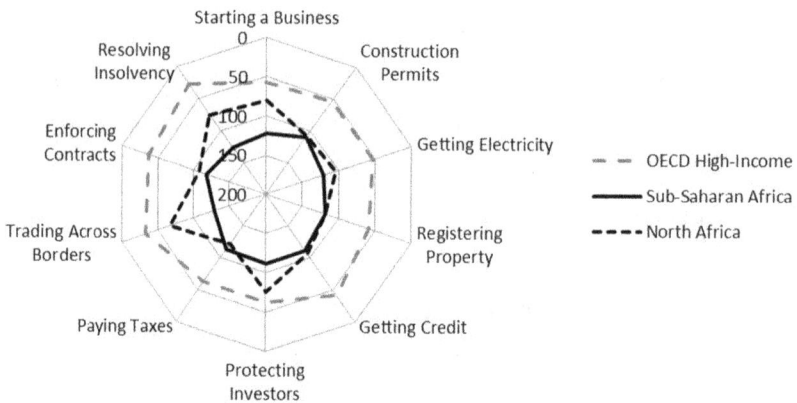

Ease of Doing Business in Sub-Saharan Africa, North Africa, and OECD. Data: Doing Business Report, Graph: Trans Africa Invest

However, there are distinctive differences between several groups of African countries. Culture and the colonial heritage have decisive influence on the ease of doing business today on the continent. History tells us the origin of some of these differences.

In order to find out if there are differences of statistical significance, African nations have been divided into four different groups on the map below, according to the dominant language.

African Countries by Official Commercial Language. Source: Trans Africa Invest

Ethiopia is the only country on the African continent that has never been colonized by European powers. Therefore, no European language is commonly spoken there. This is also true for Eritrea, which was a part of Ethiopia until 1991 when the nation became independent. The occupation of the area by the Italians from 1935 until 1941 was just a short intermezzo.

Within Sub-Saharan Africa, English-speaking countries are the most competitive as in the chart on the next page. In nine of ten parameters, the average ranking is considerably higher than the average ranking of the

French-speaking countries. In eight of ten parameters, English-speaking countries are more competitive than the Portuguese speaking countries.

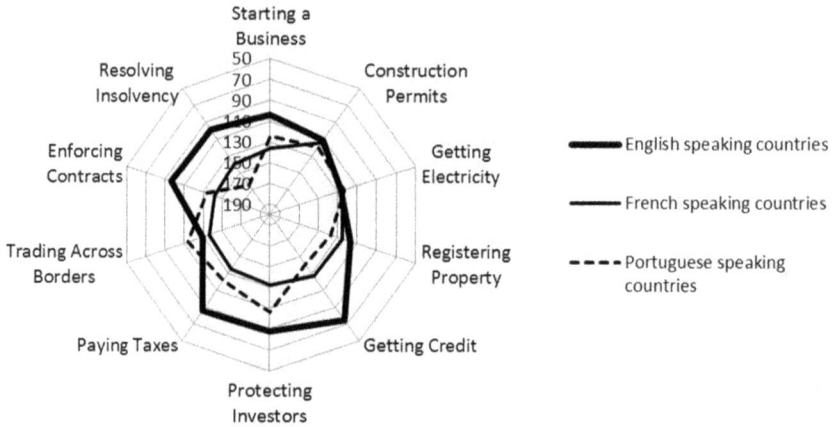

Doing Business Comparison between English-, French-, and Portuguese-Speaking Countries. Data: Doing Business Report, Graph: Trans Africa Invest

One of the reasons for the big differences is the code of law. The British legal system is more business friendly, while the French system is more bureaucratic. Also, British colonialists have equipped and trained local people, allowing them to take management posts in the colonial administration in the low and middle hierarchic levels. In the French colonies, all key persons in the administration were French citizens, or, in the case of the Democratic Republic of Congo, which was a Belgian colony, Belgian administrators. This behavior prolonged a high dependency on the colonialists. When the Portuguese left their colonies in 1975, education of the local people had been very low. In the whole country of Mozambique, there were just seven academics when the nation was dismissed into independence.

In the former French colonies, many key positions in public administration, banking, and industrial companies are still occupied by French people. It is not surprising that the ties between these countries and France are still very strong.

From a practical point of view, it is easier to start businesses in the English-speaking countries, unless the entrepreneur's mother language is French or Portuguese. Most companies from the German-speaking countries that are already doing business in Africa started in South Africa, which is considered as being the most developed market and the gateway to Sub-Saharan Africa. Additionally, Kenya, Ghana, and Nigeria are interesting destinations for them. Also, the North African countries are attractive because of their proximity to the European markets.

Risk of Doing Business: Some of the Best and Worst Environments in Africa

It is amazing how fast some African countries have reformed over the last couple of years. According to the Doing Business website[79], in Sub-Saharan Africa 36 of 46 governments improved their economy's regulatory environment for domestic businesses in 2010/11 - a record number since 2005. This is good news for entrepreneurs in the region where starting and running a business is still costlier and more complex than in any other region of the world. Many countries are still lagging behind, making it very difficult for investors and entrepreneurs to support economic development by doing business.

---

[79] International Finance Corporation. (2012). *Doing Business Report 2012.* http://www.doingbusiness.org/reports/global-reports/doing-business-2012. (Accessed online on January 16, 2012.)

Rwanda and Burundi

Rwanda is the world's second-top reformer in creating a business-friendly environment, according to the Doing Business 2012 report. This small landlocked country in East Africa, which suffers from limited natural resources, high population, and very high transportation costs to the world markets, wants to position itself as a hub for ICT services, according to the will of President Paul Kagame.

Kagame runs the country more like a CEO than as a head of state. Consequently, he initiated measures making it easier for companies and individuals to do business. Since a one-stop shop was introduced, it is possible to start a business within three days, and it takes only two procedures. This brings Rwanda's rank to 8th in the world in this category.

As Rwanda is a landlocked country, it is logical that it has pursued a strong policy of integration with the East African Community Customs Union, which also includes Kenya, Uganda, Tanzania, and Burundi. Newly independent South Sudan has also joined. The new nation, which is desperately short of managerial capacity in most aspects of business and governments, has already asked Rwanda to assist on how to make South Sudan more business and investment friendly.

On the contrary, it is more difficult to start a business in the neighboring country of Burundi. There, it takes nine procedures to complete a company registration, and the whole process takes 14 days. The cost is 117% of the average yearly income per capita, compared with just 5% in Rwanda. As a result, Burundi ranks 108th in the discipline of starting a business.

Although Burundi is still lagging, the country has managed to belong to the top reformed countries in 2010/11. From the top ten reformers, five are from Africa (Morocco, São Tomé and Principe, Cape Verde, Sierra Leone, and Burundi).

These astounding differences are hard to understand since both countries are similar in size and population and have at least one official language (French) in common. They also have the same ethnic groups (mainly Hutu and Tutsi) and share the same sad history (genocide in 1994).

One key difference is that Rwanda has developed sound government policies and clear market-oriented goals to boost economic activity. And, Rwanda has chosen English as the preferred commercial language since 1994. This significant change will help Rwanda better exploit the huge opportunities arising from being a member of the East African Community (EAC). English is the common language in Uganda, Tanzania, and Kenya, as well as Kiswaheli.

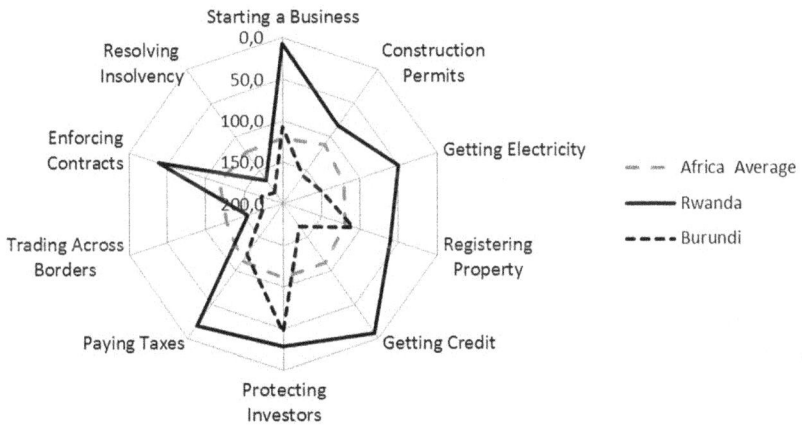

Doing Business Comparison between Rwanda and Burundi. Data: Doing Business Report, Graph: Trans Africa Invest

The previous graph underlines huge differences in the ease of doing business in Rwanda and Burundi. Not only in starting businesses are the two countries playing in different leagues, but in all other disciplines as well. It must be noted, however, that Rwanda still has to work on business factors such as trading across borders and resolving insolvency.

We hope that Burundi will continue its reforms in order to further catch up with its neighbor.

Botswana and Zimbabwe

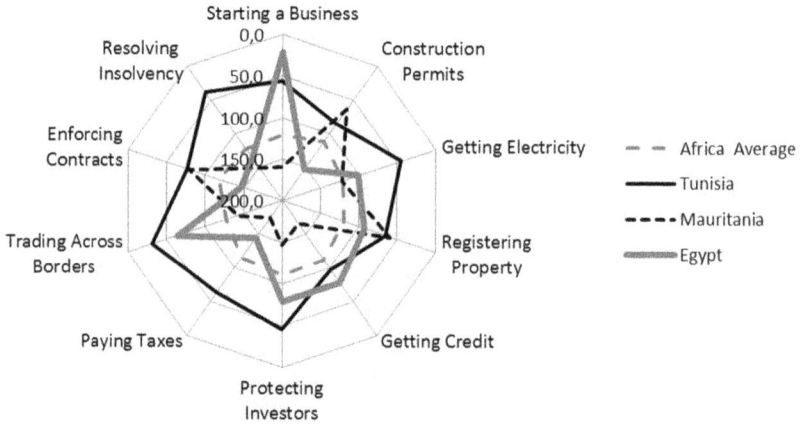

Doing Business Comparison between Botswana and Zimbabwe. Data: Doing Business Report, Graph: Trans Africa Invest

Let's look to another pair of countries. Botswana and Zimbabwe are both landlocked countries in Southern Africa. They share the same border, but have a very different history. Botswana, which is considered as the least corrupt country in Africa, has strategically used its wealth of natural resources, especially diamonds, to develop its economy and the social standards of its single tribe population without misusing proceeds from diamond exports for personal enrichment, as was the case in many other resource-rich African nations. As a result of this exemplary governance, Botswana became the fastest-growing country over a period of 40 years after independence.

Zimbabwe, on the other hand, has a lot more natural resources, including platinum, chromium, gold, and diamonds. Additionally, the colonial heritage of former Southern Rhodesia included a highly developed agricultural sector and a considerable industrial base. Sadly, the country's economy has been run down over several decades due to a negative political climate, culminating in a total destruction of the country's assets, hyperinflation and a complete financial collapse that led to a currency reform in 2009. The political situation in Zimbabwe is still unclear and highly unpredictable, which is, among other factors, responsible for missing economic and judicial reforms. One bright spot is a draft of a new constitution was released in July of this year, which will hopefully lead to democratic reforms.

It is not surprising that both countries are very different regarding doing business. However, big problems often mean big opportunities. Many anticipate positive political change as the current regime ages in Zimbabwe, so some investors are positioning themselves for future opportunities.

North Africa: Egypt, Tunisia, and Mauritania

Differences are also big among North African countries. Tunisia offers a very favorable environment for investors and business people, followed by Egypt. The revolutions in Tunisia and Egypt have already started to affect commercial, financial, and legal conditions.

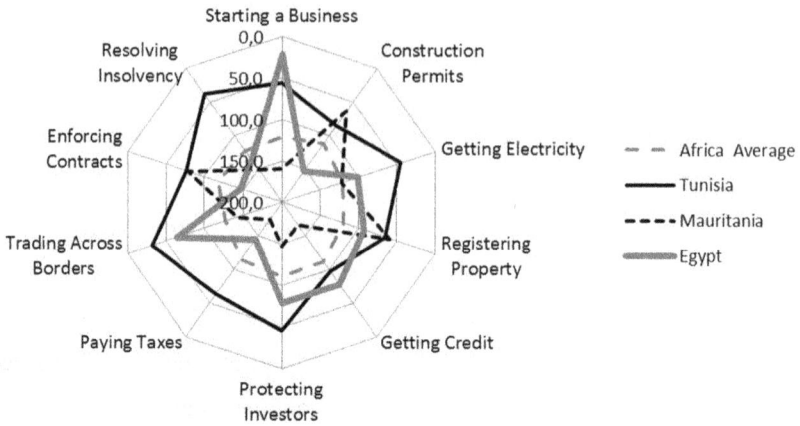

Doing Business Comparison between Egypt, Tunisia, and Mauritania. Data: Doing Business Report, Graph: Trans Africa Invest

The changes are mirrored in their rankings. While Tunisia went up from 55 to 46, Egypt fell from 94 to 110. On the other end of the scale, Algeria (ranked 148) and Mauritania (ranked 159) pose a hard environment for business people.

Oil-Producing Countries: Angola, Ghana, and Nigeria

The major oil countries of Nigeria, Angola, and Algeria have attracted a lot of foreign direct investments in recent years. In 2011, Ghana joined the club of oil-producing countries, and will probably be followed by Uganda some years later.

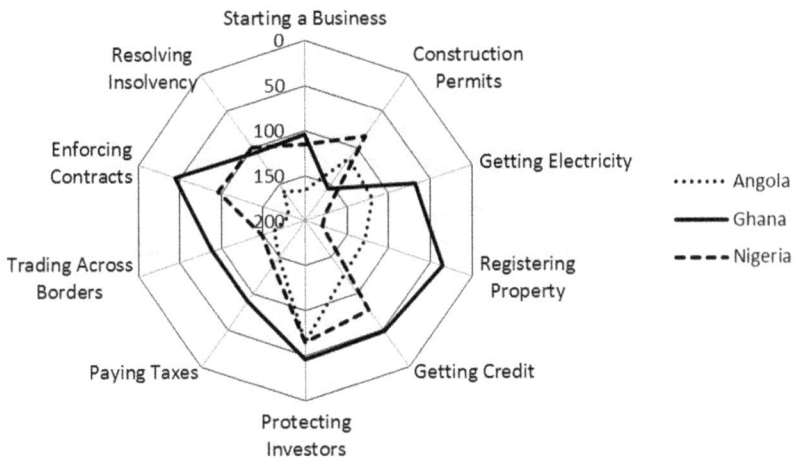

Doing Business Comparison between Angola, Ghana, and Nigeria. Data: Doing Business Report, Graph: Trans Africa Invest

The business and legal environment in Ghana is much more favorable for investors than Nigeria and Angola. Angola, a Portuguese-speaking country in southern Africa, is known for its harsh environment, high costs, and high levels of corruption. A new investment law was instituted in 2011, which requires capital injections of at least US$1 million from investors that want to benefit from various incentives. Obviously, government policies do not focus on fostering small-scale entrepreneurial activities in that country. Although the medium-term prospects for Angola are bright, the conditions of doing business are unfavorable.

However, the good news for investors and business people is: there are many countries in Africa that they can choose between, offering outstanding opportunities in many economic sectors.

Island Nations: Mauritius and São Tomé & Principe

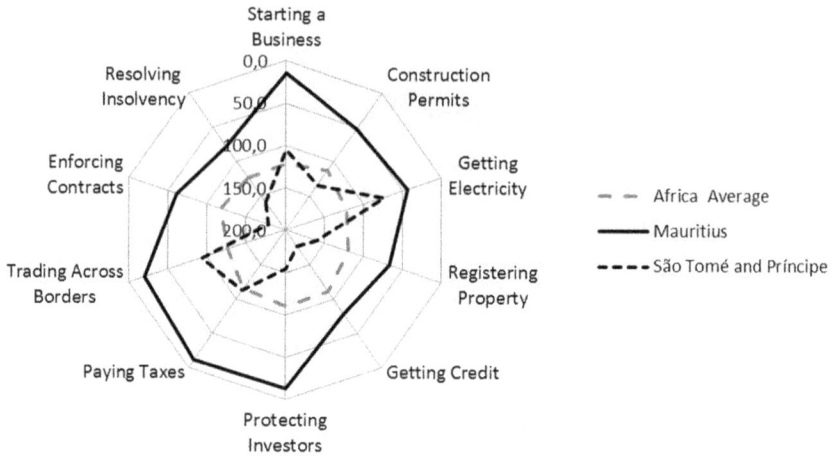

Doing Business Comparison between Mauritius and São Tomé & Principe. Data: Doing Business Report, Graph: Trans Africa Invest

According to the Doing Business indicators, Mauritius is the best place in Africa to do business. The small island in the Indian Ocean ranks number 23 worldwide. Besides its attractiveness as a pleasant tourist destination with beautiful beaches, Mauritius' specialty is an advanced and favorable legal and tax environment for investment companies, positioning it as a well sought after offshore financial center. Compare the ease of doing business in Mauritius and another small African island, São Tomé & Principe in the Gulf of Guinea - the differences could hardly be greater.

Population Powerhouses in Sub-Saharan Africa: DR Congo, Ethiopia, Nigeria, & South Africa

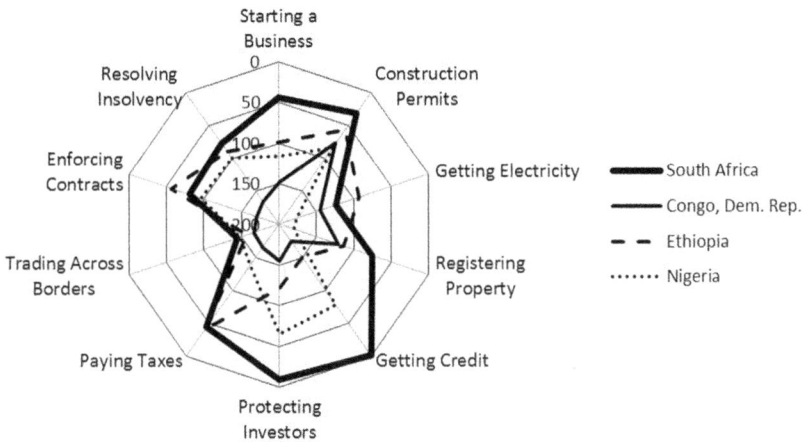

Doing Business Comparison between DR Congo, Ethiopia, Nigeria, and South Africa. Data: Doing Business Report, Graph: Trans Africa Invest

Finally, we take a look at the population powerhouses of Sub-Saharan Africa (which can translate to economic powerhouses in the future). South Africa is the most advanced economy on the continent. Nigeria has the largest population of approximately 155 million people, followed by Ethiopia (91 million) and the Democratic Republic of Congo (72 million).[80] The graph shows big differences between those nations with South Africa leading and the DR Congo lagging far behind.

---

[80] Central Intelligence Agency. *World Factbook.* https://www.cia.gov/library/publications/the-world-factbook/wfbExt/region_afr.html. (Accessed online on January 13, 2012.)

Regardless of the current political, commercial, financial, and social conditions, these are the places where both investors and companies have to be.

However, it is no longer enough for European or U.S. companies to install a launchpad in South Africa trying to penetrate the other African countries from there. What is required now is to have a physical presence in each target country.

Conclusion: The Biggest Risks and Opportunities

According to the famous German entrepreneur, Reinhard Mohn, the denial of a risk is the biggest risk of all for a company. People who are afraid of making the wrong decision might choose not to make any decision. Many employees in the financial industry are following this strategy in these unstable times. Sure, a wrong investment decision might cause them to lose assets. However, they will never excel with this attitude. Entrepreneurs are of a different caliber. They are entrepreneurs because they can make decisions and are ready to take responsibility.

Business life is an endless journey of making decisions. Successful entrepreneurs know that not making a decision is also a decision.

Not all existing paradigms about risk will change. One fundamental truth is the correlation between risk and opportunity: the higher the return on investment, the bigger the risk, and vice versa. This basic rule will never change. However, there are times where the prevailing perception of risk and opportunity by the market is skewed in one direction or the other. Right now, we have this situation. As risk is overestimated in Africa, asset prices there are mostly cheaper than they should be. The higher the perceived risk, the cheaper the asset is. For example, outstanding deals are still possible in the cash economy of Zimbabwe, even given the high political risk in that country. At the other end of the scale, Ghana is a stable country with a booming economy and newly found oil reserves have become much more expensive for deal hunters.

Finally, there is the risk of missing the right time. He who comes too late will be punished by life, according to former Soviet president Gorbachev. This is especially true for Africa today, since business has changed. If you have the right business model and the right product or service to offer, you should enter the African markets soon, even if just to create a small, initial footprint. If you do it right and invest the capital that is necessary for starting operations, you can succeed and bring value. If you wait too long, you will find yourself locked out of opportunities within the next five to ten years.

Don't miss the greatest opportunities that the global village is offering in this decade.

4

Regional Integration and Infrastructure in Africa
Lauri Elliott

Shortly after the independence era in the late 1950s and into the 1960s, African nations turned to regional economic integration. In 1991, a formal agreement was made to establish the African Economic Community (AEC). The aim of the AEC is to increase economic growth and development across the continent. Integration will:

- Unify and enlarge African markets.
- Foster intra-Africa trade.
- Reduce barriers to free flow of labor, capital, goods, resources, and services.
- Permit economies of scale.
- Provide access to a larger trade and investment environment.
- Provide frameworks for unified responses to international and geopolitical issues, e.g., climate change, trade agreements.

Existing regional economic communities (RECs) are considered the building blocks to the AEC and should establish the African Common Market between 2019 and 2023. The RECs that are recognized by the African Union (AU), the intergovernmental body of the continent, are:

- **Arab Maghreb Union** (UMA)[81] – Members are Algeria, Libya, Mauritania, Morocco, and Tunisia. In 2011, UMA's population was estimated at 84 million, which is similar in size to Germany, Egypt,

---

[81] Official website: http://www.maghrebarabe.org/en/

and Ethiopia, according to the *World Factbook*.[82] Its annual GDP was estimated at $599.7 billion in 2010.

- **Common Market for Eastern and Southern Africa** (COMESA)[83] – Members are Burundi, Comoros, Democratic Republic of Congo (DR Congo), Djibouti, Egypt, Eritrea, Ethiopia, Kenya, Libya, Madagascar, Malawi, Mauritius, Rwanda, Seychelles, South Sudan , Sudan, Swaziland, Uganda, Zambia, and Zimbabwe. COMESA's population was estimated at 476 million in 2011, which is similar in size to the European Union. Its annual GDP was estimated at just over $1 trillion ($1,012 billion) in 2010.[84]

- **Community of Sahel-Saharan States** (CEN-SAD)[85] – Benin, Burkina Faso, Central African Republic, Chad, Djibouti, Egypt, Eritrea, Gambia, Libya, Mali, Morocco, Niger, Nigeria, Senegal, Somalia, Sudan, Togo, and Tunisia. CEN-SAD's population was estimated at 442 million in 2011. Its annual GDP was estimated at $1.4 trillion ($1,445 billion) in 2010.

- **East African Community** (EAC)[86] – Members are Burundi, Kenya, Rwanda, Tanzania, Uganda, and South Sudan (final approval pending as of January 2012). Sudan has also requested membership after many years of shunning the EAC. The EAC's population was

---

[82] Central Intelligence Agency. *World Factbook*. https://www.cia.gov/library/publications/the-world-factbook/index.html. (Accessed online on January 10, 2012.)
[83] Official website: http://www.comesa.int/
[84] Data for South Sudan not included as it was not officially independent until July 2011 and data is not yet available.
[85] Official website - http://www.cen-sad.org
[86] Official website - http://www.eac.int

estimated at 140 million in 2011. Its annual GDP was estimated at $182.2 billion in 2010.[87]

- **Economic Community of Central African States** (ECCAS)[88] – Members are Angola, Burundi, Cameroon, Central African Republic, Chad, Congo Brazzaville, Democratic Republic of Congo, Equatorial Guinea, Gabon, Rwanda, and São Tomé & Principe. ECCAS' population was estimated at 149 million in 2011. Its GDP was estimated at $274.8 billion in 2010.

- **Economic Community of West African States** (ECOWAS)[89] – Members are Benin, Burkina Faso, Cape Verde, Côte d'Ivoire, Gambia, Ghana, Guinea, Guinea-Bissau, Liberia, Mali, Niger, Nigeria, Senegal, Sierra Leone, and Togo. ECOWAS' population was estimated at 301 million in 2011. Its annual GDP was estimated at $593.0 billion in 2010.

- **Intergovernmental Authority on Development** (IGAD)[90] – Situated in the Horn of Africa and includes member states of Djibouti, Eritrea, Ethiopia, Kenya, Somalia, South Sudan, Sudan, and Uganda. IGAD's population was estimated at 227 million in 2011. Its annual GDP was estimated at $305.9 billion in 2010.[91]

---

[87] Data for South Sudan and Sudan not included as of yet

[88] Official website - http://www.ceeac-eccas.org (in French)

[89] Official website - http://www.ecowas.int

[90] Official website - http://www.igad.int

[91] Data for South Sudan not included as it was not officially independent until July 2011 and data is not yet available.

- **Southern African Development Community** (SADC)[92] – Members are Angola, Botswana, Democratic Republic of Congo, Madagascar[93], Malawi, Mauritius, Mozambique, Namibia, Seychelles, South Africa, Swaziland, Tanzania, Zambia, and Zimbabwe. SADC's population was estimated at 270 million in 2011. Its annual GDP was estimated at $861.8 billion in 2010.

Being able to harmonize visions, missions, goals, objectives, policies, protocols, and practices is a huge undertaking, but is required to see the eventual economic and developmental unity of the continent. This process is further complicated by several nations, e.g., Burundi, Democratic Republic of Congo, and Zimbabwe, being members of more than one REC.

For business, investment, and trade, regional and continental integration can be a boon if done right. If a business sets up in one country, in a free trade area, it then has access to a larger regional market and can move labor, capital, and resources more readily across borders.

Right now, the EAC is a very good example of regional integration progress. The EAC established a customs union and a common market in 2010. It is also a good example of spillover benefits, such as economies of scale, wider trade and investment agendas, and attracting interest in local markets, for small and landlocked countries (e.g., Burundi and Rwanda)

---

[92] Official website - http://www.sadc.int
[93] Madagascar is currently suspended because of the political uprising in 2009.

AU/NEPAD

The African Action Plan (AAP) 2010-2015[94] of the AU/NEPAD[95] outlines a series of priority sectors concerning regional integration and development. For businesses and investors, it is important to note the projects and priorities in which the AU, or a REC, are involved, as this indicates where they are willing to put their resources; strong institutional frameworks are being developed; likely involvement of large donor organizations and banks; potential bankable projects for investors; opportunities for contracts for businesses; and eventual spin-off benefits and opportunities as the projects get underway. However, businesses and investors need to still make sure that the project is viable according to their own needs.

NEPAD has fourteen priority sectors, including agriculture and food security, development corridors, tourism, trade facilitation and private-sector development, and infrastructure. Many of the priority sectors ultimately impact business, but these examples may be of particular interest because of their highly visible opportunities and/or support for business.

For each priority sector, RECs will have bodies aligned with those at the AU level concerned with each of these areas. It is important for businesses and investors to note the influence that these structures have on the business environment in Africa, particularly large projects. For example, African countries are turning away from a focus on just generating revenues and turning more towards development. So, in the case of mining,

---

[94] African Union. *Africa Action Plan.*
http://www.nepad.org/system/files/AAP%20Rev%20-%20Final%20Report.pdf.
(Access online on January 17, 2012.)
[95] African Union/NEPAD. (2011). *Report on the Programmatic Activities of the NEPAD Agency for the Period: January to June 2011.*
http://www.nepad.org/system/files/Activity%20report%20Jan-
June2011%20english%20Final%20version.pdf. (Accessed online January 17, 2012.)

ministers of mining from across the continent have set a new agenda called Africa Mining Vision[96], which focuses on development versus revenues. Therefore, firms in the mining sector will see a wave of changes in national agendas as well.

From the business opportunity perspective, we can also look at the AAU plan as each of the priority sectors has major projects being driven through the AU. There are a total of 76 projects within these 14 priority sectors. The following are examples of infrastructure-related projects as they might be of particular interest.

Project Title Description	Description
Kenya-Ethiopia Interconnection	Interconnect power systems of Ethiopia and Kenya with a 400 KV transmission network over a distance of 1,200 km.
Nigeria-Algeria Gas Network Connection	The project involves construction of a 4,300 km gas pipeline from Nigeria to Algeria to interconnect the gas networks of the two countries, and to export 20 billion cubic meters of gas to Europe, starting in 2016.
Water Resources Planning and Management in the Nile River Basin	Program to build a common technical foundation to facilitate integrated water resources planning and management.
Missing Links of Djibouti-Libreville Transport Corridor	Pre-feasibility studies are required for the missing links of the Djibouti to Libreville highway.

---

[96] Website for Africa Mining Vision - http://www.africaminingvision.org/

Project Title Description	Description
Maghreb Highway Project (Nouakchott – Nouadhibou, Nouakchott – Zouerate and Nouakchott-Pont Rosso)	The project involves upgrading the missing links of the Mauritanian network. It is part of the substantially complete Cairo – Dakar Corridor Highway 1 (8,636km), which involves modernization of the whole Maghreb network, including the construction of a four-lane highway from Tripoli to Casablanca (3,400 km).
Beira Port Development	Upgrading the infrastructure of Beira Port in Mozambique, including further dredging.
AfricaRail	AfricaRail is a project to rehabilitate and construct 2000 km of new railway to link the railway systems of Côte d'Ivoire, Burkina Faso, Niger, Benin, and Togo, including a train service linking the ports of Lomé and Cotonou.
NEPAD ICT Broadband Infrastructure Network (UHURUNET Submarine Cable)	The program ultimately aims to encircle the entire continent with an undersea cable, UHURUNET. The network, together with the UMOJANET, will link 54 African countries.

These projects are at different stages of development. However, many have major backers including the AU, RECs, African national governments, multilateral institutions, international development organizations, AfDB, and commercial banks. In some projects, you will find that institutions, like the African Development Bank, minimize risk by being a project sponsor. These types of projects are often the types that large companies and investors seek out as long as they are viable. However, they also afford opportunities in contracting and spinoff opportunities for smaller firms.

The key question a business or investor should ask on any of these projects is, "What opportunities does it afford him or her?" It's important to probe the possibilities – not just focus on the project itself, unless you find it to be a good fit. Think about the benefits a project might bring to your existing business or investments in Africa. Think about the spinoff opportunities that will be created as the project develops. These projects, in several instances, are chosen for their strategic value, so that means there are many ways that they can be leveraged to do business and invest in Africa. In particular, infrastructure projects are considered the most bankable of the projects at this time.

The following sections provide highlights of regional integration in North, Central, East, West, and Southern Africa from an infrastructure perspective.

North Africa

2011 turned out to be a tumultuous year for North Africa with forced regime changes in Tunisia, Egypt, and Libya, as well as unrest in Algeria. Elections have occurred in Tunisia and Egypt, and Morocco held a constitutional referendum to shift more power from the monarchy to the people. With national issues in the spotlight, the push for regional integration has taken a back seat for the moment. However, it should not be overlooked. Even before 2011, little had been done in UMA concerning integration when compared with the other RECs.

The main RECs at work in North Africa are the UMA, COMESA, and CEN-SAD. All North African countries, except for Mauritania, belong to the Greater Arab Free Trade Area (GAFTA) along with other Arab nations. GAFTA primarily focuses on agricultural and animal trade. All of the North African countries are also members of the Arab League.

The North Africa region is home to the Cairo-to-Dakar highway (spanning the Mediterranean Sea and Atlantic Ocean coasts) of the Trans African Highways system, connecting the continent. Other highways extending from North Africa into Sub-Saharan Africa include Algiers – Lagos, Tripoli – Windhoek – Cape Town, and Cairo – Gabarone – Cape Town.

ICT development in North Africa is relatively strong, particularly in Egypt. The countries struggle, like other African countries, to extend broadband access throughout each nation.

North Africa has several undersea cable systems connecting the region to international broadband. The undersea cables include Atlas Offshore, SAS-1, EA-ME-WE-4, I-ME-WE, and EIG, which offer close to 12,000 gigabits.[97]

---

[97] Source is http://manypossibilities.net/african-undersea-cables/

Central Africa[98]

This region's geography is characterized by the Congo Basin, but includes the Gulf of Guinea, starting at the bottom tip of Nigeria and extending to the top of Angola. This region is rich in oil and mineral resources.

The main RECs in this region are ECCAS and CEMAC although countries are members of other RECs, e.g., DR Congo has membership in COMESA and SADC. ECCAS growth between 1999 and 2009 averaged about 6.2%, according to the African Development Bank (AfDB).[99] These resources, particularly oil, have helped to finance non-oil activities.

Unfortunately, this region is behind other African regions in terms of infrastructure development. There are serious problems with electricity and water infrastructure, which impede the development of the private sector.

In ECCAS, nations have not fully developed mutual understanding for integration, making it more difficult to develop. Several countries like Democratic Republic of Congo are considered fragile states.

CEMAC presents a different picture, representing French-speaking Central Africa. CEMAC is already an economic and monetary union. Therefore, in terms of regional integration, CEMAC is ahead of other RECs

---

[98] Major source of information for this section is: Ranganathan, R. & Foster, V. (2011). ECCAS's Infrastructure: A Continental Perspective. *Policy Research Working Paper*, 5857. World Bank: Washington, DC. http://www-wds.worldbank.org/servlet/WDSContentServer/WDSP/IB/2011/10/25/000158349_20111025144312/Rendered/PDF/WPS5857.pdf. (Accessed online on January 8, 2012.)

[99] Another source of information for this section is: African Development Bank. (February 2011). *Central Africa Regional Integration Strategy Paper 2011-2015*. http://www.afdb.org/fileadmin/uploads/afdb/Documents/Policy-Documents/RISP%20CENTRAL%20AFRICA-ECCAS%20English%20FINAL.pdf. (Accessed online on January 8, 2012.)

who have not yet formed monetary unions, so there is great potential for CEMAC to drive development in Central Africa as discussed in the chapter, *Economic Landscape in Africa.* There are efforts to harmonize the ECCAS and CEMAC trade areas to boost inter-country trade.

Even though Central Africa is the least developed region, when compared to other regions of Africa, its strategic, geographic position lined with mineral, water, and agricultural resources raises the interest in developing this region as a preferred transit zone, according to the AfDB. Some of the regional integration donors for this region are the World Bank, African Development Bank, European Union, France, Germany, United Kingdom, and United Nations.

In terms of road infrastructure, the main Trans-African Highways that pass through Central Africa are Tripoli (Libya) – Windhoek (Namibia) – Cape Town (South Africa), Lagos (Nigeria) – Mombasa (Kenya), and Beira (Mozambique) – Lobito (Angola). The Central African Consensual Transport Master Plan (PDCT-AC)[100], which covers all forms of transport – road, rail, air, sea, and inland waterways, is a master plan being implemented for the region. It aligns with the framework of NEPAD.

---

[100] Kinfemichael, M. (2008). *Transport Infrastructure Database for Central African Sub-Region.* http://www.mcli.co.za/mcli-web/events/2008/ 23jul2008/PPP%20Workshop.pdf. (Accessed online on January 8, 2012.)

In terms of energy, ECCAS is at the center of the West African, West Southern African, East Southern African, Central African, and Central African – North African power lines, which converge at the Inga Dams in the DR Congo. Central Africa has a power pool called the Central Africa Power Pool (CAPP)[101].

Just like other African regions, ICT has had a positive impact on business in the region. However, ICT development in the region is lagging behind. To address the lack of broadband access, the Central Africa Backbone (CAB)[102] project is being sponsored by international organizations like the World Bank.

Central Africa has recently been connected to international bandwidth through the undersea cables of EACS and ACE (late 2012). The region will have access to over 10,000 gigabits of international bandwidth by the end of 2012.[103]

While regional payments systems in Central Africa are not strong, there is strong financial integration between the CEMAC countries as they have one central bank – Bank of Central African States (BEAC)[104]. In a recent announcement, BEAC and the Central Bank of West African States (WAEMU), the other economic and monetary union in Africa, will work to

---

[101] Infrastructure Consortium for Africa. *Central Africa Power Pool Overview.* (Presentation) http://media.globalbizconcierge.com/externaldocs/jan2012/ica-central-africa-power-pool-overview.ppt. (Accessed online on January 17, 2012.)
[102] Website for CAB - http://web.worldbank.org/external/projects/main? Projectid=P108368&theSitePK=40941&pagePK=64283627&menuPK=228424&piP K=73230
[103] Source: http://manypossibilities.net/african-undersea-cables/
[104] Official website - http://www.beac.int/

integrate their two financial systems. This integration can help increase competition and innovation, develop a wider pool of bankable projects, and diversify risk profiles in the two regions.

East Africa[105]

The thirteen countries of East Africa – Burundi, Comoros, Djibouti, Eritrea, Ethiopia, Kenya, Rwanda, Seychelles, Somalia, South Sudan, Sudan, Tanzania, and Uganda – have overlapping memberships of varying degrees in six of the eight RECs recognized by the AU. Thus, this makes harmonization quite complex.

The countries of Burundi, Kenya, Rwanda, Tanzania, and Uganda of the EAC have not experienced major conflict in many years, except for the election violence in Kenya in 2007 and the ongoing, but diminished attacks of the Lord's Resistance Army (LRA) in Uganda. However, the EAC, which has made tremendous strides in regional integration, is surrounded by other countries – Somalia, Sudan, Southern Sudan, Eritrea - in East Africa that have not done so well in managing conflict. In addition, the current drought conditions in the Horn of Africa and piracy off Somalia's coast are heightening concerns in the region. Moves are being made to mitigate the rise of these conflicts and the spill over into other countries, e.g., Uganda allowing U.S. troops to hunt down the remaining LRA members, Ethiopia and Kenya sending troops into Somalia to fight Al-Shabaab.

---

[105] Major source of background information for this section is: Ranganathan, R. & Foster, V. (2011). East Africa's Infrastructure: A Continental Perspective. *Policy Research Working Paper*, 5844. http://www-wds.worldbank.org/servlet/ WDSContentServer/WDSP/IB/2011/10/13/000158349_20111013121848/Rendered /PDF/WPS5844.pdf. (Accessed online on January 8, 2012.)

While there are several reasons for taking stronger offensive moves to avoid conflict spillovers, one key driver is economic development. In the case of Kenya and Ethiopia entering Somalia, both countries are involved with a newly planned development corridor called the Lamu Port – South Sudan – Ethiopia (LAPSSET) transport and economic development corridor. Some areas through which this corridor will pass have recently seen more evidence of Al-Shabaab crossing over the border, including the kidnapping of Western tourists.

This is a key corridor as it will give Ethiopia and South Sudan, two landlocked countries, access to the sea. This will help boost trade and investment potential for both countries. In addition, it will eliminate oil-rich South Sudan's reliance on the pipeline through Sudan.

Even with remaining security concerns in the region, the economic growth of the region is in full bloom. The average annual growth rate for East Africa was 6.6% from 2000 to 2009.[106] Ethiopia is expected to be one of the fastest growing economies in the world and the fastest in Africa between 2011 and 2015, according to the Economist. [107]

The main regional strategy frameworks impacting East Africa are the tripartite agreement between COMESA, EAC, and SADC and the EAC protocol framework. The major development partners in the region include the AfDB, World Bank, U.S. Agency for International Development

---

[106] Another source of information for this section is: African Development Bank. (2011). *Eastern Africa Regional Integration Strategy Paper 2011-2015.* http://www.afdb.org/fileadmin/uploads/afdb/Documents/Policy-Documents/East%20Africa%20-%20Rev%20RISP%20.pdf. (Accessed online on January 8, 2012.)

[107] The Economist. (January 6, 2011). *Africa's Impressive Growth.* http://www.economist.com/blogs/dailychart/2011/01/daily_chart. (Accessed online on January 8, 2012.)

(USAID), Norway, Holland, Germany, Denmark, European Commission (EC), Japan International Cooperation Agency (JICA), UK Department for International Development (DFID), and the multi-donor funded agency, TradeMark East Africa (TMEA).

The major transport corridors that pass through East Africa are Central, Northern, North-South, and Dar es Salaam (Tazara) corridors. Both COMESA and EAC have agreed to jointly work together on infrastructure development with a strong focus on corridor development as insufficient infrastructure is also a problem in East Africa. There is also strong programming to develop One Stop Border Posts (OSBPs) to make cross border transport more efficient and seamless.

The EAC was close to finalizing the EAC Transport Strategy and Regional Road Development Programme document in 2011. There is also an East African Railway Master Plan[108], which covers the revitalization of rail lines in all EAC countries with proposed rail lines reaching into Ethiopia, South Sudan, and the DR Congo.

In terms of energy, East Africa has various energy resources, including oil, hydro, gas, coal, and renewable energies like wind and solar. Most countries have energy policies and frameworks, but gaps in the frameworks keep more investment from occurring in the region. In 2011, the Regional Power Master Plan process was initiated to develop a regional power

---

[108] CPCS Transcom International Limited. (January 2009). *East African Railways Master Plan Study.*
http://media.globalbizconcierge.com/externaldocs/jan2012/The%20East%20African%20Railways%20Master%20Plan.pdf. (Accessed online on January 8, 2012.)

strategy for Burundi, DR Congo, Djibouti, Egypt, Ethiopia, Kenya, Rwanda, Tanzania, and Uganda.[109] Like in Central Africa, there is also a power pool called the Eastern Africa Power Pool (EAPP)[110].

In terms of ICT, East Africa is creating a second wave of mobile growth, including handsets and applications. However, broadband still significantly lags behind as it does for most of Africa. The landing of the SEACOM cable was a tremendous boost for this region in terms of Internet access and has helped drive down costs and catalyzed the local ICT industry. SEACOM[111] is currently connected to Kenya, Tanzania, Uganda, Djibouti, and Ethiopia. Rwanda's connection will provide access to Burundi and eastern DR Congo. SEACOM is also expected to make connections available to South Sudan and Somalia in the near future, which will bring coverage to almost all of East Africa.

Other undersea cable systems that have arrived in East Africa include EASSy, TEAMs, SEAS, and Lion 2 (late 2012). The region will have access to slightly over 10,000 gigabits of international bandwidth.

There is still the issue of national ICT backbone infrastructure development. The EAC has successfully developed a regional ICT backbone, which connects all five countries. However, each country in the EAC is at a different state of development in their national ICT backbone deployment.

---

[109] Website for EAPP Master Plan and Grid Code Reports -
http://www.eappool.org/eng/publications.html
[110] Website for EAPP - http://www.eappool.org
[111] Website for SEACOM – http://www.seacom.mu

In terms of financial integration, there is no regional central bank. However, there is strong cooperation between the central banks in the EAC. For example, in the last quarter of 2011 all five central banks agreed to tighten monetary policies to address the rising inflation in the region.[112]

The commercial banks, particularly in Kenya, fortunately have regional business models which means they are ahead of the opportunity presented in the region. Several Kenyan banks have established themselves in other East African countries and Pan-African banks, like Ecobank and Standard Bank, can be found in several East African countries. There are also plans to establish a regional stock market. Currently, there are stock exchanges in Kenya, Tanzania, Uganda, and Rwanda.

The EAC is working on a financial integration scheme to harmonize all countries into one financial services market.[113] Thus far, the EAC countries have been able to integrate regional payments systems and improve interconnectivity between payment card switches, which will help regional trade moving forward.

---

[112] Tentana, P. (October 17, 2011). *Central Bank Governors to Tighten Cash Flow.* http://allafrica.com/stories/201110171574.html. (Accessed online on January 8, 2012.)

[113] Wagh, S., Lovegrove, A., & Kashangaki, J. (July 2011). Scaling-Up Regional Financial Integration in the EAC. http://siteresources.worldbank.org/INTAFRREGTOPTRADE/Resources/EAC_financial_integration_07_14_11.pdf. (Accessed January 8, 2012.)

West Africa[114]

Unlike the EAC, which includes only about half of the countries in East Africa, ECOWAS includes 15 member states. However, until the last few years regional integration has been slow. It started to gain steam in 2010 with the formation of the ECOWAS Commission, as well as the development of Vision 2020[115] and a Regional Strategic Plan (2011-2015)[116].

ECOWAS has also undertaken several key initiatives to develop regional development strategy and institutions. Along with WAEMU, it developed a regional poverty reduction strategy paper (PRSP)[117], which is actually a development strategy that highlights priority sectors for the region. In this case, infrastructure, industrial, financial, trade, and agriculture sectors were noted priorities.

---

[114] Major source of information for this section is: Ranganathan, R. & Foster, V. (December 2011). *ECOWAS's Infrastructure: A Regional Perspective.* World Bank: Washington, DC. http://www-wds.worldbank.org/external/default/ WDSContentServer/WDSP/IB/2011/12/05/000158349_20111205145616/Rendered /PDF/WPS5899.pdf. (Accessed online on January 8, 2012.)
[115] Economic Community of West African States. *ECOWAS Vision 2020.* http://www.spu.ecowas.int/wp-content/uploads/2010/03/ECOWAS-VISION-2020- THEMATICTIC-PAMPHLETS-in-English.pdf. (Accessed online on January 8, 2012.)
[116] Economic Community of West African States. *Regional Strategic Plan 2011- 2015.* http://www.spu.ecowas.int/wp-content/uploads/2010/06/Final_Draft- SP_doc__24_09_10.doc. (Accessed online on January 8, 2012.)
[117] Economic Community of West African States. (December 2006). *Regional Integration for Growth and Poverty Reduction in West Africa: Strategies and Plan of Action.* http://www.ecowas.int/publications/en/macro/srrp.pdf. (Accessed online on January 17, 2012.)

ECOWAS has re-established the Federation of West African Chambers of Commerce and Industry (FEWACC) and the Federation of West African Manufacturers Association (FEWAMA), as well as established the Federation of Women and Women Entrepreneurs (ECOWAS -FEBWWE).

ECOWAS growth reached a rate of 6.7% in 2010, making it the highest of Africa's five major RECs – SADC, ECOWAS, COMESA, EAC, and ECCAS.[118] This growth has been primarily driven by Nigeria's oil and gas sector with demand for the commodities.

The agriculture sector in ECOWAS also did well in 2010 due to good rainfall. The manufacturing base, which is critical to economic development, is weak in the region.

Key partners in West Africa's integration efforts include AfDB, France, United Kingdom, United States, Germany, European Commission, Canada, World Bank, and Denmark. The financial and technical capacity assistance ranges from capacity building to agriculture to transport to peace and security.

Road transport in West Africa is amongst the weakest on the continent. One issue is that the existing structures reflect the old colonial north-south structure used to tap minerals, instead of an east-west structure that would facilitate trade inclusive of landlocked countries. The region is also looking at river transport to augment road transport.

---

[118] Another source of information for this section is: African Development Bank. (March 2011). *Regional Integration Strategy Paper for West Africa 2011-2015.* http://www.afdb.org/fileadmin/uploads/afdb/Documents/Policy-Documents/RISP%20for%20West%20Africa%20-%20REV%202.pdf. (Accessed online on January 8, 2012.)

The Trans-African highways that pass through West Africa include Dakar – Lagos, Lagos – Mombasa, Algiers – Lagos, and Dakar – Ndjamena. The Dakar – Ndjamena highway connects with the Tripoli – Windhoek – Cape Town highway. The Dakar –Lagos highway connects with the Cairo – Dakar highway.

There is an ECOWAS Railway Master Plan focused on establishing over 15 interconnections to bring together the railways that exist in 11 of the 15 ECOWAS countries. This has been hampered by rail lines being of different gauge sizes.

Port infrastructure and air transport are also weak in the region without any immediate regional strategies to address. The key issue for West African ports is that they cannot handle the depth required by large container ships. However, Maersk lines has indicated that they intend to put into service smaller container ships that will work in African ports as it has seen the greatest growth in the last few years in the Africa region.

A regional air carrier has emerged within the last few years called ASKY.[119] It flies into capital cities in both West and Central African countries, including Benin, Cameroon, Côte d'Ivoire, DR Congo, Gabon, Liberia, Nigeria, Sierra Leone, and Togo.

Energy consumption in ECOWAS is the lowest in the world with only 20% of urban households and 6% of rural households having access to electricity. The region has great energy potential from oil and gas in Nigeria, Côte d'Ivoire, and Ghana to hydro in Guinea, Benin, and Togo. The World Bank is sponsoring the development of the West African Power Pool (WAPP)[120], which has a master plan.

---

[119] Website for ASKY - http://www.flyasky.com
[120] Website for ECOWAPP - http://www.ecowapp.org/?page_id=8

The region is also suitable for solar and wind energy. The Regional Centre for Renewable Energy and Energy Efficiency (ECREEE)[121] has been established to catalyze this market.

Many West African countries have been strong on implementing ICT infrastructure, though there is no regional strategy at present. However, ECOWAS is working on a regional strategy (INTELECOM II) that will harmonize ICT policies, develop alternative broadband infrastructure, and rollout of undersea cables.

Undersea cable development, for access to international bandwidth, is well under way with MAIN ONE, SAT3/SAFE, GLO-1, WACS, and ACE (late 2012). By 2013, West Africa should have close to 17,000 gigabits of international broadband.

ECOWAS is in the process of developing both a Regional Investment Policy[122] and Regional Competition Policy[123] to harmonize across all countries. This will be a boon for businesses and investors to have a common framework in which to tap all 15 ECOWAS countries.

Financial integration is not strong in West Africa as a whole. However, there is the West African Economic and Monetary Union (WAEMU), similar to CEMAC in Central Africa. WAEMU is an economic and monetary union joining together the French-speaking countries in West Africa who share history and institutional structures. Guinea-Bissau, a

---

[121] Website for ECREEE - http://www.ecreee.org/

[122] Aremu, J. The Process of ECOWAS Investment Policies Harmonization. (Presentation) http://www.privatesector.ecowas.int/en/III/Process.pdf. (Accessed online on January 13, 2012.)

[123] Economic Community of West African States. *ECOWAS Regional Competition Policy Framework.* http://www.ecowas.int/publications/ en/actes_add_commerce/1.Regional_Competition_Policy_Framework-final-P.pdf. (Accessed online on January 8, 2012.)

Portuguese-speaking country, is the exception. WAEMU countries have a common currency, CFA Franc, and a common monetary policy, so WAEMU has been able to make more progress toward economic integration than the rest of ECOWAS.

There is an attempt to form a second monetary union made up of non-WAEMU countries called the West Africa Monetary Zone (WAMZ). WAMZ would eventually merge with WAEMU.

There is also a regional stock exchange called the Bourse Regionale des Valeurs Mobilieres (BVRM). It includes the countries of Benin, Burkina Faso, Côte d'Ivoire, Guinea-Bissau, Mali, Niger, Senegal, and Togo.

Southern Africa[124]

All Southern African countries are part of SADC, also extending to the DR Congo and Tanzania. Of the 15 member states, six are landlocked countries; two are islands; six have populations below ten million; ten economies bring in less than $10 billion annually; and there is a mix of low- and middle-income countries. The region's growth declined when the economic crisis hit in 2009, but rebounded in 2010.

There are two major channels of intense economic activity in SADC. The first one is from Durban, South Africa to Lesotho to Gauteng Province in South Africa to Zimbabwe to the Copper Belt in Zambia. The second, but less intense, channel is from northern Angola to southern DR Congo to Zambia to Tanzania.

---

[124] Major source of information for this section is: Ranganathan, R. & Foster, V. (December 2011). SADC's Infrastructure: A Regional Perspective. *Policy Research Working Paper*, 5898. World Bank: Washington, DC. http://www-wds.worldbank.org/external/default/WDSContentServer/WDSP/IB/2011/12/05/00 0158349_20111205143855/Rendered/PDF/WPS5898.pdf. (Accessed online on January 8, 2012.)

The major partners in regional integration in Southern Africa include the European Investment Bank, World Bank, U.S. Agency for International Development (USAID), United Nations Development Programme (UNDP), AfDB, Development Bank of South Africa (DBSA), European Union (EU), United Kingdom, Germany, Norway, Sweden, Finland, Denmark, Austria, and Japan.

While Southern Africa's infrastructure is weak in places it is significantly better than other African regions. The Trans-African highways that are in Southern Africa include Tripoli – Windhoek – Cape Town, Cairo – Gabarone – Cape Town, and Beira – Lobito. It is also home to spatial development corridors built around the surface corridors, including Maputo, Walvis Bay, and North-South.

The North-South corridor is the main trade artery, starting in South Africa and passing through Botswana, DR Congo, Malawi, Zambia, and Zimbabwe. The link corridors include Lobito (Angola), Maputo, (Mozambique), Beira (Mozambique), Nacala (Mozambique), and Mtwara (Tanzania). The regional road network on the North-South corridor is well-developed and mostly paved.

Southern Africa's rail system is extensive with over 50,000 km of rail, compared to about 19,000 km in North Africa and around 10,000 km in other African regions. The rail system competes directly with road transport. The gap in this system is crossing borders due to lack of coordination between nations.

With ports and air transport, Southern Africa also does well compared with other Africa regions. The key port is Durban in South Africa with Dar es Salaam considered to be a distant second. SADC has the largest air transport market with Johannesburg as the hub.

Southern Africa also has more power generation capacity than any other region in Africa. However, as evidenced by the power shortages in South Africa from 2007 on, capacity is not enough even with low access levels to power by households in the region. This is likely due to the mining and industrial operations in the region, which require large capacities, particularly in South Africa. Demand is expected to increase at least 40% in the next decade. The Southern Africa Power Pool (SAPP)[125] has been established to develop a regional trade market for power.

In ICT, Southern Africa is also well developed compared to the other regions with South Africa being the most connected and capacitized country. Over 100% of the population has mobile phones and the country has the highest international bandwidth available on the continent. However, the cost of ICT is still relatively high.

Even with better infrastructure overall, it is anticipated that better infrastructure will contribute a little over 3% to economic growth per capita. Shared infrastructure to achieve economies of scale is very important for the regional development of SADC. As noted earlier, it has several landlocked countries and small economies.

SADC also has a master infrastructure plan in place.[126] It is estimated at over $100 billion and developing Public Private Partnerships (PPPs) to execute it is a significant attraction for businesses and investors.

---

[125] Website for SAPP - http://www.sapp.co.zw
[126] Southern Africa Development Community. (September 2009). *SADC Infrastructure: Development Status Report for Council and Summit.* http://www.sadc.int/cms/uploads/K-7543%20RTFP%20SADC%20 Infrastructure%20brochure_English_V11_LR.pdf. (Accessed online on January 8, 2012.)

In terms of financial integration, the process has been slow. Each country has its own central bank and the monetary union deadline is looming in 2016.

Like in East Africa, a few commercial banks have adapted a regional business model, which helps with trade and places them in good position when regional integration does occur. Standard Bank has a strong presence in SADC. SADC stock markets are also looking to integration.

COMESA and Tri-Partite Agreement

The 19 member states of COMESA include countries from North, Central, East, and Southern Africa. Therefore, there is strong geographical overlap with the EAC and SADC. Like the EAC and SADC, COMESA also has an infrastructure master plan.

The key movement with COMESA is the tri-partite agreement with the EAC and SADC to create a free trade area between 2014 and 2016. In doing so, there would be a free trade area of 26 countries, representing over 50% of the GDP and population of the African continent.

As each of the three RECs is working on integration within their boundaries, all of them are also working for integration at the tri-partite level. That means that for every regional master plan, there is one being harmonized to represent the tri-partite.

International Organization Membership and Multilateral Agreements

While regional integration is being driven on the continent, businesses and investors also need to be cognizant that each African country, each REC, and the AU may have agreements with international organizations, as well as multilateral and bilateral agreements with other countries and regional economic groups. The harmonization process involves a complex network of institutions and governments, so it will take a while.

Most, if not all African countries, have membership or observer status in the International Monetary Fund, African Development Bank, World Bank, World Trade Organization, United Nations, etc. In addition, African countries are increasing their bi-lateral trade and investment agreements with other countries. This is not about Africa becoming a single, unified economic region, but about Africa becoming a major global economic, trade, business, and investment pole like Europe, the United States, and China.

A positive note is that institutions in the RECs, the AU, international bodies, and multilateral/bilateral agreements represent key ecosystems that businesses and investors can tap to further opportunities for themselves on the continent at least from an information resource perspective.

Conclusion

Regional integration is key to increasing Africa's share of global trade, investment, and economic activity. The system to unify Africa as an economic union started decades ago, but is now making significant progress even amid major challenges.

For businesses and investors, this will mean larger markets, common frameworks for doing business and investing in the region, free movement of capital, labor, and resources, etc. While not a centralized country like China or a unified union like the United States, integration should mean significant benefits to both foreign and domestic firms.

A simple strategy for businesses and investors to prepare for taking advantage of regional integration is to set up in one of the major economic hubs in which a small footprint can be established and develop a regional business model like African commercial banks and multinational firms have done. It's important to not only think about the first market of operation from the start, but the regional market.

Sectors & Markets

5

Natural Resources in Africa

Hartmut Sieper

Africa is blessed with an abundance of natural resources. Commodities as an asset class for investors started a major bull market about ten years ago. Since then, this trend has increased in strength, despite a temporary break in 2008/2009 during the preliminary climax of the world financial crisis. It can be expected that the secular bull market in commodities will continue for at least the next ten years. Accelerated population growth and the dynamic development of emerging economies, especially China, and many frontier markets are the major driving forces on the demand side, while limited resources of many commodities and higher energy prices are the most important factors on the supply side. The gap will continue to exist even though the major recession, or even depression, of the Western economies might alleviate the pressure for a while.

While the developed world has been living beyond its (financial) means for several decades, the opposite is true for Africa. The continent has not lived up to its potential, because of both internal and external influences. This is subject to change. Major shifts that can be observed in the world will clearly allow Africa to realize its catch-up potential. Some of them are mentioned in the opening chapter while others are described in *Redefining Business in the New Africa*. Existing yet dormant wealth will be released and activated, and new wealth will be created. Business people that are willing to invest now will be able to benefit tremendously in the future.

In this respect, the natural resources of Africa will play a key role. The continent is incredibly rich because it is endowed with a large variety of natural resources. Some resources are already known while others are still to be discovered. As Africa is still heavily under explored, a lot of surprises and some big findings can be assumed for the future. However, this will not happen automatically. A lot of investments have to be made to uncover the hidden resources and to unleash their economic potential. Geologists, engineers, financiers, and many workers are needed.

The universal law of sowing and reaping that is described in the Bible and many other pieces of world literature should be respected. Only those that are sowing into Africa now, i.e. by doing research, employing people, sending managers, founding local companies, installing production facilities, building networks, and investing money, will be able to reap the fruits that will grow over time based on their initial measures and ongoing activities. Companies that just want to sell their products and services without a willingness to invest, which means they want to reap without having sown, will not succeed. One cannot grow rich in the New Africa by focusing on short-term success and immediate returns only. This is not only true for the exploration and mining businesses, but also for agriculture, manufacturing, and service industries.

New Ways to Wealth

As a former investment banker and stock market trader, I learned to understand the importance of sound, long-term strategies and sustainable business models. I am deeply convinced that business is changing. It is changing much faster and more dramatically than the majority of market players realize.

A new understanding of wealth, and how it will be created, released, built, leveraged, protected, stewarded, and transferred, will be needed if you not only want to financially survive the challenges of the coming years, but to prosper despite economic and financial turmoil.[127] Huge paradigm shifts are evolving and influencing business and investments, as well as all other spheres of life. In order to become successful in Africa, it is of utmost importance to fully understand the impact of the changing rules and shifting paradigms at an early stage and to act proactively.

Natural resources will still have a role to play in this new paradigm. So, the following sections will introduce you to Africa's natural resources, distinguishing resources above the ground and resources under the ground. Above the ground assets include renewable energies such as hydro power, solar energy, and biomass. Tropical rain forests and woodlands also represent high value.

Unused land can be transferred to arable land, which is a primary process of wealth creation. Please see chapter 6, "*Real Estate*," for further information.

Forests
Many different kinds of forests can be found in Africa. According to the Food and Agriculture Organisation (FAO)[128], Africa's forests and woodlands can be classified into nine general categories including; tropical rain forests, tropical moist forests, tropical dry forests, tropical shrubs,

---

[127]In 2013, look for our new book called "Warring for Wealth" to learn about new wealth strategies.
[128] Food and Agriculture Organisation. http://www.fao.org/forestry/en/. (Accessed online on January 23, 2012.)

tropical mountain forests, subtropical humid forests, subtropical dry forests, subtropical mountain forests and plantations.

There are two regions in Africa that have large resources of tropical rain forests that can be used for wood production:

- The Congo Basin in Central Africa, comprising of areas of the Democratic Republic of Congo, Republic of Congo, Gabon, Equatorial Guinea, and parts of Cameroon and Central African Republic.
- The West African countries of Guinea Bissau, Liberia, Sierra Leone, and parts of Guinea, Côte d'Ivoire, and Ghana.

North and South of these areas of tropical rain forests there are zones where different kinds of less dense forests exist. While most areas in Northern Africa are mostly overused by a growing population, vast areas of the thinly populated countries south of the Congo basin, e.g. Angola, Zambia, and Mozambique, are virgin territory for forestry and agriculture.

Most of the other countries in Africa have little or no forests. In South Africa, less than 2% of its land is covered by dense forests. Some reforested areas are used for commercial wood production. Deforestation is a major problem in many countries, as wood and charcoal is being used as fuel for cooking by many low-income people. Deforested areas are exposed to erosion and land degradation. The following chart depicts the forest areas (including woodlands) as a percentage of total land area.

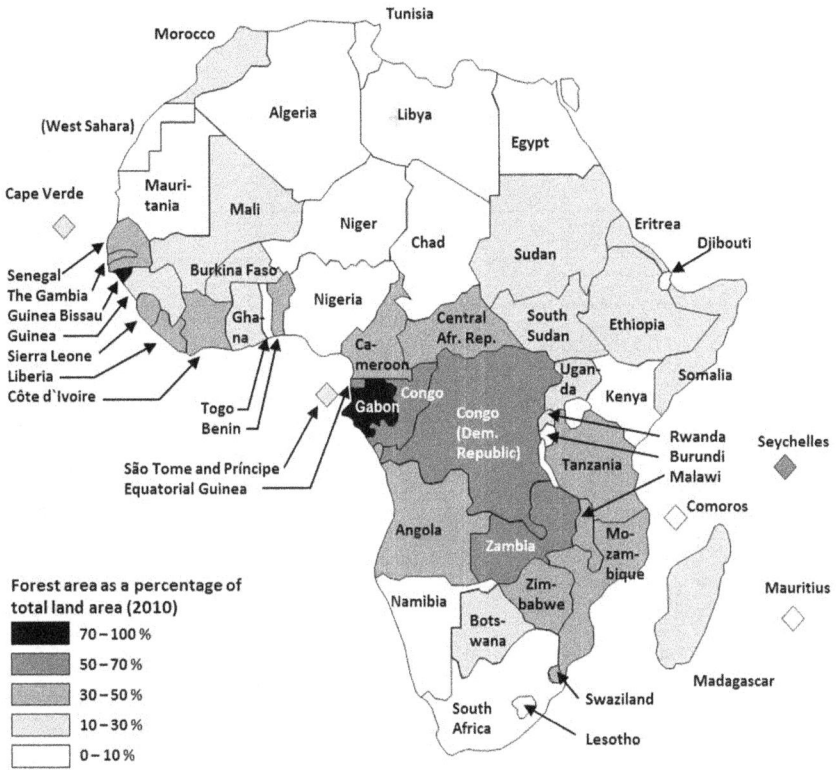

Tunisia
Morocco
Algeria
Libya
(West Sahara)
Egypt
Cape Verde
Mauri-
tania
Mali
Niger
Chad
Eritrea
Sudan
Djibouti
Senegal
The Gambia
Guinea Bissau
Guinea
Sierra Leone
Liberia
Côte d'Ivoire
Burkina Faso
Nigeria
Gha-
na
Central
Afr. Rep.
South
Sudan
Ethiopia
Ca-
meroon
Togo
Benin
Gabon
Congo
Congo
(Dem.
Republic)
Ugan-
da
Kenya
Somalia
Rwanda
Burundi
Malawi
Seychelles
São Tome and Príncipe
Equatorial Guinea
Tanzania
Comoros
Angola
Mo-
zam-
bique
Zambia
Mauritius
Zim-
babwe
Namibia
Bots-
wana
Madagascar
Swaziland
South
Africa
Lesotho

**Forest area as a percentage of
total land area (2010)**

- 70 – 100 %
- 50 – 70 %
- 30 – 50 %
- 10 – 30 %
- 0 – 10 %

Source: Trans Africa Invest

In absolute terms, the following countries have the largest forest cover:[129]

Country	Total forest (in 1,000 hectares - 2000)
Democratic Republic of Congo	135,207
Angola	69,756
Sudan	61,627
Tanzania	38,811
Zambia	31,246
Mozambique	30,601
Cameroon	23,858
Central African Republic	22,907
Congo	22,060
Gabon	21,826

There are several opportunities in the timber value chain. First is logging and exporting. However, countries are beginning to prohibit exporting of raw timber. When the current President of Gabon, Ben Ali Bongo, came to office, he stopped exports of raw timber in order to develop a process industry in the country. Recently, the Gabonese government established a special economic zone at Nkok for the purpose of producing wood products. The National Wood Company of Gabon is building a processing facility for timber. So, processing will be a growing industry on the continent, pushed in part by government regulations altering the existing value chain.

---

[129] United Nations Environment Programme. (2006). Africa Environment Outlook 2. http://www.unep.org/DEWA/Africa/docs/en/aeo-2/chapters/aeo-2_ch06_FORESTS_AND_WOODLANDS.pdf. (Accessed online on January 22, 2012.)

Also, as reforestation projects are key elements of environmental programs in many African nations, they offer excellent opportunities for long-term investors. Growing wood is an attractive natural dividend. In addition, in the short to medium term, re-forestation projects can be developed as climate change initiatives, which earn revenue from carbon exchanges. The Nile Basin Reforestation Project, an initiative of Uganda's National Forestry Authority (NFA), is doing just that while creating local jobs.

On the whole, as wood reserves are limited and forested areas are still in decline in Africa while its population is rapidly expanding, it is safe to say that wood prices and the value of forests as a commercial asset will appreciate over time.

Water

Africa holds about 9% of the world's water, according to the FAO.[130] However, North Africa and the Sudano-Sahelian region only contribute 1.2% and 4.1% to Africa's total share of world water resources. These regions include the Sahara, which is the world's largest desert; and some dry countries at the Horn of Africa (Somalia, Djibouti, and Eritrea). Other relatively arid areas exist in Namibia, Botswana, and parts of South Africa. The following table highlights the top ten countries in terms of total natural, renewable water sources[131] between 2008 and 2012.

---

[130] Food and Agriculture Organisation. (2003). *Review of World Water Resources by Country.* ftp://ftp.fao.org/agl/aglw/docs/wr23e.pdf. (Accessed online on January 20, 2012.)

[131] Definition of Total Natural, Renewable Water Sources can be found at http://www.fao.org/nr/water/aquastat/data/popups/itemDefn.html?id=4189.

Country	Total Natural, Renewable Water Resources (in km3/year)
DR Congo	1,283
Congo Brazzaville	832
Madagascar	337
Nigeria	286.2
Cameroon	285.5
Liberia	232
Guinea	226
Mozambique	217.1
Gabon	164
Sierra Leone	160

Hydropower

Africa has quite a number of big streams that have massive potential for being used as a source of hydropower. The Congo River is the third largest river in the world by volume of water discharged. If the ambitious Grand Inga project were ever realized, it would bring the maximum output of the facility to 39,000 megawatts, twice that of China's Three Gorges Dam. In November 2011, the project was reactivated after South Africa's President Jacob Zuma signed a memorandum of understanding with the DR Congo's President Joseph Kabila for South Africa to facilitate the funding and construction of the Grand Inga Dam. The outcome is still vague, as the project will cost a lot of money (approx. $80 billion, conservatively estimated), and South Africa's Eskom must get together with its Congolese counterpart to agree on how the project will be implemented.[132]

---

[132] Allison, S. (November 16, 2011). Africa: The Grand Inga Dam – Can it Really Happen? *DailyMaverick*. http://allafrica.com/stories/201111160521.html. (Accessed online on February 2, 2012.)

The Zambezi River also has more potential to generate hydro power. This is in addition to the existing Kariba Dam at the border of Zambia and Zimbabwe and the Cahora Bassa Dam in Mozambique.

The hydropower potential of the Blue Nile, which is one of two major tributaries of the Nile, the world's longest river, is enormous. Ethiopia has announced that it will construct the Grand Millennium Dam, a controversial multibillion-dollar dam that could supply more than 5,000 megawatts of electricity for itself and its neighbors.[133] Together with the Gibe III project, another large dam on the country's Omo River that is currently under construction, Ethiopia will be able to become a major power hub for Africa. It will then become a net exporter of electric power, supplying its neighbors Kenya and Uganda with excess energy.

However, the new dam projects challenge an existing water agreement from 1929 that gives Egypt and Sudan, now presumably including South Sudan, rights over all of the Nile's water. Egypt, which is totally dependent on the Nile, is threatened by the vision of receiving less water. It has yet to be seen how this conflict of interest will play out.

Finally, there are some huge lakes in East Africa with big economic potential. Lake Tanganyika, which is 673 kilometers long, is the second deepest lake in the world and the second largest in terms of sweet water volume (after Lake Baykal). Lake Malawi is known for its biodiversity; it contains more fish species than any other lake. Lake Kivu, at the border of

---

[133] Than, K. (July 13, 2011). Ethiopia Moves Forward with Massive Nile Dam Project. *National Geographic News.* http://news.nationalgeographic.com/news/ 2011/07/110713-/ethiopia-south-sudan-nile-dam-river-water. (Accessed online on February 2, 2012.)

Rwanda and the DR Congo, has huge amounts of methane gas that could be utilized for power generation. The economic potential of these lakes are - unlike Lake Victoria - still largely untapped.

Other than as a source of power, water, like land, represents the essence of what is needed to sustain life. Therefore, there is also huge potential in providing access to clean drinking water. As the world's population grows, demand for water may ultimately make it a tradable commodity as in the case with Lesotho, which supplies water to its neighbor South Africa.

Natural Beauty

Wilderness areas with wildlife represent a unique asset that can only be found in Africa. The travel and tourism industry is exploiting these areas in East Africa and Southern Africa already, but there is still huge potential. Africa has 16% of the earth's land mass, but records only 3.2% of international tourism receipts (i.e. in-country expenditure by foreign tourists).[134] Tourism development is skewed regionally in Africa. While North Africa (including Egypt) is attracting more than half of all tourism receipts, Sub-Saharan Africa is still lags behind.

Madagascar has a unique fauna and flora, with the majority of the species being endemic. There is a great potential for additional tourism once the necessary infrastructure (roads, accommodation, services, and flight connections) is put in place. However, developing this infrastructure will require a lot of investments that cannot be managed by the State of

---

[134] Tokyo International Conference on African Development. (December 2009). *Overview of Tourism to Africa.* http://www.ticad.net/documents/Overview%20of%20Tourism%20to%20Africa%20with%20reference%20to%20the%20Asian%20and%20Japanese%20outbound%20markets.pdf. (Accessed online on January 31, 2012.)

Madagascar, which is among the poorest countries in the world. Support by the private sector is urgently needed for exploiting these opportunities.

A long chain of wildebeest in the world famous Ngorongoro Crater, Tanzania. Source: Wikipedia

In East Africa, Kenya is a well-established tourist destination with trained personnel. Future potential still exists in the less known yet attractive areas of the country, i.e. the Great Rift Valley. Tanzania is known to have more animals and less traffic in their national parks than their counterparts on the Kenyan side, offering higher upside potential. The Great lakes along the rift valley (i.e. Lake Victoria, Lake Kivu, Lake Tanganyika, and Lake Malawi) offer good potential as well.

In Southern Africa, Zimbabwe is a prime destination that has yet to reclaim its former share in the travel and tourism business. Before the land deteriorated significantly, it was ranked 2nd after South Africa. When I visited the second highest waterfall in the world in the Eastern highlands of Zimbabwe on a weekend trip two years ago, I did not notice any tourists other than myself and my companions. Our guide told me that the 800-meters high, almost vertical, wall has not yet been climbed by mountaineers. This has so much potential as a tourist site!

However, entrepreneurs that want to engage in the travel and tourism sector, i.e. by operating a resort hotel, running a lodge, acting as a tour operator, should be aware of the risks. If the economic and financial crisis in the industrialized nations deepens, less tourist arrivals can be anticipated which will negatively affect many businesses. On the other side, Asian tourists represent an attractive and fast growing target group that is still neglected by many players. This consumer base might even over compensate a possible decrease of incoming tourists from the U.S. and Europe. Entrepreneurs and tourism managers who can address the specific needs of Asian tourists successfully will be able to excel. Domestic tourism is also a potential market as Africans still visit their tourist sites far less than foreigners on average

Minerals

Africa is known the world over for its mineral, gas, and oil resources. The following table gives an overview of the most important metals and minerals that can be found in Africa.[135]

Mineral	Main Producing Countries	Other Producing Countries	Countries with Potential
Platinum	South Africa	Zimbabwe	
Gold	South Africa Ghana Tanzania Mali	DR Congo Burkina Faso Côte d'Ivoire Egypt and many more	Nigeria Liberia Sierra Leone
Bauxite	Guinea	Ghana	Madagascar
Diamonds	Botswana DR Congo South Africa Namibia	Angola Liberia Sierra Leone Central Africa Republic	Zimbabwe
Copper	Zambia	South Africa DR Congo	
Chromite	South Africa	Zimbabwe	Madagascar
Manganese	South Africa	Gabon, Ghana	
Cobalt	DR Congo	Zambia, Morocco	
Tantalum	DR Congo	Rwanda, Uganda	
Phosphate	Morocco	Tunisia	Togo Niger Uganda
Coal	South Africa	Botswana, Zimbabwe	Mozambique

[135] Source is Trans Africa Invest – www.trans-africa-invest.com.

Mineral	Main Producing Countries	Other Producing Countries	Countries with Potential
Oil	Nigeria Angola Algeria Libya	Sudan, South Sudan, DR Congo, Republic of Congo, Gabon, Equatorial Guinea	Namibia, Kenya, Tanzania, Uganda, Côte d'Ivoire, Somalia, São Tomé and Principe
Natural Gas	Algeria Egypt	Nigeria Libya	

The following table gives an overview of some important resource-rich African countries and their major resources.[136]

Country	Main Resources	% of World Production[137]	Resources Rank Worldwide
Algeria	Oil	2 %	17
Angola	Oil Diamonds		15
Dem. Rep. of Congo	Tantalum Cobalt Copper Gold Diamonds	17 % 40 % 3 %	
Democratic Republic. Rep. of Congo	Tantalum Cobalt Copper Gold Diamonds	13 % 40 %	
Ghana	Gold		8
Guinea	Bauxite	20 %	1

---

[136] Ibid.

[137] Source is MBendi Information Services - http://www.mbendi.com.

Country	Main Resources	% of World Production[137]	Resources Rank Worldwide
Liberia	Iron Ore		
Libya	Oil	2 %	20
Mali	Gold		
Morocco	Phosphate	75 %	1
Nigeria	Oil	3 %	12
South Africa	Gold Platinum Chromite Manganese Coal	 75 % (2010) 42 % 15 % 4 %	1 1 1 (70 %) 1 (80 %) 5 (4 %)
Tanzania	Gold		
Zambia	Copper	4 %	8
Zimbabwe	Platinum Chromite		3

Investments in Mineral Resources in Africa

Investors and business people can benefit from mineral resources in Africa in two ways. One option is to buy stocks of resource companies. The other option is to directly invest into exploration or mining projects. Both possibilities can be very rewarding yet include many risks.

Portfolio Investing in Exploration and Mining Companies

The majority of listed companies focused on mining in Africa are international corporations with headquarters and stock listings in Johannesburg, London, Toronto, or Sydney. Only very few of them are listed on African stock exchanges.

Depending on the life cycle of an exploration company, analysts focus on different parameters. For example for early-stage exploration companies, the quality of the company very much depends on having experienced managers with proven track records on board and the amount of cash, as they have not generally found resources to mine.

The more advanced the producing company becomes, the less important the financial strength and the quality of management is considered by financial analysts. Instead, they focus more on key figures like enterprise value divided by production, price earnings ratio, price cash flow ratio, and dividend yield.

Artisanal and Small-Scale Mining

Artisanal and small-scale mining (ASM), which is prevalent in Africa, exploits a wide range of minerals, for example gold, copper, tantalum, tin, and diamonds. It sustains basic livelihoods for the miners and their families. Their contribution to national economies is still small, but has the potential to become much more.

Most small mines could greatly increase their output and profitability if the miners had access to financial and technical support. Western investors can help convert ASMs into viable operating enterprises by offering such support. By bridging that gap, investors create win-win scenarios for all stakeholders. Many miners would be happy to offer participation in their mines by entering into joint venture agreements with serious and honest entrepreneurs and investors.

Different permits, or licenses, are required for starting exploration or mining activities. This is handled differently by each country. In most cases, subsequent licenses have to be applied for, each consecutive license having more rights, covering less acreage, and becoming more expensive. For example, the Ghanaian Mining and Minerals Law, which was passed in

1986 lists three types of license that are applied equally to Ghanaians and foreigners except for the provisions relating to artisanal mining and exploitation of construction minerals, which is reserved for Ghanaians. The following chart[138] provides highlights of these licenses.

License type	Purpose	Area	Duration
Reconnaissance license	Regional exploration, not including drilling (remote sensing only)	No limitation on size	12 months renewable
Prospecting license	Search for minerals and valuation	150 km²	2 years renewable with reduction of area to not less than half
Mining license	Extraction of minerals	50 km² per lease up to maximum of 150 km² per company	30 years renewable

Mineral Sector Risk Assessment

Business people that want to engage or invest in exploration and mining projects in Africa, are advised to do as much research as possible before they take the first step.

When it comes to gold, a psychological mechanism has to be considered carefully. The bright, shining, yellow metal has fascinated man over several thousand years. Many people become greedy when they get close to gold. If you have to assess gold mining projects, wishful thinking is

---

[138] Source is MBendi Information Services -
http://www.mbendi.com/indy/ming/af/gh/p0005.htm.

another common trap. Gold mines can be very tempting as they hold the promise of getting rich quickly. It is very helpful in such situations to have check lists readily available and to complete them tenaciously.

When you assess a project in the mineral sector, you should be able to deal with the following risk parameters: commercial, financial, counterparty, reputational, social, political, location, health and safety, environmental, construction, strategic, operational, and technical risk.

For example, commercial risk can be covered by asking the following questions:

- Is the project commercially viable?
- Is the grade of metal in the ore big enough for covering all costs and allowing a considerable surplus?
- Is the business case robust enough that the venture remains cash flow positive even if the metal's price decreases significantly?

I honestly believe that the price of gold will continue to climb over the next several years, as the economic and financial crisis will unfold its full potential. Access to gold mining assets will be sought after by many banks, hedge funds, institutional investors, and high net worth individuals. Parabolic price advances that usually occur at the end of great bull markets have not yet been observed.

However, when the average person starts buying gold mining stocks, you should think of selling and moving to another asset class. This will still take some time before this tipping point will be reached. Investing in natural resources will remain to be one of the best asset classes that you can have exposure to, for many years to come.

The New Multipolar World Involved in Africa's Resources

The first big race for exploiting Africa's natural resources happened when ruthless slave traders from Portugal, Spain, Great Britain, France, and some other nations caught young African men and women and "exported" them to the colonies in the New World. The next dark episode started in the late 19th century when the above-mentioned European powers, including Germany, Italy, and Belgium began to colonize Africa and took large quantities of natural resources from the continent.

The enclave structure of the African mining sector must be seen as a colonial legacy. Most of the mining industry has very weak links with the rest of the national economy leading to structural deficiencies. For example, railway lines were built to connect major mining areas with the next port, instead of connecting the large cities with each other.

The chase for resources continued after the colonies became independent in the 1960s and 1970s. Soon after the great bear market in commodities began in 1980, the chase cooled down.

At the beginning of the 21st century, when the new super cycle of commodities started to unfold, foreign powers again turned their attention toward Africa. When the People's Republic of China "discovered" Africa as a valuable source of commodities, Chinese state companies invested heavily in resource-rich countries like Angola, Sudan, Chad, Zambia, and Nigeria. Their primary focus was, and still is, on oil, but soon other commodities like copper, cobalt, and coal captured their interest as well. China quickly became the most dominant foreign player in Africa.

Whenever U.S. or European companies want to get access to large infrastructure projects in Africa, they have to compete with Chinese corporations. The problem is that it is not possible to successfully compete with the Chinese on price.

However, the predominance of Chinese players in Africa is about to change. Large emerging countries, such as India and Brazil, are expanding in Africa's mineral resource sector. Vedanta Resources from India has massively invested in the Copper Belt in Zambia while the Brazilian company, Vale do Rio Doce, and the Indian Tata Steel group are competing for the gigantic coal resources in Mozambique.

Land grabbing has become a concern in the agricultural sector. Asian countries are looking for huge pieces of arable land that they can cultivate and export the produce to their own countries. Dominant players in this neo-colonial game are South Korea, China, the United Arab Emirates, Qatar, Saudi Arabia, Libya, Pakistan, and India. The preferred target countries are Sudan, South Sudan, Ethiopia, and Madagascar, but Tanzania, Zambia, Zimbabwe, the DR Congo, Cameroon, and Liberia are also seeing significant interest for their land resources.

However, not every major project involved in huge land deals is grabbing for land. These projects, if implemented correctly, can help local economies, create jobs, and even serve the local markets. In doing so, project developers are more likely to create sustainable ventures, as has been the case with Feronia in the DR Congo. Feronia has consistently operated there for 100 years.

The increasing demand from foreign countries and multinational companies for natural resources in Africa is boosting the opportunities for governments of resource-rich African countries to negotiate more favorable licensing and tax regimes. Unprecedented demand, driven by large developing-country industrialization, particularly China, will continue to create an anxious global environment over security and reliability of metals and minerals supply.

It can be hoped that the intensifying competition as the new normal of a multipolar world will lead to introducing and strengthening policies of fair mining and farming in Africa. This would create another big shift in Africa that must be considered by entrepreneurs and investors.

Conclusion

Africa is tremendously rich in natural resources above and under the ground. Export of raw materials, especially crude oil, gold, diamonds, and platinum, has been and still is the major driving force of the continent's long-term economic upswing. However, the best is yet to come, because many regions are still deeply underexplored, allowing the opportunity for mining companies and oil firms to make further discoveries. As governments of African countries are trying to renegotiate better deals with international resource companies, it can be anticipated that a high number of resource projects will remain in Africa, benefiting local communities and businesses which will lead to better living conditions and prosperity.

The same is true for resources above the ground like forests and water. The natural resources of Africa are a major key to creating, releasing, building, leveraging, and preserving wealth - not only for Africa and her people, but also for bold and responsible companies and individuals from the developed world that will help develop these resources.

6

Real Estate in Africa

Hartmut Sieper

Real estate is one of the major asset classes for the creation and preservation of wealth, and Africa offers a host of opportunities in the real estate sector. This is especially true if you compare the current situation and outlook of African markets with the developed markets of the Western world. In order to fully understand the competitive advantage of African property markets, we should start with a global overview.

Since 2007, investors have experienced dramatic price changes in stocks and bonds, currencies and derivative instruments, commodities, and real estate. The major themes for 2012 and thereafter are:

- Changes in risk perception of major asset classes
- Hard assets are sought after by smart investors, while financial assets (paper assets) will be disposed of
- Rising concerns of market participants, politicians, and regulatory authorities that financial markets may become dysfunctional
- Development of a multipolar world with increasing divergence between industrialized countries, emerging markets, and developing nations regarding economic growth, financial health, and change of global relevance
- Intensified attempts to "manage" the international debt crisis by treading water and tackling the symptoms rather than by solving the problems
- Negative real interest rates in the developed world that undermine wealth preservation

- International diversification of assets in order to mitigate country and currency risks
- The safety of investments has decreased, e.g., bond markets, because risk has surged.
- On a macro scale: more control and regulation versus protection of financial, economic, and personal freedom
- Boom and bust cycles: What is next?

Asset Classes under Attack

In the current, unstable environment for financial markets, more and more people are looking for safe havens, and fleeing risky asset classes in favor of financial instruments that are considered risk free.

The dilemma is that many traditional safe havens have lost their aura of being a secure place for building and storing wealth. U.S. property prices started to collapse in 2007, leading to the subprime crisis which marked the first stage of the financial troubles from which we are yet to emerge. The banking crisis was the second stage that commenced in 2008 and culminated with the default of the U.S. investment bank, Lehman Brothers. The subsequent deep recession and collapsing commodity prices in 2009 can be seen as the third stage. After a temporary respite in 2010, the fourth stage unfolded when the financial problems of several European countries triggered the sovereign debt crisis, and the Euro crisis followed suit.

There are many indications that the fifth and the sixth stages will be a new banking crisis which will be greater and more dangerous than the last, and the breakup of the European Monetary Union is a potential. Some banks from Italy, France, Austria, and Germany with less capital may have to be nationalized if part of sovereign debts of Greece and other Southern

European countries cannot be cancelled, or if a bank default were to cause a sudden crash of the derivatives market as counterparty risk becomes relevant with immediate effect.

The writing on the wall cannot be overlooked. A silent bank run is in full motion in Greece and has started in Italy, too. Italy represents the second largest sovereign bond market in the world. The country is too big to be bailed out, even with the financial help of the combined Euro zone countries. This would send shock waves around the globe. However, Italy is not the only candidate for a default. 8 trillion of sovereign bonds of the most important industrialized countries need to be refinanced by 2014. On the other hand, bond markets have already priced in Greece's sovereign default, and the majority of market participants are waiting for Greece to abandon the euro and return to the drachma.

Therefore, many investors and politicians are hoping that the European Central Bank will start unlimited quantitative easing (newspeak for printing money). If that happens, it would be just a matter of time before the exploding money supply triggered major inflation. The excess money would have to leave the banking sector (which has so far proven to be a bottomless pit for absorbing it), and enter the real economy. Once the circulation of money finally accelerates, the onset of hyperinflation would be inevitable.

The financial world has been turned upside down. We are experiencing the worst and most dangerous crisis since the Great Depression of the 1930s. Authors of some famous financial newsletters have already heralded this as the "Greater Depression" for the developed economies.

Within the space of only two years, formerly "risk-free" assets became first "a little risky" and very soon "toxic." The speed of deterioration is unprecedented in the history of financial markets. In addition, developments on the markets and decision making processes in the political arena are so intertwined that even the most talented analysts are unable to give reliable forecasts. The lifecycle of the validity of official announcements, political decisions, and financial statements has shortened dramatically.

Uncertainty and fear that have become the new normality among investment strategists, portfolio managers, and traders have now reached the man in the street. Even the average person is starting to ponder which value will last and which will not. Hard assets come to mind: having something solid that will withstand the storms ahead is becoming desirable for many ordinary people.

The Investment Case for Real Estate

This would normally be a good environment for rising property prices, making real estate an attractive economic sector and preferred asset class for institutional and individual investors.

However, most real estate projects in the West are highly leveraged, as they are financed with very little equity, if any at all. Instead, they are used as collateral for huge loans from mortgage banks. A special situation can be observed in Austria and Hungary, where most private real estate investors have financed their houses with foreign exchange loans, mostly denominated in Swiss Francs and Japanese Yen. Both currencies have appreciated against the euro and the Hungarian forint, respectively, thus increasing the amount to be paid back.

Properties that are debt financed are not considered a hard asset, but rather a financial asset. Only debt-free property used for one's own residence can be seen as a hard asset that preserves value for an individual or family.

In addition, national economies facing recession will see a shrinking of private household income and falling purchasing power, leading to lower property prices. Rising interest rates (which may result from falling bond markets) will put additional pressure on the owners of highly leveraged property. If they are forced to sell into a falling market, prices will fall further. Foreclosures become inevitable thus further fuelling the vicious circle. Increasing supply and lack of demand will derail the market as a whole. On a macro level, the negative demographic trend of rapidly ageing populations in Europe, Japan, and China will not support the demand side of the equation. This indicator will remain negative for decades to come.

The development of continuously falling property prices that was experienced in the United States (despite record low interest rates) could well be repeated in parts of Europe. Real estate markets in Spain, Ireland, and the United Kingdom are heavily exposed to such chain reactions.

In a nutshell, investing in real estate is not necessarily a good idea, at least if you live in the United States or Europe.

The Investment Case for Real Estate in Africa

The situation in rapidly expanding emerging and frontier markets is, however, very different from the gloomy scenario described above. Macroeconomic growth translates into higher national, corporate, and personal income. On a macro level, both rapidly rising population and the major trend towards urbanization are leading to high demand for residential housing, especially in the cities.

Many countries in Africa are experiencing a construction boom that is set to last for years to come. High pent-up demand for residential housing and rising incomes of the rapidly growing middle class offer an interesting playing field for property developers. The demand for office buildings and new city hotels will remain strong on the back of solid macroeconomic growth and the rising interest of international companies in accessing African markets.

Inflation rates in most African countries are significantly higher than in the developed world. Inflationary periods are generally good for the appreciation of real estate prices.

The price level for buying or renting properties depends on a broad range of factors, the most important being the relationship between supply and demand, location, purchasing power, availability, terms and conditions of financing, and type of use.

Mortgage financing is still in the early stages of its development in Sub-Saharan Africa except for South Africa, which is a developed market. Where access to mortgage loans is limited and interest rates are punitively high, very few people are able to obtain finance for their homes. As a result, most local property markets are far removed from any risk of a bubble developing.

In markets like Zimbabwe and the DR Congo, where little credit is available, the majority of house purchases are self-funded, so that buyers are able to dictate terms.

The real estate market can be divided into several sub sectors:

- Office buildings and business parks
- Residential housing
- Industrial buildings
- Shopping centers
- Hotels (city hotels, resorts)
- Lodges
- Farms
- Land (municipal, agricultural, forestry)

Each sector has its own pros and cons and depends on distinctive customer groups. The current situation and outlook may also differ from country to country.

Commercial Property

Office buildings, business parks, and industrial buildings address the needs of both local and international companies. The latter primarily tend to focus on a country's capital, or else its financial/economic center. The following table lists countries where the political and economic capitals are different.

Country	Capital City	Economic Capital
Côte d'Ivoire	Yamoussoukro	Abidjan
Cameroon	Yaoundé	Douala
Nigeria	Abuja	Lagos
Tanzania	Dodoma	Dar es-Salaam
Malawi	Lilongwe	Blantyre
South Africa	Pretoria	Johannesburg

Countries with different political and economic capital cities

The following graph demonstrates that commercial rents are heavily dependent on how the property is being used. Retail outlets provide the highest returns per square meter. Therefore, retail companies have to pay a higher rent than for offices or industrial buildings.

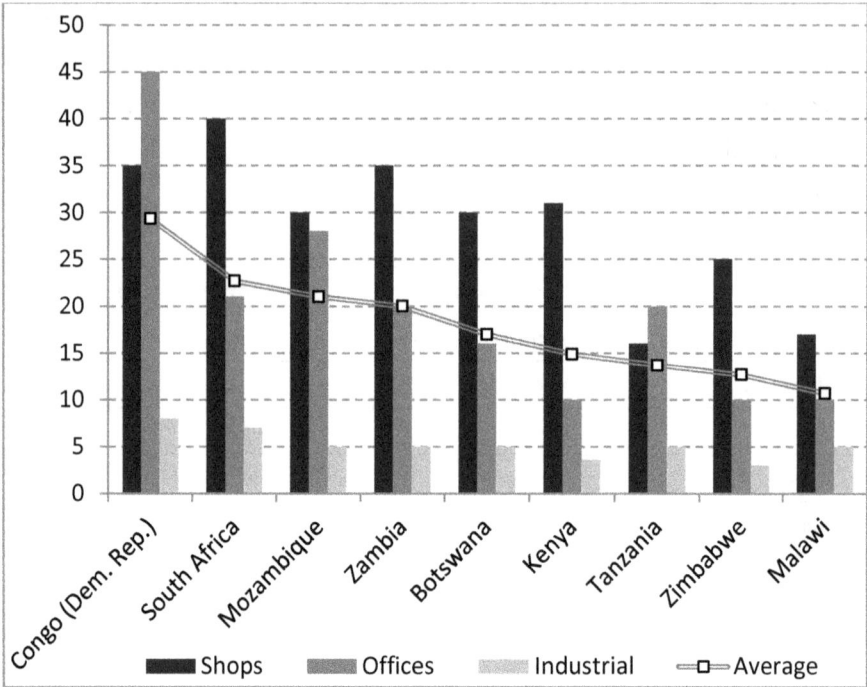

Regional rental rates for commercial property 2010 (US$/square meter). Source: MMC Capital Research

Although the prices of commercial property in Zimbabwe appear to be quite inexpensive compared with other countries, prices were even lower three years ago. Since the currency reform of 2009 and the subsequent dollarization of the Zimbabwean economy, rental rates exploded. From 2009 to 2011, prices in Harare rose from 5 to 25 US$/square meter for shops, from 3 to 8 US$/square meter for offices, from 4 to 10 US$/square meter for business parks, and from 1 to 3 US$/square meter for industrial buildings.

Looking back from here, it seems to have been an excellent time to buy property in Zimbabwe. However, the country was in a deeply depressed state, characterized by high levels of uncertainty and political risk. Bold investors prepared to take such a risk could have made a fortune.

Even in the same city, markets can be very different. The office market in Zambia is a good example. In Lusaka's Central Business District (CBD), most existing offices are regarded as obsolete as they do not meet modern occupier requirements. Most tenants require an open-plan, flexible space with plenty of car parking plus back-up solutions for electricity and voice and data communications. In addition, occupants want to have the capacity for future expansion. So, rent for top quality accommodations are expected to rise in the short to medium term.

The attraction of industrial areas increases if they have been designated as Free Trade Zones (FTZs) or Special Economic Zones (SEZs). In many cases, the government assigns specific incentives, such as tax holidays, duty-free imports of capital goods, or tax exemptions, to companies located in such areas. Therefore, property prices can be higher than in other industrial areas without such privileges. Companies and investors that want to set up production plants, logistic centers, or office buildings are advised to carefully examine if such special zones already exist or are planned.

Hotels and Resorts

Prices of hotels correlate to the profits that the owner can generate from them. While occupancy rates of city hotels mainly depend on economic activities in the city and the country, because most guests are travelling for business purposes, resort hotels focus primarily on tourists. Occupancy rates of resorts and prices per room per night usually vary depending on the season, and will also be affected by changes in country risk as a result of unrest (e.g., Kenya after the last elections, Egypt after the revolution) or if such a situation has ended (e.g., Côte d'Ivoire). Asset prices of hotels can fall significantly if tourists fail to appear.

Conversely, prices of such assets can rise if the region becomes more attractive to visitors. A good example is the Kavango Zambezi Trans Frontier Conversation Area (KAZA TFCA), soon to become the largest national park in the world. It will cover parts of five countries (Zambia, Zimbabwe, Botswana, Namibia, and Angola) and includes more than ten existing national parks and game reserves (Chobe NP, Makgadikgadi NP, Nxai Pan NP and Moremi Game Reserve in Botswana; Kafue NP and Sioma Ngwezi NP in Zambia; Hwange NP, Matusadona NP and Chizarira NP in Zimbabwe; and Bwabwata NP, Khaudum NP, Muduma NP and Mamili NP in Namibia).

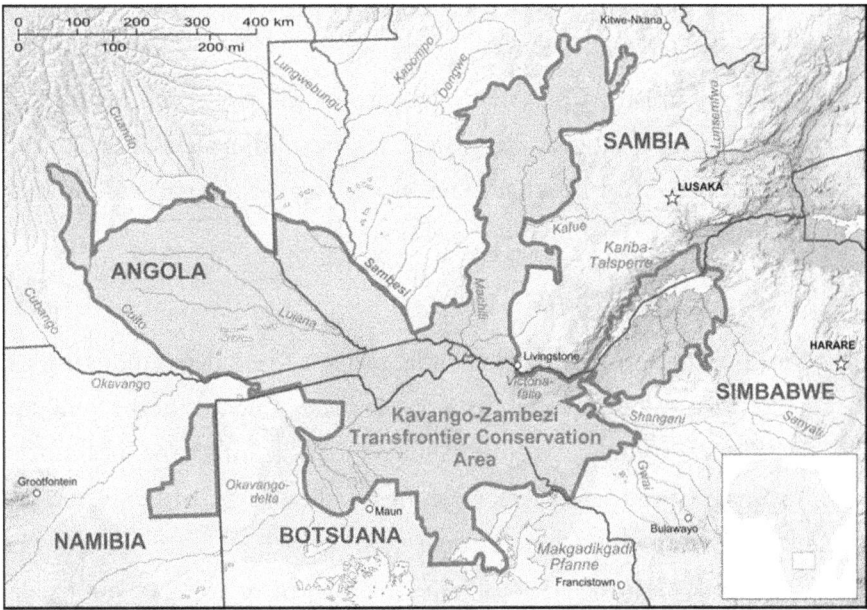

The Kavango Zambezi Trans Frontier Conversation Area. Source: Wikipedia

Clearly, the most attractive location in this setting will be that surrounding the world-famous Victoria Falls, including the cities of Livingstone, Zambia and Victoria Falls, Zimbabwe.

Resorts, lodges, and camping grounds in the Kavango Zambezi TFCA should become more attractive when tourism levels to the area increase, thereby driving up occupancy rates and demand for more accommodation. On the other hand, a prolonged recession in the developed world would negatively impact the flow of visitors.

Nevertheless, the tourist industry in Africa hopes for more visitors from Asian countries that might well more than compensate for the possible loss of visitors from Europe and the United States. In order to benefit from the shift towards Asia, local companies and entrepreneurs from the hospitality sector need to adjust their business models and marketing activities accordingly, as well as offer added value to their guests, e.g. by hiring Chinese interpreters.

However, infrastructure challenges have to be overcome before this positive scenario can unfold. In particular, a new bridge has to be built to span the Zambezi River in order to better connect various parts of the area. Financing for this has yet to be secured.

Residential Property

Prices for buying and renting residential property vary depending on size, location, neighborhood, habitat density, technical standards of the building, and the distance to the city center. Prime locations attract the local upper class, expatriates, and foreigners while the middle classes tend to be located in midmarket properties. Low-income groups dwell in areas at the lower end of the market. However, boundaries of this segmentation are not fixed.

Large numbers of the urban poor live in informal settlements that can stretch over large areas of African cities. The property's vicinity to such settlements also affects the price for purchases and rents. Long-term investors wishing to invest in residential properties should keep a careful eye on informal settlements and how they are likely to develop in the foreseeable future. As long as average personal incomes grow faster than the urban population, the social situation should be stable and even allow for poverty alleviation in the city.

When urban population growth (determined by the general demographic trend and the speed of urbanization) starts to exceed the increase in personal incomes of new city dwellers, informal settlements can be expected to increase as fewer people can afford housing, and more of them will be impoverished. This will lead to a degradation of property assets and falling prices. It may also undermine the value of existing properties in adjacent areas.

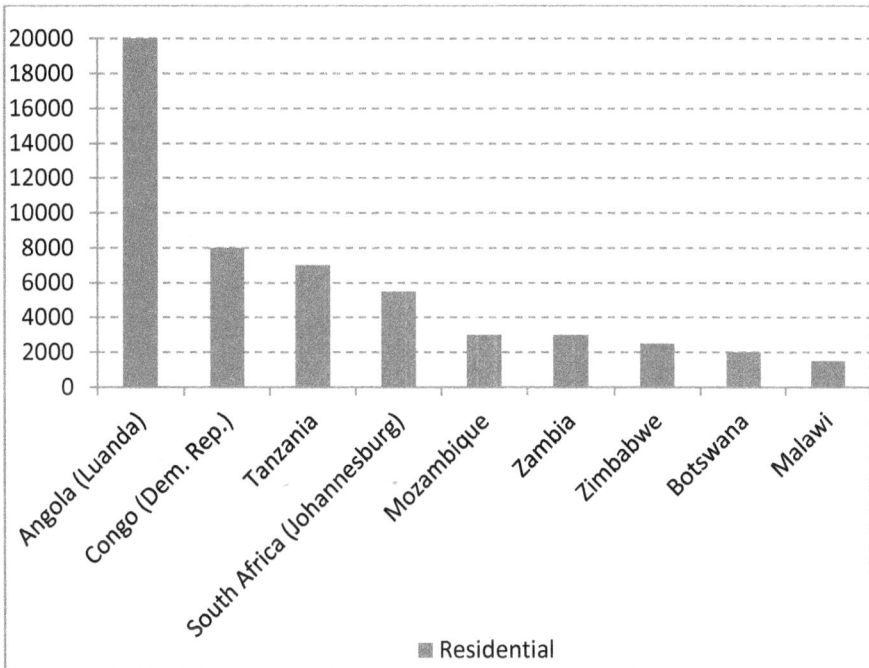

Regional rental rates of residential real estate 2010 (Upmarket, low density areas; US$/month). Source: MMC Capital Research

Prime residential estates in low density areas are most expensive in those countries and cities where supply is very tight, and where the upper classes control a disproportionate amount of the wealth. In the DR Congo and Tanzania, rental rates are very high, despite the extremely low average purchasing power in these countries.

In terms of prime residential rentals in the region, landlocked countries, such as Zimbabwe, Botswana, and Malawi, offer fairly competitive monthly rates compared with other regional counterparts, such as Angola, the DR Congo, South Africa, and Tanzania.

Availability, quality, and security of properties of the highest standard, as well as provision of electricity and Internet access, are other parameters that need to be factored in.

Luanda, the capital and largest city of Angola, is the most expensive city in the world for expatriates, according to Mercer's Cost of Living surveys. It is followed by Tokyo and N'Djamena, Chad.

In terms of location, it is important to distinguish between macro and micro locations. The bigger and more important the city, where an office, industrial building, shopping mall, condominium, or villa is located, usually means the higher the price. Zimbabwe provides a good illustration. The capital, Harare, is far more expensive than the secondary cities of Bulawayo, Beitbridge, Victoria Falls, Gweru, Masvingo, and Mutare. In Harare, tenants have to pay about 2.5 times the prices in the other cities. This pattern of properties in the largest city having the highest prices applies to most countries in Africa.

The number of monthly rentals that a tenant has to pay in advance to the lessor gives a good indication of how great the imbalance is between demand and supply. In many cities in Nigeria, Cameroon, and other West African countries, tenants have to pay 24 months' rent in advance in cash. When the initial period of two years is over, the rent for the next 24 months has to be put on the table. These rules apply when huge demand meets limited supply. Obviously, this situation is very different from that in developed countries.

New City Developments

As I have outlined in 2011's *Redefining Business in the New Africa*, urbanization is a megatrend that has a particularly pronounced impact on Africa. Millions of people are migrating from rural to urban areas for a variety of reasons. While the percentage of people living in urban areas has already reached very high levels in the Western world and Latin America, some parts of Asia and most parts of Africa lag far behind. The urban population in Africa accounts for about 40% of the continent's total population, 60 years behind Latin America where 80% of the people now live in cities.

From 2000 to 2030, Africa's urban population is expected to grow from 294 million to 742 million people, an increase of 152%.[139]

Urbanization is taking place in different ways:

- Expansion of existing cities
- Upgrading villages to cities
- Development of suburbs to form the core of new cities
- Planning and building new cities

Most existing cities in Africa will grow randomly, as new migrants arrive and settle somewhere in the city or its periphery. Only a few city councils have implemented a strict process of spatial and urban planning. One example is Kigali, the capital of Rwanda.

Some large cities are planning specific extensions of their outskirts, e.g. Eko Atlantic City which will be built on a new artificial island adjacent to Victoria Island, Lagos. The new city will meet the needs for financial, commercial, residential, and tourist accommodation with a state-of-the-art, high-tech infrastructure in line with modern environmental standards. Eko Atlantic City will also offer its residents an independent source of energy generated specifically for the city. This added value is especially important in the Nigerian context of constraints in power supply.

---

[139] UN-HABITAT. (2010). *The State of African Cities 2010: Governance, Inequalities and Urban Land Markets*. http://www.unhabitat.org/documents/ SACR-ALL-10-FINAL.pdf. (Accessed online on January 8, 2012.)

Abuja is a planned city that was built mainly in the 1980s. It replaced Lagos as Nigeria's capital in 1991.

In Côte d'Ivoire, Yamoussoukro benefited from becoming the capital in 1983. It still appears to be more of a large village than the political and administrative capital. The far bigger city of Abidjan remains the economic and financial center and, therefore, has the highest real estate prices in the country.

Juba, capital of the new nation of South Sudan, acquired political and administrative functions overnight. The existing infrastructure of roads, buildings, and utilities is totally inadequate for future needs. Many problems and challenges lie ahead, offering numerous opportunities for risk tolerant entrepreneurs and investors. Most likely, however, lack of capital will not be among the challenges as the new nation is likely to be supported by international organizations and development agencies. Multinationals wanting to participate in the country's huge oil reserves are already active in South Sudan.

Much is going on in and around Nairobi, the capital of Kenya and also the main economic hub of East Africa. Kenya's national development agenda includes the Nairobi Metro 2030 Strategy and its ambitious project of Tatu City[140]. This planned community is aimed to become the prototype of the African city of the future and a replicable model in Kenya and across Sub-Saharan Africa. The vision for Tatu City is the creation of a world-class, mixed-use new city for an estimated 62,000 residents, situated directly in the path of a continuously growing urban development extending northwards from Nairobi. Tatu City will not only provide homes and jobs for thousands of Kenyans, but will also offer unparalleled economic and business opportunities, including real estate investments. It is also a

---

[140] Official website - www.tatucity.com

fascinating case study for efficient and effective urban development and management in the 21st Century and the mobilization of private resources for the development of urban infrastructure and services.

Konza Technology City is another decentralized development area designed to alleviate the congestion within Nairobi. The Konza Technology City (initially called the Malili Technopolis) will be located approximately 65 km southeast of Nairobi – "where Africa's silicon savannah begins."[141] The Kenyan government is currently looking for a master developer for the 5,000 acre site.

Both Tatu City and Konza Technology City will be run by semi-autonomous, parastatal authorities that will help oversee the continuity of the projects and non-interference by the politicians. The planned communities will provide a comprehensive mix of land uses to cater for all the needs of residents and visitors. These will include residential developments, retail, commercial, tourism, social facilities, and recreation.

Tete is the capital city of the Tete Province in northwestern Mozambique. This place offers the most interesting business opportunities in the country's real estate sector. The dynamic development of the commercial and residential market is based on the gigantic coal resources that have been explored recently. The Moatize deposit is one of the biggest in the world, attracting large mining companies and many exploration- and mining-related business activities. Demand for accommodation is vast and rising while supply is still very limited. Savvy investors find excellent investment opportunities there. The biggest challenge for entrepreneurs at such remote places is the lack of skilled workers.

---

[141] Official website - www.konzacity.co.ke

A similar development can be anticipated for the port city of Takoradi in southwestern Ghana, which is the nearest commercial port to the Jubilee oil fields. Business and leisure travelers are increasingly demanding quality, affordable accommodation and conference facilities in the country's new oil and gas hub. The tourism sector is growing at a rate of 25%, and the demand for accommodation is rising. The expectation of an oil boom has pushed up real estate prices in the city and also caused a lot of activity in the construction sector.

Yield of Real Estate Investments

The following table shows the yields that property investors can achieve in various countries and cities in Africa. [142] Yields vary, but differences are less than might be expected.

Country	Offices	Retail	Industrial	Residential
Angola	8%	10%	8%	6%
Botswana	9%	10%	13%	10%
Cameroon (Douala)	11%	10%	14%	9%
Côte d'Ivoire	10%	9%	12%	8%
Dem. Rep. of Congo	12%	15%	13%	10%
Egypt	10%	8%	11%	8%
Ghana	10%	9%	12%	9%
Kenya	9%	11%	13%	7%
Mauritius	9%	9%	11%	7%
Morocco (Rabat)	10%	10%	14%	8%
Mozambique	9%	9%	11%	8%

[142] Knight Frank Research. *2011 Africa Report.* http://www.knightfrank.com. (Accessed online on February 1, 2012,)

Country	Offices	Retail	Industrial	Residential
Namibia	10%	10%	12%	8%
Nigeria (Lagos)	10%	9%	12%	8%
Rwanda	10%	12%	14%	6%
South Africa (J'burg)	9%	8%	10%	5%
Tanzania	10%	10%	10%	7%
Uganda	10%	11%	13%	8%
Zambia	11%	10%	14%	12%
Zimbabwe (Harare)	10%	9%	13%	8%

Real Estate Ownership

Countries with liberalized property markets are the most attractive to foreign investors. They have a long tradition of private property ownership. The legal framework is quite sophisticated offering high investment security, compared with other African countries.

The following sections show how foreigners can acquire real estate in Africa. Restrictions apply in some countries, depending on the type of land.

Countries with Liberalized Property Markets

There are only five countries out of 54 that have liberalized property markets. The following table describes them.[143]

South Africa	South Africa has one of the world's most accessible property markets. Foreigners may acquire and own property, including agricultural land.
Botswana	Freehold land ownership is available and encouraged for foreigners.

---

[143] Source is http://www.cheaplandregistry.com

Namibia	Foreigners may acquire and own property in Namibia, except agricultural land. Land is typically held in freehold title. There is an adequate land registration system in Namibia.
Morocco	The property market in Morocco is quite active and foreigners may acquire and own it. Morocco follows French law with reference to title and title deeds. Title insurance is available.
Egypt	Foreigners may own property. International title insurance is available. There are adequate controls over land records to create a comfort level with ownership. 99% of the real estate in Egypt can be owned by freehold title. Real estate in the South Sinai and Sharm El Sheikh can only be acquired via a 99-year lease.

Countries with the Most Restricted Property Markets

Countries that had, or still have, systems based on socialism generally do not allow private ownership of land. Land usually belongs to the state, or the government, and will be available for usage only on long-term leases. Registration processes are often complicated and ownership rights are not well protected. The following table highlights countries in this category.[144]

Angola	All land belongs to the state and may only be used by permit on long-term leases.
Mozam-bique	The government owns all land in Mozambique. Land is controlled by 99-year leases. Foreigners may obtain control and use of land through these long-term leases.

---

[144] Ibid.

Democratic Republic of Congo	All property belongs to the State, but this is controverted by individuals, tribal communities, and local cities and governments. As there is no effective system for land ownership and transfer in place, issues around ownership are very complicated.
Ethiopia	Foreigners may not own freehold land in Ethiopia. Ethiopian citizens may own land in freehold. However, most of the land is only available on leases. The land registration system is not well developed and can be very tricky.
Nigeria	All property belongs to the State. Foreigners cannot acquire or own real estate in Nigeria. Properties can be leased for terms of 99 years.
Tanzania	The Government owns all the land in Tanzania. Foreigners can acquire an interest in Improved Property with a lease with terms of between 33 and 99 years. Properties in and around Zanzibar typically have shorter term leases, and there are no automatic renewals.
Zambia	Foreigners may not acquire or own land in Zambia. However, there are a few exceptions.

Countries with Free Property Market

In some countries, there are certain restrictions that may depend on the type of land (i.e. freehold land, tribal land, community land, urban land) or its classification, respectively. With agricultural land in some countries, there may be political and social issues around land ownership, which might even prevent land from being properly developed, as is the case in most parts of Zimbabwe. The following table highlights countries in this category.[145]

Ghana	Foreigners may acquire and own property, depending on the type of land. The main land category can be accessed easily. Land owned by the Government can also be acquired upon application and approval.
Cameroon	The right of ownership of real estate is granted by the Constitution. No reference is made to a citizenship requirement. Cameroon's laws are affected by the differences between British and French laws. Cameroon still lacks reliable national cadastral land register.
Kenya	Foreigners may own property which is classified as commercial or residential. Land can by "used" via a 99-year lease. Neither foreign individuals nor foreign controlled corporations can own agricultural land.
Rwanda	Foreigners must make Bank Deposits of 500,000 U.S. dollars for a period of six months. Foreigners may acquire and own real estate above the ground. They may not acquire any interest in the land which is owned and controlled by the government. Land leases can be obtained for periods of between 50 and 99 years.
Mauritius	Foreigners may purchase real estate in Special Approved Projects and also receive a residency permit, at a minimum price of 500,000 U.S. dollars.

---

[145] Ibid.

Conclusion

Being one of the major asset classes for the creation and preservation of wealth, Real estate in Africa offers a host of opportunities. This is especially true if the current favorable situations and bright outlooks of many African markets are compared with the negative developments in the Western world.

While the world financial system is running into problems that can neither be mastered nor hidden by politicians and bankers any longer, hard assets are sought after by smart investors.

African property markets have a competitive advantage for various reasons. Population growth and urbanization will lead to increasing demand for residential housing for the next 20 years. Prices will be driven by widening gaps between demand and supply. Rising prices for purchase and rent can be awaited, although mortgage financing is very limited in the frontier markets.

In the commercial and industrial property sector, the attractiveness of the markets is closely related to the economic activity and the city or region. The big economic upswing of most parts of Africa in the years to come will most likely support further price advances, although some markets are no longer cheap. For example, Luanda is one of the most expensive cities of the world, and investors should not buy property at the current exaggerated price levels.

Despite avoiding certain cities and areas that have become too hot in recent years, long-term investors should think about positioning themselves right now. Africa offers a good environment for rising property prices, making real estate an attractive economic sector and preferred asset class for institutional and individual investors.

When considering African property as an investment case, one has to carefully think about the legal environment and laws regarding acquisition and ownership of property. In some countries legal ownership of property by foreigners is possible, while in other countries ownership is limited to certain types of land. In other countries, private ownership of land is not allowed, but the land can be leased for long periods.

In any case, investors are strongly advised to do a detailed legal, commercial and financial due diligence before investing any money. This is extremely important in any developing market.

7

Bond Markets in Africa

Sam Mokorosi

Globally, bond markets are an alternative vehicle for both governments and the private sector for financing long term projects, such as housing and infrastructure development, in addition to financing government deficits. Africa's bond markets are in varying levels of development. The successful development of a bond market requires a number of conditions such as a developed money market, favorable macroeconomic policies, market participation, appropriate trading systems, and a sound legal and regulatory framework. Thus, developing bond markets requires huge investment in institutional building.

Experience also shows that development of a government bond market is crucial for paving the way for the development of a corporate bond market. The development of bond markets widens the financing options for firms and enables the government to shift its domestic debt to longer-term securities.

Indications are that the African macro-economic environment is becoming more favorable for bond markets. According to the International Finance Corporation (IFC), lower inflation rates, lower interest rates, and more stable exchange rates are all facilitating the development of bond markets across the continent. Over the long term, African bond maturities are extending and yield curves are flattening.

In tracing the development of the African bond market landscape, we will discuss the types of bonds in issue across the continent, issuance by African governments and government controlled entities, and bonds issued by the private sector. We examine the amount of bonds in issue and the yields offered by the various issuers across the continent. Our focus will be on Africa's regional centers which include South Africa in the South, Egypt in the North, Nigeria in the West, and Kenya in the East.

Bonds in Issue across Africa

Apart from South Africa, the size of the bond market is typically smaller than the equity market, and the bond market is typically dominated by national government issuance. The International Finance Corporation (IFC) notes that bond markets across the continent still need much development, with only seven markets having treasury bonds above US$1 billion. The table below compares bond issuance across the continent, in comparison to the size of economy, and the equity market, according to the IFC.

Country	Equity		Bonds		
	Equity Market Capitalization to GDP (%)	Number of Listed Companies	Gov. Bonds Outstanding (US$ Mn)	Gov. Bonds Outstanding (US$ Mn)	Non-Gov. Bonds to GDP (%)
South Africa	29.3	410	53,752	45,201	19
Nigeria	21.4	216	15,982	847	1
Kenya	36.6	55	4,753	767	3
Mauritius	75.7	89	2,244	0	0
Zambia	48.0	20	1,094	6	0
Ghana	73.7	35	1,341	4	0
Tanzania	18.4	15	557	103	1
Uganda	20.9	11	739	40	0
Mozambique	3.3	9	147	55	1
Botswana	29.8	31	465	608	5

Treasury, or government, bonds are by far the largest types of bonds in issue across the continent. They are medium- to long-term debt instruments issued by the government to raise money in local, or foreign, currency for a period of more than one year. Maturities range from 1 to 30 years.

Investors in African government bonds are typically institutional investors, such as commercial banks, pension funds, and mutual funds. Central banks across the continent are also active in the government bond market as monetary policy instruments. Increasingly, government bonds are available to retail investors who can purchase government bonds with relatively low minimum investment amounts – for example, the minimum in Kenya is roughly US$500.

International investors are also a key part of African bond markets. Foreign currency bonds are issued by governments in the larger economies in leading currencies, such as the U.S. dollar, the euro, and the Japanese yen. These foreign currency bonds are referred to as Eurobonds. International investors can also purchase local currency government bonds, but they often require local bank accounts.

Types of Bonds in African Markets

The following are types of bonds available in Africa:

- **Fixed coupon bonds** bear predetermined fixed coupon (interest), which is usually semi-annually based on the face value held during the life of the bond. When bought at a discount, investors benefit from the discount (capital gain, which is critical for secondary market trading) and regular interest payment.
- **Floating rate bonds** pay semi-annual interest based on a benchmark rate. For example, an average rate of 91-day, or 182-day, treasury bill plus some margin. Some floating rate bonds are

linked to the prevailing inflation rate. They are usually in high demand in high inflationary environments.

- **Infrastructure bond** proceeds are used to fund specific infrastructure/projects specified in the prospectus.
- **Zero coupon bonds** are those in which no regular interest payments are made. The government issues the bond at a deep discount and redeems the bond at par value. The difference between the discount and the par value redemption offers the investor his or her return.

Funds raised in African bond markets are used for a fairly wide range of purposes. The following tables show some examples provided by the IFC.

Infrastructure	Housing	Sub-National
<ul><li>Water Utilities – Botswana</li><li>Road Fund Administration – Namibia</li><li>Port Authority – Senegal</li><li>Ferry Operations – Cape Verde</li><li>KenGen Energy – Kenya</li><li>Comunaute Electrique – Benin</li></ul>	<ul><li>Shelter Afrique – Kenya & West Africa</li><li>SEMA – Mali</li><li>Botswana Housing Corp</li><li>Home Finance – Ghana</li><li>Famers House – Zambia</li><li>IFH – Cape Verde</li></ul>	<ul><li>Lagos State – Nigeria</li><li>Niger State – Nigeria</li><li>City of Doula – Cameroon</li><li>Municipality of Sal – Cape Verde</li><li>Municipality of Praia – Cape Verde</li><li>City of Dakar – Senegal</li></ul>

Telecommunications	Agribusiness	Microfinance
• Safaricom – Kenya • Mcel Cellular – Mozambique • Gt Ghana Telecom – Ghana • Uganda Telecom – Uganda • Onatel – Burkina Faso • Celtel – Burkina Faso • CITelecom – UEOMA • Telcel Faso – UEOMOA • Togo Telecom – Togo	• Botswana Vaccine Institute • SOCAPALM – Cameroon • Sasini Tea – Kenya • Fan Milk – Togo • Nesko – UEOMOA • Palci – Côte d'Ivoire	• Faulu – Kenya • Pride – Tanzania • Bayport Financial – Zambia

Although eclipsed by national government bond issuance, there exist small, but growing, non-national government bond markets across Africa. The term non-national-government relates to bonds and asset-backed securities issued by entities other than the federal/national government, including corporations, states/provinces, municipalities, and project finance companies created for specific infrastructure projects.

According to the IFC, benefits of non-national-government bond markets include better risk management for borrowers/issuers via the ability to reduce currency mismatch and obtaining lower interest rates. These markets allow for the diversification of the financial sector and accelerated private sector development. Ultimately, growth is generated, jobs are created, and poverty is reduced.

Current African Bond Market Dynamics

The Standard Bank of South Africa (Standard Bank) tracks the performance of African government bonds. The graph below shows the performance of the bonds on a total return basis from 2007 to 2011. The graph compares global emerging market bond performance to the performance of African bonds including and excluding South Africa (ZA).

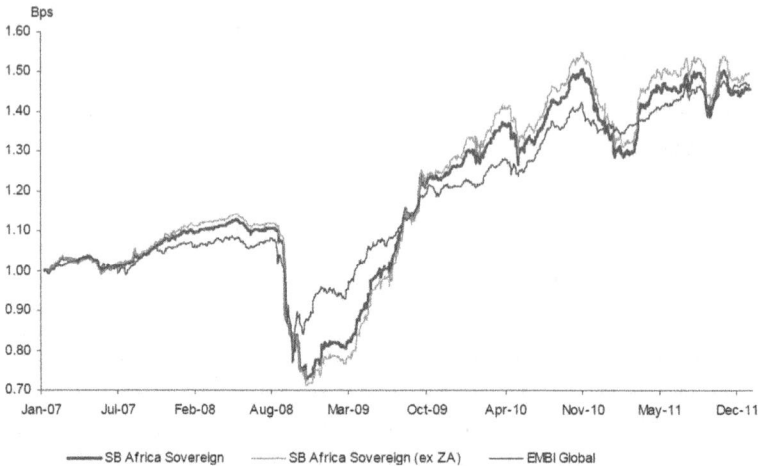

Performance of African bonds from 2007-2011. Source: Standard Bank

The graph shows a general positive performance over the last four years. However, the effects of the global financial crisis are clearly seen from the under-performance of late 2008 and 2009.

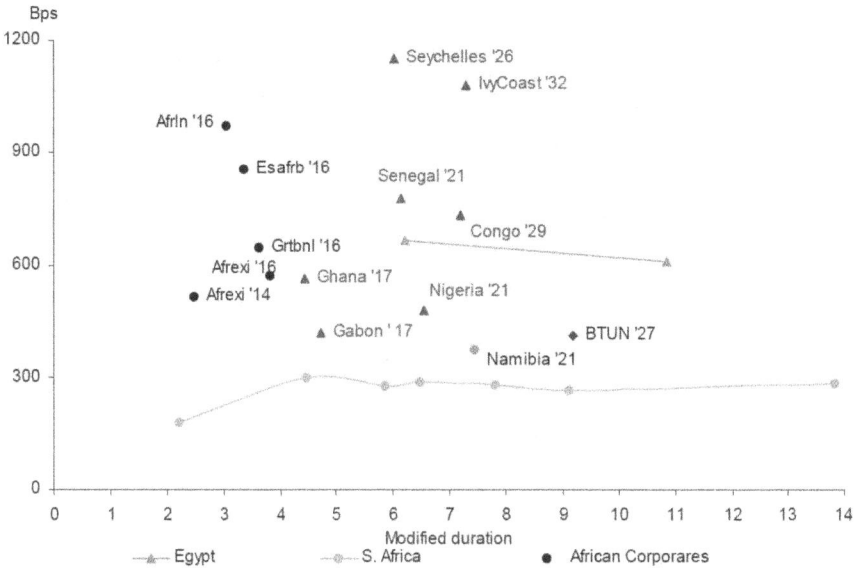

African Government and Corporate Bond Trading Compared to U.S. Treasuries. Source: Standard Bank

The graph above shows where various African government and corporate bonds were trading in January 2012 relative to U.S. Treasuries. As illustrated, the South African government pays around 3% more than the U.S. government to borrow in international bond markets. At the other end of the scale is the government of the Seychelles, which has a 2026 bond trading at approximately 12% above U.S. Treasuries. A select amount of African corporates are also indicated in the graph.

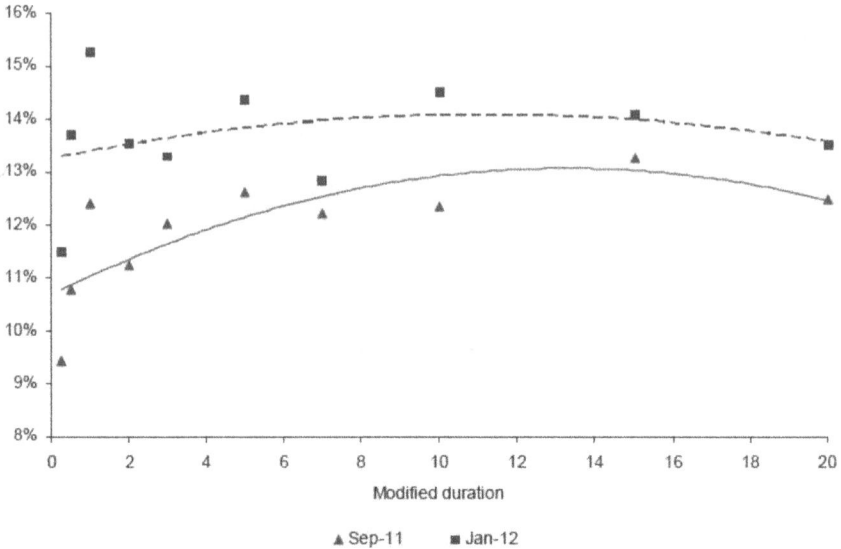

Liquid African Currency: Local Currency Average Bond Yield Curve. Source: Standard Bank

Africa's simple average local yield curve, as measured by Standard Bank's AF10 currencies (the continent's most liquid currencies) above, shows increased yields in the last quarter of 2011 due to increased global financial uncertainty and inflationary pressures on the continent. Standard Bank expects yields to decline in 2012 as markets stabilize and central banks reduce benchmark interest rates.

Sovereign African Eurobonds are also expected to perform relatively well in 2012. Low U.S. Treasury yields for most of 2012 are expected to support the African Eurobond asset class.

The South African Bond Market

The South African bond market is the most established on the continent, with a history spanning more than 100 years. As the leading issuer in country, the Government of South Africa has an investment grade rating from each of the major international ratings agencies. The table below indicates the agencies' ratings.

	2009	2010	2011	2012	2013
S&P	BBB+	BBB+	BBB+	BBB+	BBB+
Moody's	A3	A3	A3	A3	A3
Fitch	BBB+	BBB+	BBB+	BBB+	BBB+

By November 30, 2011, the South African government had outstanding international debt of approximately US$15 billion, which equates to 4% of the country's GDP. These bonds are purchased by leading institutional investors across the globe.

Domestic issuance by the South African government stood at approximately US$130 billion. Local bonds are issued in the South African rand and are purchased by mostly local South African investors.

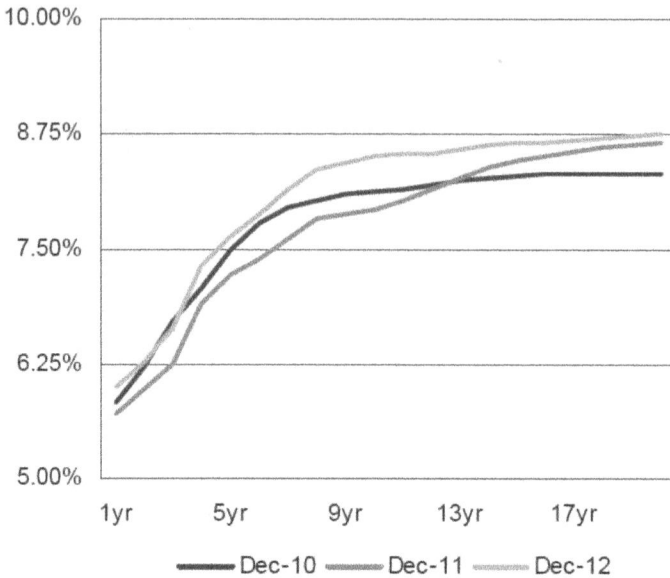

South African Domestic Government Bond Yield Curve. Source: Standard Bank

The graph above shows the domestic government bond yield curve. The graph indicates that the South African government can raise capital in the domestic bond markets at 5.6% for one-year funding, and between 7.5% and 8% for eight-year funding and beyond.

According to Standard Bank, South African bond yields were range-bound during 2011, although the range was relatively broad at about 1.10%. South African Reserve Bank (SARB) rates are expected to remain flat during 2012, with the result that the bond market will continue to trade within the same 1.10% range for at least the first half of 2012. Standard Bank expects that within the range, the yield curve will steepen, while inflation accelerates and government bond issuance increases. Inflation is expected to be 6.5% in the first quarter of 2012 (from 6.1% year-on-year in Nov 2011) and remain at, or above, the upper end of the SARB's 6.0%

inflation target ceiling throughout 2012. Inflation risks are fuelled by the recent spike in local food prices and the on-going weakness of the South African rand, which is expected to continue.

South African state-owned entities (SOEs) are also fairly active in the domestic bond market. Some of the larger bond issuers include the electricity utility, Eskom, and the manager of freight rail and the national ports, Transnet. To support its large infrastructure renewal program, Eskom's bonds are guaranteed by the national government for more than US$40 billion. Despite the government guarantee, bonds issued by SOEs still typically trade at higher yields (lower prices) than similarly dated national government bonds. For example, Eskom's 3-year bond yield trades approximately 0.7% higher than equivalent national government issued bonds.

The South African Corporate Bond Market

The South African corporate bond market is smaller and less established than the government and SOE bond markets. South African corporates began to tap the bond market in earnest in the mid-1990s. 2001-2002 saw the entrance of asset-backed securities into the corporate bond market. Securitization grew fairly quickly as home loans, car loans, and corporate debtors' books were all bundled into securitized bonds. The 2008 global financial crisis put the brakes on this growth, but the South African market has begun to rise from the ashes with new post-crisis securitizations.

Two such securitized bond issues for 2011 were two bonds by Toyota Financial Services totaling R760 million (about US$100 million). The first bond, a four-year floating rate note of R260 million has a maturity date of 2015 and was substantially oversubscribed, receiving bids in excess of R700 million. This note was issued at a rate of 85 basis points above the 3 month JIBAR (the Johannesburg interbank agreed rate).

The second note issued was a five-year R500 million note with a spread of 130 basis points over the R157 million government bond resulting in a coupon of 8.7%. The fixed rate note was also substantially oversubscribed, receiving bids of more than R1 billion.

The Egyptian Bond Market

As the leading issuer of bonds in Egypt, the government's external debt stood at US$35 billion in 2010, while domestic debt reached US$170 billion. Government bond issuance is supported by the ratings assigned by international credit rating agencies. The table below shows some ratings volatility due to the political unrest in the country since the start of pro-democracy demonstrations across the Arab world.

	2009	2010	2011	2012	2013
S&P	BB+	BB+	B+	BB	BB
Moody's	Ba1	Baa1	B2	B1	Ba3
Fitch	BB+	BB+	BB-	BB	BB+

The table shows Standard Bank's expectation that ratings will rebound overall in 2012 and improve further in 2013 as the political climate improves with the conclusion of the electoral process in late 2012.

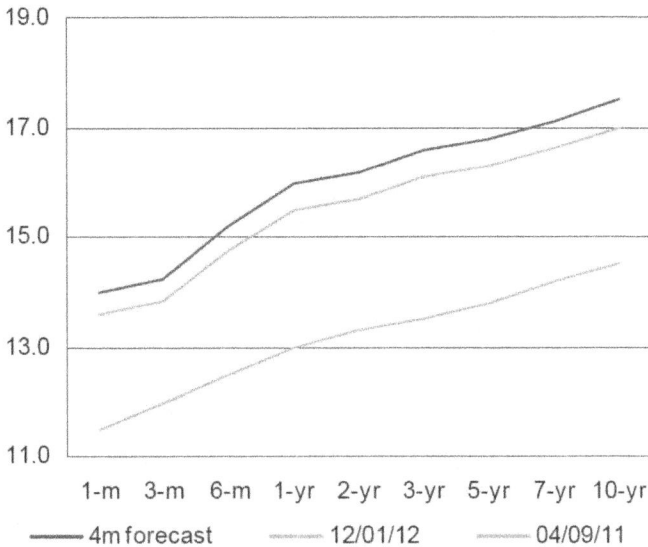

Egyptian Domestic Government Bond Yield Curve. Source: Standard Bank

The graph above depicts how Egypt's domestic government bond yield curve has pushed significantly north between September 2011 and January 2012 despite relatively low inflation. The increase in bond yields has been in response to the Central Bank of Egypt increasing benchmark rates to support the local currency – the Egyptian pound. As the currency regains some strength due to political stability, Standard Bank expects that yields will subsequently decline, with longer dated bonds tipped to show the greatest move. This will only happen in late 2012 though, hence the four-month (4m) forecast in the graph, showing further increase from the current (January 2012) yield curve.

The Nigerian Bond Market

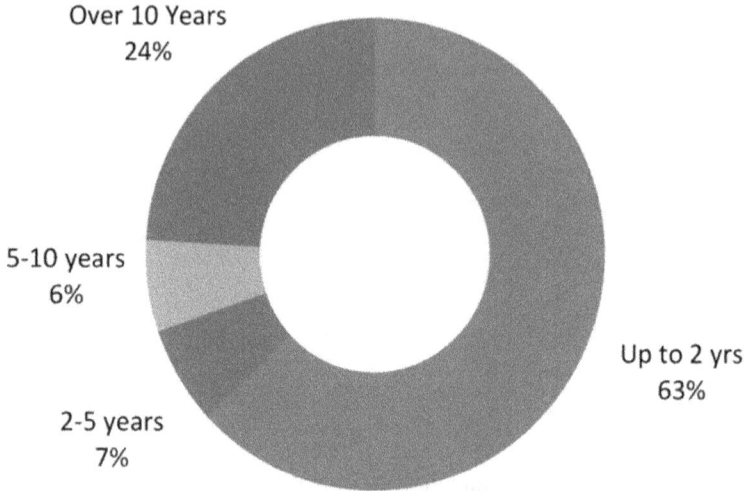

Over 10 Years
24%

5-10 years
6%

Up to 2 yrs
63%

2-5 years
7%

Nigerian Profile of Domestic Government Debt in 2003. Source: Central Bank of Nigeria

The federal government of Nigeria is a dominant player in the Nigerian bond market. According to the IFC, the government restructured its external and domestic debt in 2003 with the first federal government bond issued in 2003.

By 2005, regular monthly federal government bond issues had commenced. By 2008, government bond tenors had increased to 20 years. Total outstanding government bonds equaled US$16 billion in 2009.

The domestic yield curve has been inverted (i.e., short-term rates are higher than long term rates) since the sharp increase in policy rates at the October 10, 2011 Monetary Policy Committee (MPC) meeting of the Central Bank of Nigeria. While short term rates have remained exceptionally high, bond rates dropped in late 2011, driven by institutional demand, notably after the neutral interest rate decision at the November 21, 2011 MPC meeting.

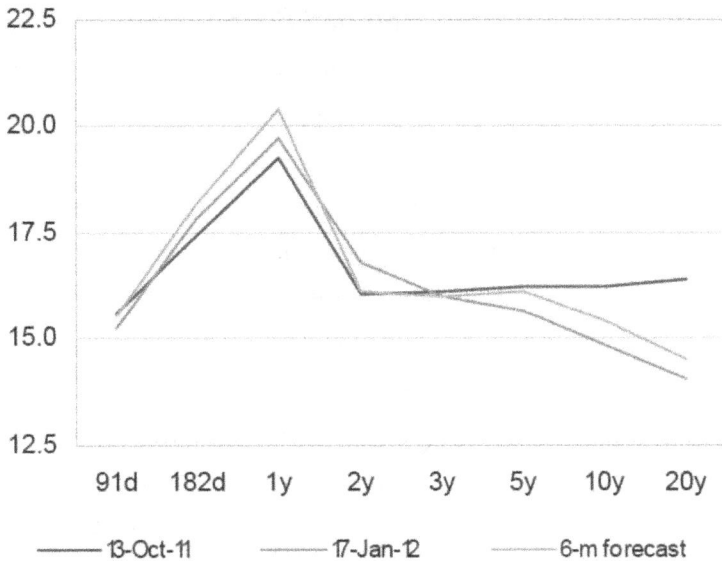

Nigerian Domestic Government Bond Yield Curve. Source: Standard Bank

As shown in the graph above, Standard Bank expects the domestic Nigerian bond yield curve to remain inverted for the next six months due to the inflationary pressures still faced by the economy.

Apart from the government debt restructuring discussed earlier, pension fund reforms in 2004 also assisted in the development of the Nigerian bond market. Assets under management have grown rapidly (average 30% per annum) to US$13.3 billion in 2011. With assets under management expected to reach US$30 billion by 2016, pension funds have become an important investor base for the Nigerian bond market, holding 6% of the market in 2008 and growing to 22% of the market in 2009. With new investment guidelines introduced in 2010, pension funds will be expected to increase funding for infrastructure and corporate bond issues in the coming years.

The Growing Nigerian Sub-National Bond Market

The recent growth of the Nigerian sub-national bond market has been more of a necessity than deliberate design. Since 2002, several states in Nigeria have taken the option of approaching the capital market to seek funds, especially by issuing bonds as a stop-gap following falling international oil prices, which led to a reduction in their allocations from the Federation Account. The states thus looked for cheaper and longer-term funding from the bond market as banks were unable to fulfill this need.

For investors, the attractiveness of state bonds includes their tax-1%exempt status, and the payment guarantee provided by the Federal government (except for bonds issued by Lagos State which don't have the guarantee). However, there has been virtually no participation from foreign investors in state bonds as of yet.

With the growing interest of the states in the bond market, Nigeria looks set to overtake South Africa as the continent's biggest issuer of sub-national government debt. In South Africa, the banking sector is more consolidated and has more capacity to lend to municipalities. South Africa's business center, Johannesburg, became the first local authority to tap the bond markets in 2004 and has since been joined by neighboring, Ekurhuleni, and the port and tourism capital of Cape Town.

So far, over a dozen Nigerian states have accessed funds from the market, raising more than US$2.3 billion in nine years. This surpassed South Africa's $1.9 billion in municipal bonds in 2011. Outstanding municipal issues account for only about 1% of South Africa's bond market, but in contrast, Nigerian state bonds account for 7% of the overall bond market.

Though the Nigerian states initially sought these funds for budget shortfalls to meet developmental projects, there is evidence to indicate that they apply the funds nowadays for everything from roads to luxury resorts.

The Nigerian Corporate Bond Market

The growth in the Federal government and State government bond markets over the last decade or so has sparked interest in the corporate bond market in Nigeria. According to securities firm, Dunn Loren Merrifield, additional tail winds for the Nigerian corporate bond market include the government's desire to strengthen the corporate bond market through the granting of tax waivers and the revision of pension funds guidelines to accommodate corporate bonds as approved investment instruments. Growth in this market has been further driven by increased awareness among firms of the need to match long-term financing requirements with long-term funds.

Dunn Loren Merrifield estimates that corporate bond issues increased to N105 billion (US$700 million) in 2011, representing a 41.9% increase over 2010 volumes and a 182% compound annual growth rate (CAGR) from 2009 to 2011.

The Kenyan Bond Market

The government of Kenya is an active issuer in the local Kenyan bond market with approximately US$7 billion of bonds in issue. A similar amount of debt has been issued in external markets. Purchasers of the bonds include commercial banks, the Central Bank of Kenya, non-bank local investors, and some international investors.

According to the IFC, the Kenyan bond market dates back to 1997 when the first floating rate Treasury bond was issued. Kenyan government debt maturities began to increase from a maximum of six years in 2002 to 30 years in 2011. The mix of local to external debt has also shifted over the years. The share of domestic debt to total debt rose from 33% in 2000 to 54% in 2010. Treasury bonds, as opposed to treasury bills, also increased from 28% in 2000 to 82% in 2010. The table on the following page illustrates the relatively stable credit ratings of the Kenyan bond market.

	2009	2010	2011	2012	2013
S&P	B+	B+	B+	B+	B+
Moody's	Not rated	Not rated	Not rated	Not rated	Note rated
Fitch	B+	B+	B+	B+	B+

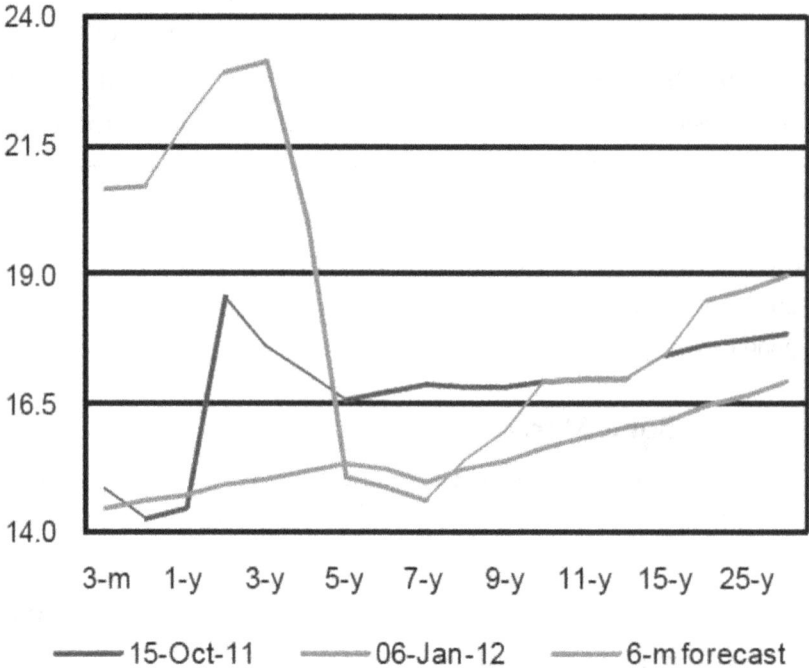

Kenyan Government Bond Yield Curve. Source: Standard Bank

The graph above shows the domestic bond yield curve for the government of Kenya. The current high inflation rate in the country (about 19% in January 2012) has resulted in an inverted, or downward sloping, yield curve. The government thus pays relatively high rates of over 20% for shorter term funding, but a much lower 13% for ten-year funding. The market is thus anticipating a long-term decline in the inflation rate for the next ten years. The curve also shows a more normal increase in rates from years 10 – 30 (upward sloping yield curve). 30-year bonds are currently costing the Kenyan government 16%.

Standard Bank expects that Kenyan Treasury bill yields are likely to compress some 600 basis points in the first half of 2012, as monetary policy is gradually eased, resulting in a normalization of the yield curve. Inflation has probably peaked, and is about to fall significantly. Market expectations of this were evident in the Treasury bill auctions held in early January 2012.

Most auctions since July 2011 were significantly undersubscribed, but the 91-day and 364-day auctions held on January 4 and 5, 2012 were 25% and 102% oversubscribed respectively. Once the authorities have decreased benchmark rates, they will look at issuing further down the curve, where the market expects to see some yield compression into 2012.

The Kenyan Corporate Bond Market

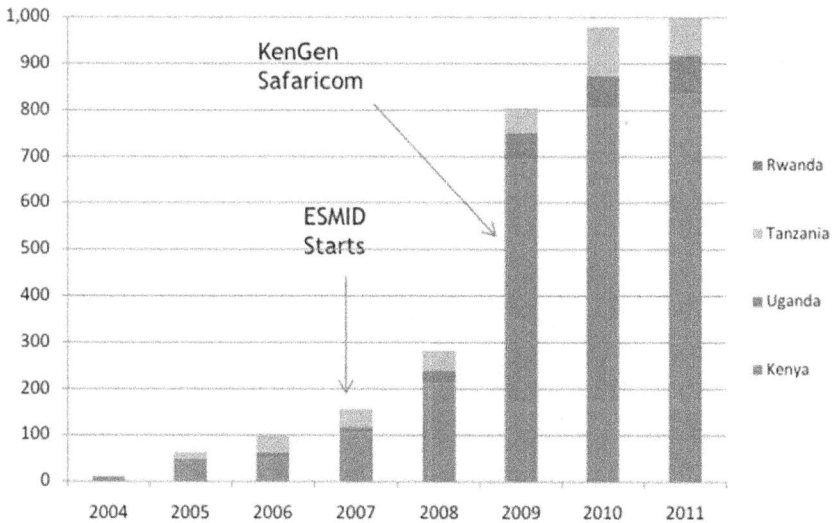

East African Cumulative New Corporate Bond Issues (in US$ Millions). Source: IFC

The Kenyan corporate bond market has been a leader in the East African region. 2009 marked a significant jump in issuance, with cumulative new corporate bond issues climbing from US$200 million in the preceding year to US$700 million. The graph above depicts this increase.

According to the IFC, the Kenyan corporate bond market equates to roughly 3% of GDP, indicating significant headroom for growth.

Conclusion

This chapter provided an introduction to bond markets across Africa. It should come as no surprise that the markets are still developing.

Great strides have been made in building the institutional frameworks for efficient bond markets across South Africa, Egypt, Nigeria and Kenya. However, the headwinds of currency fluctuations, high inflation, global financial market turmoil, and in Egypt's case, political unrest, have meant that the return performances of African bond markets has been sub-optimal in 2011. 2012 is expected to be a more stable year, which should prove positive for bond market performance, the issuance of new debt, and the general development and maturity of African bond markets.

8

ICT Innovations across Sectors in Africa
Lauri Elliott

While the majority of African households may still not have PCs, they are increasingly accessing the Internet using mobile phones. Mobile phone usage is growing faster in Africa than anywhere else. John White, Business Development Manager with Portio Research, observes that, "Of all the regions we look at ..., Africa holds the most promise in terms of the largest as yet untapped potential. By the end of the decade, there will be eight mobile phones for every 10 people on the continent."[146]

Developed nations, like most of Western Europe and the U.S., have gone through a technological evolution: from fixed phones, to dial-up networks, then cable Internet, high speed, 3G and now 4G. Other nations that haven't gone through these progressions, like many countries in Africa, are leapfrogging the first stages and moving straight into high speed mobile networks.

Helping out this cause, companies like Google are selling low-priced smart phones to developing nations where the larger cities are already set up for the population to start using 3G technology. According to White, "For companies looking for that last great bastion of growth in the mobile space, Africa is the place to be over the next decade. Nowhere else still holds the offer of that much growth."

---

[146] Interview with John White of Portio Research conducted by Lauri Elliott in 2011.

But mobile technology isn't just changing the ICT sector nor is it the only technology changing the continent. As a whole, technology will help the continent leapfrog the development cycle across sectors. In a series of articles written for Brainstorm Magazine[147], I explored evidence of how technology is, and has the potential of, changing the continent. In the follow sections, I share some of those articles covering education, travel, manufacturing, and mining. I want to acknowledge Hilton Tarrant[148], co-author on all of the articles except for education.

Educating Africa Through the Use of Mobile Technology

As mobile market penetration grows across Africa and "mobile" becomes more ubiquitous, mobile learning is gaining ground. Mobile learning, also known as m-learning, is simply the delivery of learning over mobile platforms. Earth-shattering? No. Essential to delivering education in Africa? Yes.

Says Elliott Masie, visionary for the Masie Institute: "Mobile devices will evolve to be the primary computing device in the Third World, as well as in the Second and First Worlds, over the next four years."

Merryl Ford, research manager: Emerging Innovations Group at the Meraka Institute feels strongly that, "[South Africa and Africa] are very well positioned to make a huge impact and contribution with regard to new and innovative service platforms," in the m-learning market.

Africa "leapfrogged" the global mobile phone market in growth and innovation, and has the potential to do so in the m-learning space.

---

[147] Official website - http://www.itweb.co.za

[148] Hilton Tarrant - https://www.twitter.com/hiltontarrant

According to Dr. Tom Brown, an expert in m-learning in Africa: "Africa is actually leapfrogging from an unwired, non-existent e-learning infrastructure to a wireless e-learning infrastructure. It (m-learning) will become the learning environment of choice."

This presents new and expanded opportunities for ICT and educational entrepreneurs in Africa who provide content, applications, and services for the m-learning market. Sam Adkins, chief research officer of Ambient Insight, says the learning content market in the U.S. will grow about 25 percent per year while services will grow about 36%, even during this economic downturn. In fact, the economic downturn has helped fuel the global market for m-learning because companies want to reduce travel required for learning, according to Masie.

The key is to understand what this market looks like, the opportunities available, and challenges facing it, then explore sustainable business models. The primary market in Africa is the mass consumer market, including rural and poorer populations.

Says John Traxler, director of the Learning Lab at the University of Wolverhampton: "M-learning is seen as a way to bridge the gap caused by lack of infrastructure and service delivery in areas like education and healthcare, particularly for the poor or rural populations, in Africa." Since mobile phone market penetration has reached beyond 85% in South Africa, this translates to over 41 million potential m-learning consumers.

Poor populations are the primary, or largest, market segment in Africa. This market segment includes the mass African consumer market, which possesses lower income levels than those in the West.

Another market identified by Brown is the mobile workforce and more broadly the mobile society. Globally, 50% or more of the workforce work outside the office. Both Traxler and Masie see the evolution of mobility in society as important to the growing m-learning market. Says Masie:

"Mobile learning/performance will evolve at the same rate as the acceptance of the mobile device as a support tool in our lives."

In this second market segment, the vision of m-learning, coined by Traxler as "just-in-time, just-enough, just-for-me," begins to come to life. Says Masie: "We will see more mobile performance support applications rather than traditional e-learning. Mobile will connect people to expertise and to social learning aspects, as well as placing coaching and mentoring into the hands of the workforce."

The type of mobile devices used by these market segments is an important factor. ResearchICTAfrica (RIA) did a survey[149] in 2008 involving over 23,000 households across 17 countries about ICT access and usage. On average, South Africans said they were willing and able to pay $19.25 (approximately R170) for a cell phone. The highest amount respondents were willing and able to pay for a cell phone was $29.70 in Cote d' Ivoire.

Mobile handsets in this range are simple in design, more text-based and focus on providing basic services. This fits the first, and largest, market segment of the broader African population. On the other hand, the mobile workforce segment uses a broader range of mobile devices that offer more options, such as audio, video, and rich multimedia applications.

------

[149] Gillwald, A., & Stork, C. (2008). *Towards Evidence-Based ICT Policy and Regulation: ICT Access and Usage in Africa.* http://www.researchictafrica.net/publications/Towards_Evidence-based_ICT_Policy_and_Regulation_-_Volume_1/RIA%20Policy%20Paper%20Vol%201%20Paper%202%20-%20ICT%20Access%20and%20Usage%20in%20Africa%202008.pdf. (Accessed online on January 10, 2010.)

Commercial Opportunities

Besides the education industry, the healthcare industry is leading the way in m-learning. Says Adkins: "The most sophisticated innovations in mobile learning are emerging from the healthcare industry, which will have a significant impact on mobile learning in the U.S. and across the globe, particularly in the area of patient education."

Converting these opportunities to successful, sustainable and profitable business models in Africa is the trick, however. That said, there are several mobile business models that can be explored for m-learning. Ford cites MXIT's use of sponsorship, the entertainment industry's use of micro payments (e.g. ringtones, screensavers), and pre-loaded bundle packages combining learning content and a mobile device.

Traxler says there is a dearth of profitable, m-learning business models in Africa at the moment since the industry is still in the pioneering stage. Masie thinks firms may not necessarily make huge profit margins on m-learning, which may be more like e-mail, "high functional use, but low profit margin," he notes.

Traxler says a challenge to commercializing m-learning in Africa is a predominate mind-set in Africa, which anticipates government will develop and use m-learning as a means to meet its commitment for service delivery. Multinationals like Nokia and MTN, involved in m-learning research in Africa, have not been great drivers of commercial development of m-learning either. Instead, they support its development for the greater good, perhaps waiting to see how commercial opportunities will develop from the research.

Ford says other challenges are "the (perceived) complexity in developing services over this platform," as well as, "a shortage of mobile software developers in South Africa (and Africa)."

She adds that this is why the Meraka Institute is developing, "an open source, cell phone-based mobile and telephony platform with tools, sample services, and applications. It will de-skill the process of providing cell phone-based products and services by individuals, SMMEs, NGOs, government, and the private sector within the South African context." An upside to the current challenges is the planned increase in broadband availability in Africa over the next five years.

This includes the quick expansion of 3G and 4G broadband networks. This will allow many Africans to tap into knowledge already available on the internet. Knowledge is a significant factor for empowerment – and, the preferred delivery platform will not be computers or laptops but mobile devices.

M-learning obviously presents opportunities for ICT firms looking for new and emerging channels. However, they will have to overcome the challenges involved in a "pioneer" sector while staying on top of business models that will be profitable and sustainable. In the end, it will come down to how well they read and reach out in this mobile revolution.

The Business of ICT in Manufacturing in Africa

Africa lags behind its global counterparts in industrial and manufacturing development. Even when comparing the percentage manufacturing contributes to the gross domestic product (GDP) in African countries to other developing countries, manufacturing contributes about ten percent in African countries and 21% in other developing countries.

In Africa, but outside South Africa, there are pockets of manufacturing success stories. The Ethiopian leather industry has made a name for itself in global niche markets. Robert Parker, group VP of research for IDC Manufacturing Insights, says the one significant manufacturing segment in Africa is the remanufacturing of computer and electronics.

However, the picture is getting brighter. Globalization, innovation, and ICT are transforming many sectors to anywhere, anytime platforms. In the manufacturing sector, the mantra is "design anywhere, make anywhere, sell anywhere," says Parker.

One shift is product manufacturing, separated into tasks and spread across manufacturing facilities. This is seen as a huge opportunity for new, smaller manufacturing entrants in low-income countries, including those in African countries, according to the Industrial Development Report 2009 by the United Nations Industrial Development Organization (UNIDO).

Parker speaks of a similar shift from mass to micro to pod manufacturing. Historically, manufacturers built one facility to serve the world. With pod manufacturing, manufacturers can download designs and methods from anywhere to localized manufacturing equipment to serve the local economy.

Pod manufacturing has reduced cost tremendously and increased flexibility. For example, there is equipment to manufacture wine, starting at $3,500.

Parker also says that local African manufacturers will be able to "bring more diversified and custom products to their local consumers." For example, Digiskin allows customers to go online to design skins to cover gadgets, including cellphones. A company can purchase a production machine to provide some of these skins locally to customers.

For a long-term opportunity, Parker says that African governments need to leverage access to their abundant resources and require firms to develop manufacturing and processing facilities locally alongside extraction operations. In some instances, deposits in Africa may account for 80 to 90% of global deposits of certain precious minerals or metals. They need to play the leverage game like China. China recently limited the export of rare metals to boost the price. African governments can use the same principle in a different way.

In every aspect, ICT is embedded in the manufacturing value chain from infrastructure to intelligent manufacturing. Without sufficient broadband infrastructure, approaches like pod manufacturing might not be possible.

Parker also sees another opportunity with the pervasive wireless infrastructure in Africa, allowing African firms to tap into and manage the full manufacturing value chain almost anywhere with technology like remote sensing and radio-frequency identification (RFID).

While there may only be pockets of manufacturing on the continent, the global manufacturing shift opens new, even immediate, opportunities for ICT firms looking for new pastures, e.g. industrial clusters in Uganda and Tanzania, as they develop. It will be important for ICT firms to continually scan the environment to take advantage of these emerging opportunities.

Manufacturing Convergence

Further south, leveraging information, communication, control and power is helping South African manufacturers innovate and compete.

Manufacturers have two options during the global economic downturn: cut back and try to weather the storm, or take the opportunity to be more innovative and aggressive. However, because South African factories struggle to manufacture products at the same cost as is possible elsewhere in the world, and due to a strong currency, local manufacturing concerns face these two options all the time.

Rockwell Automation believes that even though convergence has become a cliché over the past decade, "today the combination of technology maturity and economic necessity has made manufacturing convergence a manufacturing reality." Manufacturing convergence sees the merging of functions and systems that have been separate. The theory is that with people, processes, and technology working together, manufacturers can perform better.

Convergence within manufacturing leverages information, communication, control, and power.

It's no use simply having systems and machines recording data. Information must be in a manageable form: the new goal is presenting information in context.

Sources of information can be, "streamlined to allow configuration, visualization, maintenance and optimization of manufacturing processes and plant assets," Rockwell says.

Immense value is created when IT and manufacturing departments are able to share information seamlessly and securely, while running multiple applications over the same network. An enterprise manufacturing approach that is particularly suited to larger distributed companies envisions the enterprise as a "virtual manufacturing network."

EOH, during an implementation at Coca-Cola's greenfields Bloemfontein plant, was able to capitalize on available technologies while the rest of the group used mostly manual or semi-automatic systems. In time, improvements to its other factories will mean that they can join the network across the Coca-Cola SABCO enterprise.

The trend nowadays sees standard, unmodified Ethernet being adopted broadly across the plant and enterprise for data collection and real-time control. Add to this newer functionality such as voice, video and mobility, which are beginning to appear in the plant environment.

However, despite these advances, manufacturing convergence is a complex environment and cannot be delivered by a single supplier. In South Africa, system integrators like Bytes and EOH implement solutions from companies as varied as Cisco, Microsoft, SAP, Wonderware, and Dassault Systems.

Beyond this, original equipment manufacturers are embracing new so-called "smart" service business models enabled through embedded software, wireless connectivity and online services. This shift has significant implications for manufacturers.

Lifecycles of products are becoming ever shorter as releases will begin to ship in "real-time" with software devices delivered to products over networks when needed. Oracle's manufacturing VP, Manish Modi, reckons it's hard to accurately predict what manufacturing operations will look like five years from now, but, "factors we experience today are likely to have a residual effect on the supply chains of tomorrow."

Modi says that many of the top manufacturers will have leading, "service-oriented architecture suites in place to enable supply chain evolution as well as needed flexibility to quickly respond to changing markets and inevitable shifts in buying patterns."

He also suggests that most manufacturing systems will support Web or Enterprise 2.0. "The future adoption of tools like wikis, blogs and mash-ups to create, store and collaborate on information by skilled manufacturing users should not come as a surprise. Touch screens and sophisticated wireless devices should be a common part of leading factory floors."

But, the biggest problem in converged manufacturing is not the availability or implementation of technology: it's changing the mindset of the people themselves.

The Business of ICT in Health in Africa

There is no question that the healthcare sector in Africa represents a huge challenge and opportunity. The question is how, and how well, ICT will meet the challenge.

Most African countries have a critical shortage of healthcare workers, and the majority of African healthcare systems are low-ranked internationally, according to the World Health Organization.

Dr. Dirk Koekemoer, Chief Executive Officer of GeoAxon, states plainly that the challenge is, "creating a healthcare system out of nothing, which can deliver quality basic primary healthcare services to those without it."

While this situation is a critical challenge, it presents a tremendous opportunity for ICT in the health sector. The opportunity is particularly good in the mobile sector (mHealth) due to the penetration of mobile phones on the continent. A United Nations report[150] says: "Mobile phones reach further into developing countries than other technology and health infrastructures."

One mantra for mHealth is, "make available the right information at the right place at the right time and in the correct form." This mantra, when actualized, translates to several benefits, according to Tyson Greer, CEO of Ambient Insights.

First, clinicians and patients can make more informed and intelligent decisions. Second, real-time data is provided for communication, consultation and notification. Third, mHealth increases efficiency and

---

[150] United Nations. (2009). *mHealth for Development: The Opportunity of Mobile Technology in the Developing World.* http://www.unfoundation.org/news-and-media/publications-and-speeches/mhealth-for-development-1.html. (Accessed online on January 10, 2010.)

speed of care, and increases productivity of healthcare workers. And finally, it provides on-demand access to information and continual learning for healthcare professionals.

There is a unique opportunity to provide ICT-based products and services to the private healthcare sector. Firstly, because private sector healthcare already represents a good portion of services provided to Africans compared to public healthcare. And secondly, African governments are using private healthcare providers to augment and enhance public healthcare systems, which are overtaxed.

This creates a sizable opportunity for ICT firms. Specific business opportunities in mHealth, according to the mHealth in Development report, include education and awareness, remote data collection, remote monitoring, communication and training for health care workers, disease and epidemic outbreak tracking, and diagnostic and treatment support. Koekemoers also says that developing centralized, electronic medical information records is a low-hanging fruit opportunity.

GeoAxon is delving into business opportunities presented in diagnostic and treatment support. Its "Tele-medicine Doctor in a Box" allows a doctor to examine a patient over the Internet, using devices the patient interacts with locally. These devices transmit data, which would normally be assessed in a face-to-face consultation with a doctor, remotely to the physician.

While mHealth seems to be gaining momentum, it still has several challenges. mHealth is still in the pioneer stage with many projects in pilot, but little empirical evidence to prove its impact. Koekemoers indicates that funding for innovative solutions is still difficult to come by. And while the technology may be there, the ecosystem for the mHealth sector is still immature.

Recognizing that mHealth is still an emerging sector in Africa with high potential, ICT firms might want to first look for low-hanging fruit opportunities and those that leverage its strengths.

Big Opportunity in South Africa

The healthcare market is huge. A recent report by research and consulting outfit, Markets and Markets, says the healthcare IT systems market will be worth $53.8 billion in five years' time.

One of the major areas of growth in the space is tele-medicine. This is by no means new technology, with policies put in place and applications created over a decade ago.

A new push, by networking giant Cisco, is through a pilot program demonstrating that tele-medicine is real and it works. The so-called Health-Presence program saw remote clinics linked up in Aberdeen, Scotland and San Jose, California.

This service provides what Cisco terms "care at-a-distance over the network." It uses Cisco's TelePresence teleconferencing technology, with patients and physicians able to see life-sized images of one another. The system also collects physiological data from a variety of linked devices such as a stethoscope, blood pressure cuff, pulse oximeter and other diagnostic equipment.

The Aberdeen trial started in January 2009 and found that 90% of the patients who used the technology were satisfied with the experience, 95% said the visit felt confidential and 93% said they would recommend it.

"In almost every case, we could accurately identify the degree of urgency and make a diagnosis," said Dr. James Ferguson, national clinical lead for the Scottish Centre for Telehealth.

He added: "Cisco Health-Presence can enable us to deal safely and effectively with 90% of the cases we see."

The Medical Research Council (MRC) in South Africa is currently running five separate tele-medicine projects around the country.

Obviously bandwidth constraints mean that the implementation of tele-medicine is difficult in both South Africa and Africa. In addition to bandwidth, the MRC identifies other obstacles such as the lack of easy-to-use, robust diagnostic instruments, and no dedicated tele-medicine center to act as a hub for tele-medicine.

The deployment of terrestrial fiber networks in South and East Africa, as well as the commissioning of SEACOM, has helped solve the bandwidth problem, however. At a recent exhibition, SEACOM showcased healthcare teleconferencing applications, and in early 2009 at GovTech, Moses Mtimunye, then acting CEO of South African State Information Technology Agency (SITA), said that in the near future, similar technologies to Cisco's TelePresence, "will make for commercially available tele-medicine projects providing people in rural areas with world-class healthcare services."

The national Department of Health says its long-term goal is to, "make tele-medicine live up to its potential as a valuable tool to improve access to high-quality and cost-effective health care services in South Africa."

Beyond structured implementation of tele-medicine systems, Cisco believes that Health-Presence could mean a revolution: "Instead of making a dash to an urgent care facility or emergency room, what if you could use your television or other networked device to connect with a medical center?"

Cisco believes this is not fantasy, it reckons it could become reality within the next three to five years.

The Business of ICT in Mining in Africa

The mining sector has been slow in its uptake of technology, but the global economic crisis and long-term issues are serving as catalysts for adoption.

The outlook for the mining sector has radically changed due to the global economic crisis. This boom and bust cycle has left many mining companies considering ways to manage operating costs in order to remain economically viable. But this is not the only challenge the sector faces, according to a Deloitte and Touche report[151]. In the long run, the sector must find ways to remain sustainable amid the sea of legal, social, economic, and environmental issues.

These challenges actually present opportunities for the ICT sector because technology can manage complex systems, streamline processes, reduce costs, and improve efficiency and productivity. Consider enterprise resource planning (ERP) software, which coordinates the entire mining value chain, from locating to divesting minerals. Think of radio-frequency identification (RFID) and global positioning system (GPS) technologies, which track the movement of minerals and equipment.

There are also examples of technology specific to the mining sector. The oil sector is demonstrating the potential of ultra-deep water drilling technology, which drills and extracts oil from greater water depths.

The technology is creating and extending market opportunities to the industry by accessing previously unreachable deposits. For example, new oil operations began pumping oil commercially off the coast Ghana at the end of 2010.

---

[151] Deloitte and Touche. (2009). *Tackling Trends 2009: The Top 10 Global Mining Issues.*

Dr. Greg Baiden, director of Penguin ASI and a global expert on automation, says: "Automation in the mining industry will follow similar trends to those in the manufacturing industry."

It starts with a person using an automated machine to handle multiple tasks and eventually evolves to artificially intelligent, autonomous machines. Baiden says the future includes intelligent machines that can heal themselves.

For now though, automation has not reached critical mass in the sector. Large mining companies like Rio Tinto and BHP Billiton are considered early adopters. Teleoperations, or telerobotics, is the operation of a machine at a distance.

Penguin ASI's wireless technology, which communicates with robotic equipment under water, gives a glimpse of the potential of telerobotics in solving some of the mining sector's sustainability issues. This wireless technology will enable mining companies to extend the life of their mining operations on land. Imagine flooding mines with water to double their mining depth, and using telerobotics equipment to run the operations.

One natural result of using better technology and innovation is cost reduction in the mining value chain. This will eventually serve the economic development of Africa well. As the cost of mining decreases, it allows smaller mining firms to establish themselves.

The business opportunities for ICT providers in the mining sector can be found in the corporate, technical, and value chain systems. Historically, ICT providers focus on mining as a niche. However, as enabling technologies provide broader benefit to the sector and new mining entities arise, there are increased opportunities for the ICT sector.

Also, the mining sector faces serious challenges to its long-term sustainability. ICT firms, which identify gaps in the value chain and create solutions that close the gaps, leverage the value chain and contribute to sustainability, will carve their own space.

Mining Data

While there is undeniably a lot of technology used in the underground ore extraction part of mining, more focus is currently being put on the processing side of productions. MD of Softline Accpac, Jeremy Waterman, says that, "inherently it's a reasonably simple business." With mining, "you're putting a whole lot of resources in and you're taking production out."

But there has traditionally been a disconnect between production and what Waterman terms the "financial side of things," particularly among smaller miners. This has been a cause of frustration within the industry and a number of solutions now seek to marry the two elements.

This is a classic implementation of an enterprise resource planning (ERP) system, but up until recently, "marrying the elements" was simply absent.

"In the past it was tended to be done more on a kind of matchbox," says Waterman. "You had a whole lot of costs and you had a lot of production and you subtracted one from the other and you made a profit."

Nowadays it's a lot more complicated. Waterman describes how workflow management systems can be used for control, and to "capture production data that's coming back" into the system. The real difference is made by the layering business intelligence on top of these systems.

Ugan Maistry, business unit head of Mining & Manufacturing at EOH, agrees: "Over the years, there's been this maturity in terms of process-control and automation systems to be able to execute. There is now maturity in business systems like ERP."

But over the past few years, Maistry says there is a newfound maturity around the systems in between the parts. He calls it 'mining execution systems,' and describes it as very similar to manufacturing execution systems.

He likens many of the processes in mining to inventory management. "Previously, people only knew what they had and what they produced if they actually stopped their operations and took stock."

"Questions like, 'Where is the actual material in their value chain?'" adds Maistry.

He says some customers have been spending considerable amounts of money in the last two or three years on exactly this: business intelligence systems, which he likens to "enterprise manufacturing intelligence."

"But," says Maistry, "what they haven't explored is how to extract value out of that information."

This is the next frontier. Now, "our customers need to mine the data, and I'm talking end-to-end," says Maistry. "It's about looking at information in context, not just in terms of volumes and quantities, but in costs as well." Waterman takes it one step further: "We [South Africa] are trend-setters in mining as a whole. There's been an explosion of midcap miners, and that is where we're seeing the real growth."

Aside from ERP and workflow management systems, the back office sees similar ICT trends to those in pretty much every industry. Working costs are being rationalized, with single vendor outsourcing one way of saving money.

Licensing rationalization is being looked at, says Maistry, and providers like Microsoft and SAP are "coming to the party."

All the Time, Anywhere Travel Resources

Online ticketing of air travel will dominate consumer e-commerce for the next five to ten years in South Africa. Information technology spending in the travel and aviation sector is increasingly focused on delivering real-time services to travelers.

Travel technology group, Amadeus has launched a mobile version of its CheckMyTrip platform that enables travelers to check the most up-to-date travel itineraries via the web. This is not only limited to pre-departure flight information; it includes hotel and local weather data at any stage of a journey.

As part of the extension of the Amadeus platform, it has also launched applications for smartphones: CheckMyTrip for BlackBerry and the iPhone.

It's tip-toeing into the social web as well with the CheckMyTrip application for Facebook. The idea here is to offer customers the ability to share travel plans with friends and family.

Locally, airlines have innovated around the booking, check-in, as well as the payment process.

SAA's low-cost airline Mango is the first airline to offer payment on its website and through its call center via retail store cards. It's also integrated with Shoprite Holdings' Computicket and Money Market operations, which made it the first to trade air travel through retail outlets.

Rival 1time debuted online check-ins on its website in 2007, and the company says that: "Information technology has been one of the cornerstones of [the] airline since its inception."

It has worked together with local developer Qualica on reservations and departure control systems. Qualica's Departure Control System (DCS) was implemented at 1time's airport operations around the country.

Says 1time: "The DCS is supplemented by an integrated baggage management system (BMS) that allows the airline to track the movement of luggage through the airport and onto the aircraft." The system also works with the airline reservation system to provide an "integrated solution for servicing passengers."

When 1time launched in 2004, 75% of its bookings were done through its website. This figure is now over 90%. Says Michael Kaminski, IT director of 1time Airline: "The internet booking engine is an important cog in our business."

World Wide Worx says online ticketing of air travel will dominate consumer e-commerce for the next five to ten years and this has led the airline to do two major website refreshes (together with user experience tweaks) since 2008.

The airline believes that "website speed, functionality, and ease of website use for our passengers" is critical. It's aiming to include making more travel products and "building customer relationship management functionality into the site."

While the front-end website sits on top of the airline reservation system, it's invested in self-service kiosks that also connect to that platform. These are currently online at OR Tambo International Airport, Cape Town, Durban, and Port Elizabeth.

The logical next step for all airlines will be for real-time flight tracking, which would layer on top of these platforms. Already SAA and the Airports Company of South Africa offer live "flight status" information on their websites.

A year ago, SAA launched a mobile website that allows passengers to track flight schedules, departure information and weather forecasts.

According to SAA, the initiative is in partnership with Star Alliance, the international airline network to which it belongs. Star Alliance developed the Common IT Mobile Platform, which SAA used to launch its own portal for customers.

Game Changer

ICT is a game changer in the global travel industry. According to the "Travel Innovation and Technology Trends, 2010 and Beyond," by PhoCus Wright, trends include discovering alternatives to global distribution systems (GDSs), expanding use of Twitter-like tools, incorporating travel information "anywhere, anytime" platforms, moving toward convergence of social media and location-based services, and increasing use of social media for monitoring.

Bob Offutt, senior technology analyst at PhoCus Wright, indicates the first major technology shift will be an open platform, Open Axis, for airline flight reservation systems, or global distribution systems (GDSs), as opposed to proprietary systems like SABRE.

To enhance the user experience, augmented reality platforms like LAYAR will continue to emerge. Augmented reality is a direct view of a physical environment augmented by computer-generated imagery. Travelers will be able to get a more realistic view of hotels, conference centers, and restaurants online.

Says Offutt: "This is an area the industry is looking for ways to monetize."

Social media will also shape the industry. Its use will go beyond reputation management to modeling products and services based on user-generated feedback and content. For example, users share information on locations and services on TripAdvisor[152], which can inform and shape the travel plans of others.

---

[152] TripAdvisor - http://www.tripadvisor.com

Travel information services, like identifying services available at airports and baggage requirements and fees, will continue to grow. On the cellphone, this becomes "anywhere, anytime" and an opportunity for continuous merchandising.

"The industry recognizes the growth opportunity is greater in sales beyond tickets," Offutt says.

Location-based services will enhance both social media and travel information. Imagine being able to visually "walk alongside" someone as he or she takes a tour. EveryTrail[153] and Google Places[154] are examples of location-based services.

But one of the greatest opportunities for the industry is the cellphone. Offutt says this opportunity is particularly suited to Africa.

Edward Bergman, Executive Director of Africa Travel Association (ATA), agrees. But is the Africa opportunity significant? Yes, it is. While Africa is the least traveled to region in the world, it has sustained growth unlike other regions, according to Bergman.

In fact, "Africa was the leading growth region (in 2009) during the economic crisis and many African governments consider it a way to stimulate economic growth," he says.

According to the World Travel and Tourism Council (WTTC), growth is estimated at 2.8% in 2011 and 6.5% in 2012 in Sub-Saharan Africa. During this period, the personal and government sub-sectors are estimated

---

[153] EveryTrail - http://www.everytrail.com
[154] Google Places - http://www.google.com/places/

to grow above 5% per year, while growth in business travel will hover around 4%. North Africa[155] will perform better in 2011 at 4.75% but is estimated to be at 6.5% with Sub-Saharan Africa in 2012.

One challenge of the African travel market is a lack of accessible local information. But, it presents a particularly open market for application developers, content providers, and others.

With sustained growth patterns, a conducive environment, and open opportunities for ICT, tourism presents a solid opportunity for the next three to five years and beyond.

ICT in Agriculture

Key drivers for the introduction of technology in agriculture are the lack of labor, higher employment costs, reduced fertility of soils, the need to raise yields, regulatory requirements relating to traceability of agricultural products, as well as green considerations.

For "greener" agriculture, farmers are looking to reduce the usage of pest- and disease-control chemicals. An obvious use for technology in agriculture is record-keeping.

ICT can be used in almost every step of procurement, production, distribution and the marketing of agricultural produce. Technology is also employed in the actual process of farming, with computerized irrigation systems, sensors for temperature and moisture, and robotic harvesting systems.

---

[155] This data was released before the political disruption in North Africa in late 2010.

The integration of ICT in agriculture allows farmers to receive detailed and largely real-time feedback. Satellite imagery and global positioning systems (GPS) are used to provide thorough information about farmland. Other technologies include aerial thermal and near-infrared imaging.

So-called "precision farming" makes use of technologies like GPS and geographic information systems (GIS) in order to collate and process large amounts of data that can be analyzed to "inform farm management decisions."

In a 2008 study, Rachel Tembo explains that precision agriculture is an, "information-and-technology-based agricultural management system that identifies, analyzes and manages site-specific spatial and temporal soil variability within a field for optimum yield, profitability, sustainability and protection of the environment."

Technologies used in precision farming allow farmers to "vary inputs, such as fertilizers, pesticides and seeding rates throughout fields based on management zones." The adoption of technology reduces redundancy and labor costs and allows for expanded hours of production.

Randall Covey, in Remote Sensing in Precision Agriculture, argues that the benefits of precision agriculture include the, "reduction in the cost of producing the crop, a reduction in the risk of environmental pollution from agrochemicals when applied at higher levels than required by the crop, provision of better information on inputs and land management, improved environmental stewardship and significant improvement in agricultural yields."

Precision farming is gaining adoption on the continent, not only in the more sophisticated South African agricultural sector.

A project in Sudan, Agadi, introduced precision farming to its commercial mechanized farming sector. The results saw, "planting times reduced by 60%, area under plant cover was improved by 3.5% and the costs of spraying herbicides were cut substantially," says Covey.

Tracking and tracing systems are another area where technology is used in farming. There is backward traceability, where the origin of a product can be found at any point in the supply chain, and forward traceability where the "locality" of products can be traced.

For example, European Union regulations mean that all agricultural products entering the union should be tracked back to the actual farm of origin.

In the local wine industry, all wine exported to the EU complies with an EU regulation instituted in 2002, which says that all, "role players in the industry have traceability systems in place for each product to facilitate its traceability." Further to this, at every point in the supply chain, participants are required to be able to identify the business or person dealt with one step forward and one step backward.

Information Makes All the Difference

Agriculture is a priority sector for the African Union and most African countries and provides a large portion of employment on the continent. The African agriculture sector involves a significant number of small-scale farmers. As mobile phone penetration increases, ICT is taking a hold and appealing to this market.

Edith Adera, senior program specialist for The International Development Research Centre (I DR Congo), says that the broad focus for ICT in agriculture is Market Information Systems (MIS) and Knowledge Management (KM) systems so that farmers can link to markets, as well as grow and manage their crops more effectively.

Examples of existing MIS providers include Drumnet in Kenya, Foodnet in Uganda, and Tradenet in Ghana. Most MIS providers are private sector organizations, but Drumnet, an NGO, remains sustainable by charging fees for services to users.

Mark Davies, MD of Esoko (formerly Tradenet), says MIS has been around for two decades. However, the information was maintained by government and academic institutions, not necessarily reaching farmers. This is how Esoko started five years ago when someone brought the idea of providing market prices to farmers.

Esoko has evolved into a "network sourcing" platform that creates a communication and exchange platform for existing agricultural and trader networks. This platform is "E-bay, Salesforce, LinkedIn, and Facebook rolled into one," according to Davies.

He explains that part of Esoko's business model is the collection of local data through the networks. As networks join, they populate and maintain information about members and transactions, which, with permission, can be shared within the network, across networks, and across countries and markets. Part of Esoko's success is that it is based on a pull versus push model, which means that the networks generate the demand for Esoko's offerings.

Esoko also has a strong deployment and support model, which Davies says is essential to its success. Esoko is currently in eight countries, including Ghana, Sudan, Cameroon, and Madagascar. Esoko's franchise model will enable rapid expansion.

Both Adera and Davies agree MIS platforms help farmers reduce transaction costs, negotiate better prices, etc. Another important ICT platform in East Africa is the mobile payment platform, M-PESA, which is popular with farmers, according to Adera.

A future benefit of these platforms is direct access between African farmers and global buyers. Buyers tend to seek out opportunities where there is transparency, data, and reliability, according to Davies. A new feature in Esoko called "scouting" allows members of networks to be polled with questions like "what are your forecasted crop yields?" potentially providing real-time data to buyers.

Like in other sectors, ICT platforms are helping to democratize the markets, increasing economic opportunities, and connecting the disenfranchised in agriculture.

This means larger market access for businesses.

Ideas for New Innovations for Mobiles in Agriculture

As shared in *Redefining Business in the New Africa,* demand for food going into 2050 has the potential to create tremendous opportunities for Africa, which has the natural resources to be a major contributor to global food chains. The report called *Connected Agriculture: The Role of Mobile in Driving Efficiency and Sustainability in the Food and Agriculture Value Chain*[156] suggests several mobile solutions that could make a significant

---

[156] Vodafone. (2011). *Connected Agriculture: The Role of Mobile in Driving Efficiency and Sustainability in the Food and Agriculture Value Chain.* http://www.vodafone.com/content/dam/vodafone/about/sustainability/2011/pdf/connected_agriculture.pdf. (Accessed online on January 13, 2012.)

difference in developing the agricultural sector in Africa. These also present opportunities for businesses and investors, so we have summarized those in the report we have not already mentioned in the following paragraphs.

Because the risk of a failed harvest can be fairly high poorer farmers tend to not take the monetary risk of purchasing high quality seeds and other tools. An idea on the horizon to help lessen this risk is micro-insurance. Farmers will be able to purchase this via their mobile phones to insure an income when Mother Nature decides not to cooperate. Unpredictable weather, animal or plant diseases and unpredictable crop yields are just a few factors that can decimate a harvest. With micro-insurance farmers will be able to insure that they will not lose everything due to unforeseeable circumstances. This peace of mind will also lead to the purchase of higher quality seeds and tools. In another ICT in Africa series done by Hilton Tarrant and myself, *ICT in the Business of Insurance in Africa*[157], we cover some of the facets of this market.

Many rural farmers in Africa today end up selling their harvest at their farms to traveling merchants. While this prevents the farmer from having to make the journey into town, he often has little negotiation power with the merchant. On top of that, inadequate storage facilities often result in the farmer taking whatever rate is offered. Using mobile phones, farmers of the not so distant future will be able to access virtual markets where they will be able to auction their goods to the highest bidder. An online market will benefit everyone involved as the farmer will get the opportunity to sell his products at a competitive price, while the buyer will get to select specific items that he wants and the consumer will receive a better product. Esoko is a platform that already taps into this potential.

---

[157] Hilton, T., & Elliott, L. (2010). *ICT in the Business of Insurance in Africa.* http://www.afribiz.info/content/ict-in-the-business-of-insurance.

Occasionally farmers will have to harvest early to make a quick buck if they run into financial troubles. This prevents them from reaping the benefits of a full harvest. A helpful, potential feature of the virtual market is micro-loans. Farmers who are in need of extra income to improve their harvest will be able to advertise for investors online. These loans can be used to purchase valuable tools like modern farming equipment, higher quality seeds, fertilizers, and pesticides. People from all over the world will be able to supply farmers with a micro-loan with a promise of interest on their investment. Investors will be able to view a farmer's profile, see what they are growing, see how past harvests faired and invest where they like. The financial aid will help to produce a more bountiful harvest which will result in better quality of product and more sales.

Advancements in ICT for use in agriculture don't focus solely on helping farmers. Using mobile devices to track the journey of produce from farm to market will create the opportunity for a more efficient transaction for everyone in the value chain, including the environment. Merchants will be able to schedule pickups in a way that maximizes the space that they have available and can significantly cut down on the number of trips they have to make. Not only will this save the shippers money, fewer trips will result in a decrease in the amount of carbon that would result from more time driving.

There is also the idea of traceability – being able to track from "Farm to Table" as it has been coined – in food value chains. While not a mature market, the Los Angeles Times[158] reports that there is major work to make

---

[158] Huffstutter, P.J. (October 3, 2011). Amid Mounting Safety Concerns, Technology Helps Track Food from Farm to Table. http://articles.latimes.com/2010/oct/03/business/la-fi-food-safety-tracking-20101003. (Accessed online on January 13, 2012.)

these technologies an everyday occurrence to help shore up safety efforts. Major producers like Dole have developed systems, which can track lettuce within 100 feet of where it was picked. Major food chains in the United States like Food Lion are requiring that suppliers be able to trace the products they sell to them.

These innovations are great for all concerned. First, farmers get more money, which helps improve the lives of farming families and communities. Second, consumers get a better product. With more income, the farmer will be able to purchase better seeds, fertilizer, and pesticides which will yield bigger harvests of higher quality produce.

Third, as many of the scenarios also result in more organization and higher efficiency for farmers, merchants, and end consumers, carbon emissions will decrease as fewer trips into the rural countryside will be needed to collect produce. And fourth, since this competitive space is still emerging there are many opportunities for entrepreneurs and investors.

Conclusion

ICT is taking off in Africa and virtually all industries are being affected. From the communication and transportation industries to manufacturing, agriculture, mining, and medical field advancements, technological innovations are changing the way business is done.

Advancement in technology leads to improvements in quality of life, to monetary gain and an improved economy, to a more educated population, and over time a developing nation becomes developed.

For business and investors, it is important to recognize that ICT is creating tremendous opportunities on the continent, catalyzing leaps in development across the board. However, ICT serves as a disruptor of existing business ecosystems so it is important to note disruptive technology, how it impacts industries, and eventually your business model. Technological disruption is just as important to consider as potential political or social disruption when looking at any emerging market.

Strategies &
Networks

9

Using Networks to Build Ecosystems for Success in Africa

Lauri Elliott

It is a misnomer that Africa is not plugged into the global economy. From ancient trade routes, which included portions of Africa, to the more recent, though tragic, African slave routes, trade has flowed through Africa early in the history of civilization.

Today, Africa is integrated into global trade systems through sectors like mining and agriculture. Côte d'Ivoire, for example, is the world's largest producer of chocolate and West Africa is connected to the global cotton trade. Botswana is at the center of the diamond trade and South Africa in several mineral trade structures. In addition, South Africa has strong mining, manufacturing, and engineering capabilities, making it a global leader. Just this month, the Nigerian strike about removal of fuel subsidies threatened to cut off the U.S. market from a crucial supply of oil. Nigeria happens to be the fifth largest oil exporter to the U.S., according to 2011 figures.[159] What happens in Africa does matter in the global economy.

---

[159] Energy Intelligence Agency. (November 29, 2011). *Crude Oil and Total Petroleum Imports Top 15 Countries.* ftp://ftp.eia.doe.gov/pub/oil_gas/ petroleum/data_publications/company_level_imports/current/import.html. (Accessed online on January 16, 2012.)

Raw materials, or commodities, are just one of the major areas in which Africa is at the forefront in global business and society. The diversity of the channels is growing from health, economics, technology, sports, etc. The best representation of this is the diverse African diaspora that is spread across the globe. There is a diversity of professionals, students, and average workers within these numbers. In the United States, the African diaspora represents an academic elite, who earn more advanced degrees than any other ethnic group. This group also represents a small, but significant, middle class consumer segment.

The question is really not whether Africa is plugged into global business and society, but how to amplify its voice and influence. Africans need to lead from their positions of authority and influence, so that Africa's embeddedness and interconnectedness on the global scene increases for the benefit of Africa and increases its impact on global affairs. We can see President Jacob Zuma of South Africa taking the U.N. Security Council to task over how it handled the Libyan crisis in 2011 and about not listening to the African Union.[160]

From a business perspective, the global networks and ecosystems in which Africa is represented present opportunities for developing necessary ecosystems to support business ventures and opportunities on the continent. One of the key success strategies we have found is developing partnerships, both local and global. In our core structure, we cover three

---

[160] Baudauf, S. (January 13, 2012). Zuma Tells the UN: Listen to African Union. *Christian Science Monitor.* http://www.csmonitor.com/World/Africa/ 2012/0113/Zuma-tells-the-UN-Listen-to-African-Union. (Accessed online on January 16, 2012.)

continents – Africa, Europe, and North America – with Africa as the center of our business. These key partnerships have helped us, a small organization, more easily and readily tap significant markets.

The networks and ecosystems to tap into are numerous – cooperatives for mining or agriculture, entrepreneurial hubs, faith, students, African professionals on the continent and in the diaspora, indigenous nations and traditional leaders, multinationals, international and development organizations, NGOs and humanitarian organizations, educational and research institutions, etc. If you look a little closer, you will probably find connections to Africa all around you.

Having said this, knowing that these channels exist to help you develop a successful ecosystem to operate in Africa is not enough. You need to understand the changing dynamics of global business that have moved from control to symbiotic structures, and that to "connect" with success you need to operate in a new paradigm. Thus, the following sections will describe one of these ecosystems – Global African Entrepreneurs – as a narrative and then discuss how you can build your own ecosystem from almost anywhere in the world to do business in Africa.

Global African Entrepreneurs

I have been watching a growing shift over many years in global business networks, which suggests a new regime is getting ready to exercise its power and influence in Africa and the globe in a visible and coordinated way. The new regime will change the very fabric of business, society, and politics. The networks of Global African entrepreneurs are about to emerge (if they haven't already) as a core system for change and development in Africa.

Who are Global African entrepreneurs exactly? They are young Africans, who have formed strong identities unique to them but blended with their African heritage and global exposure and experience. They are a subset of the Global-African Youth consumer I described in *The Rise of the Global-African Youth Consumer*.[161]

In particular, they see themselves as creators and architects of the future of Africa along all facets. While the term, "entrepreneur," is most often associated with for-profit ventures, an entrepreneur is anyone who creates.

An example of Global African entrepreneurs in the political landscape was the Arab Spring, led by youth seeking a voice in their futures and forcing change. I noted in *Redefining Business in the New Africa*, early in 2011, that this movement was also representative of a new paradigm in governance in which informal networks would gain more influence over governance at all levels of society in Africa. However, this is not just an African paradigm, but a global paradigm. Thought leaders who participated in surveys for the *Outlook on the Global Agenda 2012*[162] by the World Economic Forum recently concluded this as a major global issue, or influence.

This is the context in which Global African entrepreneurs are rapidly gaining prominence, power, and influence. While there were Global African entrepreneurs like Wael Ghonim in the Arab Spring, this movement represented a spontaneous emergence. The group of Global African entrepreneurs, however, is more strategic and organized as a whole.

---

[161] Elliott, L. (October 3, 2011). The Rise of the Global-African Youth Consumer. *Afribiz.net*. http://www.afribiz.net/content/the-rise-of-the-global-african-youth-consumer. (Accessed online on January 9, 2012.)

[162] World Economic Forum. (2011). Outlook on the Global Agenda 2012. http://www3.weforum.org/docs/GAC11/WEF_GAC11_OutlookGlobalAgenda.pdf. (Accessed online on December 17, 2011.)

In the paper, *The 'New' Generation of African Entrepreneurs*[163], Barbara McDade and Anita Spring of the University of Florida describe the group, for which I have coined the name "Global African entrepreneurs," as "business globalists who organized a system of business enterprise networks consisting of national, regional, and Pan-African organizations." They describe Global African entrepreneurs in more detail by saying:

> *Some defining characteristics of these entrepreneurs are interactive social and business relationships, use of modern management methods and information technology, trust among fellow members, transparent business practices, advocacy on behalf of the private sector, and commitment to increasing intra-African commerce. Their mission is to improve the climate for private sector business in Africa and to promote regional economic integration. They pursue cross-national commercial ventures, maintain official observer status at established regional economic organizations, sign memoranda of understanding with multilateral agencies, establish venture capital funds, and help to change government policies.*

The entrepreneurs who participated in the McDade and Spring study were members of the Enterprise Network, a pan-African organization with regional organizations like the Southern Africa Enterprise Network (SAEN). In the study, network members demonstrated a marked difference in mindset towards Africa compared to traditional African entrepreneurs:

> *Compared to network members, other African entrepreneurs interviewed seem to be just as hard-working and committed to*

---

[163] McDade, B., & Spring, A. (January 2005). The 'New Generation of African Entrepreneurs': Networking to Change the Climate for Business and Private Sector-Led Development. *Entrepreneurship & Regional Development, 17,* 17-42.

success, but they express more pessimism (or certainly less optimism). They anguish over business constraints such as the poverty in their countries, poor infrastructure, political and/or regulatory instability, inadequately trained work-force, effects of HIV/AIDS on employees, and corruption, among other things. They say that they feel powerless to change these conditions. Network members, by contrast, express an attitude of empowerment and confidence in their ability to help to improve these conditions. They do not discount the problems they face. Rather, they have challenged and changed these conditions.

Network members have a global business outlook while maintaining an inward focus that interprets Africa's economic crises (of the past) not as hopeless, but as fertile ground for business opportunities. They view the role of business on a broad scale: the ability to address the unmet demands for goods and services throughout the continent.

I was recently speaking with an African professor who was amazed at how his younger brother had gone to school, worked, and started companies successfully in South Africa, Zimbabwe, Canada, and now Ghana. He noted that his brother was at ease in many cultures and able to navigate business even with large institutions. In essence, this young man is confident, competent, and able to create his own path successfully.

McDade and Spring point out that Global African entrepreneurs, as a group, are virtually invisible to academics, which I believe is also the case with many other spheres of society. However, there are many examples now of successful individual Global African entrepreneurs – Eleni Gabri – Madhin of the Ethiopian Commodities Exchange, Ashifi Gogo of Sproxil,

Ory Okolloh of Ushahidi, and Funke Opeke of MainOne Cable. In fact, Global African entrepreneurs are no longer the exception to the rule in business circles but are part of the "new" rule.

While this group might be invisible to many elements of society, it is by no means insignificant – quite the opposite in fact. Global African entrepreneurs belong to many different, influential networks like the Frontier 100 of the Initiative for Global Development, World Economic Forum, and Desmond Tutu Fellows. In addition to leading disruptive companies, some have strategic positions in international organizations like the United Nations, World Bank, International Monetary Fund, and the International Finance Corporation. Many of them possess significant networks through their alma maters like Oxford, Cambridge, Harvard, MIT, and Yale. Many have worked for global consulting firms, such as Deloitte & Touche, PriceWaterhouseCooper (PwC), Accenture, KPMG, and Ernst & Young, as well as multinational companies.

But there is more to Global African entrepreneurs than just being a socioeconomic or general business group. They are a movement. They advocate, work together, strategize, and organize while leveraging their strengths and networks. They expect to affect change.

In a not so obvious way, they are changing the rules of development in Africa. They are influencing how both business and government drive private sector growth on the continent and helping to demonstrate the potential of trade and business over aid and charity to develop the continent in the long term.

Global African entrepreneurs represent the future. They are suited for the relationship-orientation (versus transaction-orientation) business models that will dominate the "new" economy.

In *Emerging Paradigms in International Entrepreneurship*[164], Leo-Paul Dana, Hamid Etemad, and Richard Wright indicate that small firms today are finding more success with interdependence and relationships. Firms are giving up independence to "share power and control and cooperate voluntarily to maximize efficiency and profits."

This is the changing landscape in a multi-polar world. Dana, Etemad, and Wright provide some characteristics of the multipolar network economy (a transformation of the ancient bazaar economy):

- Focuses on relationship marketing
- Prices are negotiated
- Former competitors cooperate for mutual gain
- Decision-making influenced by relationships with members of network
- Brand loyalty is influenced by preferential treatment (based on relationships)
- Power and control is decentralized

While many others are still operating in old paradigms, Global African entrepreneurs are already adept at what is called "symbiotic management." Symbiotic management is, "a collaborative effort by multiple parties, each of which benefits from the joint effort, such that added value is created," according to Dana, Etemad, and Wright.

For businesses and investors looking for good strategic partners that can connect them to both Africa and the global marketplace, Global African entrepreneurs fit the bill. At the very least, they can share successful ways to navigate business opportunities in Africa.

---

[164] Dana, L., Etemad, H., & Wright, R. (2004). Back to the Future: International Entrepreneurship in the New Economy. *In Emerging Paradigms in International Entrepreneurship*. Edward Elgar Publishing: Cheltenham, UK.

Building a Global Network for Business

Business in Africa is not just about tapping a regional market, but also a global market. The idea is to tap African markets as part of creating a global value chain that can leverage any part of the globe for your business. So, you need to see yourself as a global organization tapping a global region.

Being a global organization is not just a mantra for tapping marketplaces around the world. It is, in fact, a new paradigm shift – a new reality. For today's companies, global is not something they do but something they are.

"Born Global" firms, a term coined by McKinsey and Associates, are those that provide products or services globally from birth. According to research by McKinsey, Born Global firms see the world as their marketplace from the beginning, not as an expansion of their domestic markets. These firms will often implement their global strategy within two years of inception.

In fact, more firms than ever go global right from the start each year. Neal Gandhi, author of "Born Global" and CEO of Quick Start Global, says this is part of our business future. Gandhi says that Born Global firms are efficient. By efficient, he means use of resources is optimized. Firms place their legal headquarters, teams of talent, and capital around the globe where it makes the most sense. That means a company's legal headquarters could be in Mauritius, its development team in India, its artistic team in the United States, and sales and marketing teams spread across the globe.

These may sound like multinational firms, but they aren't. These firms often employ less than 25 people in their first few years. Another term for these firms is micro-multinationals.

In addition, Born Global firms differ from traditional multinationals in that they do not consider borders per se in their strategy. Gandhi indicates that since regulations like taxation vary from country to country and the concept of borders are still very strong as to how governments regulate business, the business environment for a Born Global can be quite complex and difficult to address as they lack the resources of a multinational. But Gandhi points out that a Born Global entrepreneur takes challenges like this in stride.

Gandhi says the one key factor for a Born Global firm is having the right people. Born Global firms need people that are passionate, trustworthy, buy into the vision, and can execute in the local context.

A Born Global Firm in Action

Ashifi Gogo is CEO of Sproxil, Inc., a Born Global firm operationalized first in Africa. Gogo indicates that Sproxil's global strategy was a natural result of the challenge Sproxil was designed to address - counterfeit products.

Sproxil's initial service to eliminate counterfeit drugs has a global value chain. Many legitimate brand and generic pharmaceuticals are manufactured in India and China, and then sold in Africa. So, its customer base spans several countries and, therefore, it does as well.

Gogo says that ICT, mobile phones, and broadband have made a significant difference in managing costs, work, and reducing the number of required visits to Africa. The Sproxil team is able to stay connected regularly with each other and clients in Africa by VOIP and video calls.

Sproxil's team is spread across the Atlantic – in the United States and Africa. When asked for a photo of the entire team, Gogo couldn't produce one as the entire team had never met in one location.

So, technology has served as a key enabler for Sproxil to operate globally. However, Gogo says it is important to also find trusted local partners who can work well remotely using ICT and understands the markets you are entering.

Addressing Challenges of Forming a Global Ecosystem

Global firms have the same challenges as local or regional firms. They need the right people, right resources, right information, and right capital to tap business opportunities. However, finding the right combination of these for a successful business strategy is more complex. As soon as you look to do cross border engagement of any type, you immediately add complexity which can seem insurmountable.

However, the key to any successful Born Global venture, as noted by Gandhi and Gogo, is people. In this connected world, you are only a few degrees from people who can help you find the right people, right resources, right information, and right capital. The right people do not need to be in your organization. You just need access to them to get to everything else.

You see, people are the owners, stewards, and gatekeepers to what you need. What you don't have, someone else can provide. That's why I say that going global is not only a matter of what you have, but also what you can tap into.

At the heart of every successful firm today, is an ecosystem, which is both internal and external to the organization. If you can build this ecosystem to provide the necessary support for your global venture, you will be well ahead of others when implementing opportunities in Africa, or anywhere is in the world.

In essence, your goal is to become the network facilitator of an ecosystem that will support your business venture. You will not own the majority of resources and assets needed for your business venture, but you will be able to marshal what's needed through your ecosystem.

James Moore, in *Predators and Prey: A New Ecology of Competition,*[165] described an ecosystem for economic pursuits as:

> *An economic community is supported by a foundation of interacting organizations and individuals--the organisms of the business world. This economic community produces goods and services of value to customers, who are themselves members of the ecosystem. The member organizations also include suppliers, lead producers, competitors, and other stakeholders...*
>
> *...Over time, they co-evolve their capabilities and roles, and tend to align themselves with the directions set by one or more central companies. Those companies holding leadership roles may change over time, but the function of ecosystem leader is valued by the community because it enables members to move toward shared visions to align their investments and to find mutually supportive roles.*

As the network facilitator, you are seen to provide key value, which then opens the door for you to access other people, resources, information, capital, etc. for your business purpose. Companies like IBM, Apple, etc. are doing this successfully, but you don't need to be big to serve in this role. You can apply the same principles to small networks.

The role of network facilitator is well-suited for global business as today's global businesses place elements of their value chain where it makes the most sense. Network facilitators connect people and build networks where it makes sense.

---

[165] Moore, J. (1993). Predators and Prey: A New Ecology of Competition, *Harvard Business Review*, May/June.

One simple example is based on advice from Dennis Hessler of Spyglass Point Productions, who helps people start small exporting businesses. Choose an industry, or product, that you understand and would be considered an expert. Find a local manufacturing firm that does little or no exporting and offer to serve as its liaison to developing markets overseas. Then, work on locating foreign buyers. However, where you add value is in managing the entire process for the firm, not just in making sales. If you create value, the firm will not want to work around you or will find it difficult to do so.

While you have started with one firm, you have developed a small ecosystem to support this client, including export and import research, market research, freight forwarders and customs experts, etc. You can use this same ecosystem to support other clients and as the ecosystem expands you can look at spin-off opportunities.

A key imperative you need to follow in order to be successful in developing powerful networks and ecosystems is creating value for people and organizations.

Building a Dynamic Network

I, myself, am a task-oriented person. This means I travelled the hard road to learn the significance of people in getting results and business success. My training ground has been Africa for close to a decade now. While expertise plays a part in my success, relationships also play a significant role.

When I started to research the notion of social networks, I learned that social networking was even important for Bill Gates. When Gates started his firm, his mother used her social connections in Seattle to provide Gates access to key business people.

One of my biggest observations is that social networks are very important when one is initiating a new idea, whether in business or covering social issues. So, just as we spend time developing the next great idea, we need to focus on developing the ecosystem that will support the idea through its lifecycle.

A network is an interconnected system of things or people. Social networks are human networks we belong to, defined by relationships.

However, social networks in their raw form are not leveraged for business. In order to produce a strong network that will lead to business results, it has to have a purpose. So, to tap the power of our networks we need to transform them from social to value (purpose driven) networks. Value networks consist of people who come together in a loose association to achieve some economic, political, or social good.

Pay special attention to two phrases – "value" and "loose association." First, our whole business and economic systems are based on value creation. People, and organizations made up of people, have the ability to take raw materials and transform them into something of value for others, including things for which people will exchange something of value, e.g., money, knowledge, land, resources.

A value chain is the series of value-added activities involved to deliver valuable products and services to the end consumer. For example, a farmer grows string beans which he harvests and sells to an agricultural processor like Del Monte. Del Monte cooks and cans the string beans, then transports the product to wholesalers and distributors. The wholesalers and distributors will finally get the product to stores where people can purchase them. In today's application of value chains, many firms refer to their supply chains and distribution channels as their value chains which can make creating value seem like just a technical exercise.

It is attitudes like this which have divorced value from business. Financial institutions create complex instruments from which they can make money, but don't represent value. Day traders cause volatility in stock markets because they make their money from finding gaps in the market, not value. It's hard to tell what value is really in the stock market today. And at some point, these attitudes and behaviors cave in on themselves, skewing markets and business.

If we take a closer look at a value network, we find that our network of people represent value because they own, have access to, or have stewardship over information, resources, capital, etc. So, we want to be able to identify the value held within it and leverage it to shape our business strategies.

In this perspective of business, it is the strengths in these loose associations in the value network, as well as your own strengths, that determine the opportunities of which you are able to take advantage.

Network Weaving

The process to build this ecosystem is based on principles, but moves dynamically. Networks, because they involve people, are fluid, dynamic, and constantly changing, so our approaches must match.

Healthy networks are like grapevines, which produce fruit. As they are cultivated, the grapevines produce new fruit every harvest – they multiply.

Healthy networks should also multiply. When they do, your access to resources, information, capital, influence, etc. grows. And just like grapevines, they need to be cultivated to yield good fruit. Cultivating can involve pruning back some relationships, cutting some relationships, grafting some relationships together, and watering some relationships.

In cultivating a network, you have an active role not a passive one. Valdis Krebs, and others, has coined the phrase, "network weaver," for this role.[166] A network weaver takes responsibility for building healthy networks.

Network weavers look like people we call "social butterflies," but they network, or cross-pollinate ideas, resources, and opportunities for people with a purpose. Social butterflies network just to network.

Network weavers also watch, weave, and wake up networks in order to create value for people. They operate out of the heart (spirit) first, then the head (mind) and hands (body). They innately see the value of people and want to provide value to people.

There are three principles for successful network weavers whether it is for business, political, or social good. First, they love what they do and love people.

Second, they serve, share with, and sacrifice for people. It is not about "I," but about "we."

---

[166] Krebs, V. & Holley, J. *Building Smart Communities through Network Weaving.* Accessed online at http://www.orgnet.com/BuildingNetworks.pdf. (Accessed online on October 17, 2011.)

Third, they create win-win situations for stakeholders, not just shareholders. The goals are to do no harm and no one needs to lose. We see the opposite of this in public companies on the stock market where there is push to increase the stock price and dividends to shareholders while communities, employees, and others are harmed by the extreme nature of pursuing stock prices and dividends.

This principle is very important in emerging markets, like Africa, where even though there are huge opportunities, most of the countries have huge development challenges like poverty, poor health, and poor education. It is not ethical to only look at how you can make money and not consider how to support the local economies. It can be as simple as working with a local partner who employs people. By working with that local company, you are supporting the local economy. In fact, you will learn later that this is one key method for you to manage and reduce risks and costs.

There are seven major activities involved with network weaving:

- **Meet and Greet** – Network and be open to meeting new people anywhere, anytime. Introduce others.
- **Manage** – Stay in touch with people. Seek them out to see how they are doing and what they are doing.
- **Mention** – Seed something useful to your network.
- **Map** – Know the people, relationships, and activities of your network.
- **Mesh** – Bring people together around a purpose or common interest (Tribes).
- **Mobilize** – Assist the network to organize around purpose or common interest.
- **Move** – Get the network to act.

The first four activities deal more with one-on-one interactions while "Mesh," "Mobilize," and "Move" deal more with developing a network as the basis for the ecosystem you need to support your business venture.

The "Meet and Greet" activity involves making new connections and connecting people. When you meet a new person, you want to listen and learn from them. You can ask yourself the following questions and take mental notes:

- Who is s/he?
- What is his/her passion, purpose, or interests?
- What are his/her strengths?
- Why is s/he here?
- Is there an opportunity to help him/her?

When you connect people, you are "leading them to the water." You are leading them to people with which you believe they can form a mutual relationship. In the process, you want to consider the following questions and take mental notes:

- Who they are?
- How do you know or how did you meet them?
- What are their common passions, purposes, or interests?
- How might they be able to help each other?

When actually making the connection between people, Jack Ricchiuto of *Designinglife.com* says there are different levels of introduction which involve varying levels of your involvement. For example, you recently met Tom and believe that there would be mutual benefit if he met Shakira, who has a common interest and complementary capacities. You have the option to introduce them in the following ways:[167]

1. Suggest Tom should speak to Shakira.
2. Suggest Tom should speak with Shakira and call Shakira to look for a contact.
3. Introduce Tom to Shakira in an email.
4. Introduce Tom to Shakira in a conference call.
5. Introduce Tom to Shakira in person.
6. Introduce Tom and Shakira in person and follow up with them to nurture connection.
7. Introduce Tom and Shakira and offer a collaboration opportunity to get Tom and Shakira off to a successful partnership.

Levels 6 and 7 are both meaningful and most productive, if you feel led to use these approaches. As your network grows, you will not be able to offer this level of interaction for everyone, but you can still connect them effectively to help nurture their networks and yours.

---

[167] Ibid.

The "Manage" and "Mention" activities are those you conduct after you have met people. Manage involves three key elements:

- Make note of the person right after you meet them. Your notes should include name, contact information, passion/purpose/ interest, strengths, and anything else you can remember of interest. Personal details about family and likes and dislikes will often help open conversations.
- Follow up in a timely manner. Acknowledge that it was nice to meet the person, and complete anything you promised.
- Keep in contact periodically.

The "Mention" activity is simply connecting people that you know with people, resources, or information they will find beneficial. This means that as you meet new people or come across new information, think about who would find this new opportunity beneficial or valuable. Don't get into the habit of sending out mass mailings, which do not reflect the personal touch of sharing something you think will be beneficial.

The "Manage" and "Mention" activities should be done with some regularity as it allows you to reach out to people that you may not see often. Checking in once a year is a good general policy, by phone, if possible. You never know what someone has been up to and what new collaborations are possible as things have likely changed in both his/her business and yours. As you will learn later, having the right people working with you can cut cost, time, and risk, so setting aside time to reach out to others is an investment that can pay off big.

The best tools for managing the "Manage" and "Mention" activities are still contact management or email programs with calendar and task features. Many of the social tools like Facebook, Linkedin, Twitter, and MySpace are nice connection platforms and can augment what you do;

however, they do not help you manage information, tasks, or resources well. Many email programs now, like Outlook, allow you to integrate your social network accounts into your inbox.

You can learn how to tap the advantage of trust to complete the remaining three activities in network weaving – Mesh, Mobilize, and Move – in a chapter in *Redefining Business in the New Africa* entitled *Leveraging Trust Networks.*

The Importance of "Personal Touch" in Building Networks

Most people I share with on how to build their networks tell me they have never thought of managing their connections this way. They go to events and collect cards that sit on a desk somewhere. I remind them that they are missing opportunities. Meeting someone is a value encounter that you do not want to waste.

The best example in my own experience was the work I did with youth entrepreneurs in South Africa. There always seemed to be some bump in the road because people didn't see the value of having youth entrepreneurs in a business ecosystem. At the time, I was working on for-profit business models that would also lead to inclusive opportunities for young entrepreneurs that didn't have much business experience but could learn and provide service with the right opportunities.

I would frequently get comments like, "Why are you working with young people? They can't offer you anything." But what many people failed to realize is that those young people understood their local communities and often had contact with important figures because of tribal affiliations. Now, I have access to the very markets everyone else is trying to tap. I looked for value where others didn't see any. This can be part of your success as well.

I hope you will approach network weaving as a means to identify the value everyone can bring and the value you can bring to others. When you are able to identify value and then shape business strategy around the unique value that your stakeholders bring to the table, you will be able to anticipate and execute where others fail. And while it does take an investment of your time and energy, once your value network is sufficiently established it will help you tap opportunities faster and with less cost and risk overall.

The process of network weaving also promotes the creation of goodwill, a social currency. The *Merriam-Webster Dictionary*[168] defines goodwill as, "a kindly feeling of approval and support," "benevolent interest or concern," or "the favor or advantage that a business has acquired especially through its brands and its good reputation." In fact, goodwill is an intangible asset that is included in accounting practices. It is the value that a company has beyond its book value. Marshall Fields said, "Goodwill is the only asset that competition cannot undersell or destroy."

When someone has goodwill toward you, he or she will more likely share his or her knowledge, assets, and connections with you. Creating goodwill leads to influence. Goodwill is also a type of trust. As mentioned before, trust can be used as the basis to create a network in which to launch successful ventures in Africa.

Conclusion

If you didn't fully understand how important networks can be before reading this chapter, then hopefully you do now. By honing your networking skills you can acquire connections that stretch around the globe and back.

---

[168] Merriam-Webster - http://www.m-w.org

Aim to be a network weaver and introduce people to each other as they have done for you. Your networks should be ever expanding and along with it your access to resources, information, capital, influence, etc. will grow. Once you develop your networks, you need to use the value held within them to shape your business strategies and develop a strong ecosystem that will support your business ventures and investments in Africa.

10

Leveraging Informal Markets in Africa
Nissi Ekpott

In Africa, just like everywhere else, businesses can only become successful if they have a substantial consumer base to sell to. Thus, every business person wants to be sure there is a market for his products or services before he spends his resources setting up.

In Africa, a casual observation does very little to reveal the size of the market and true demand for products and services. African economies offer a much larger market opportunity than most people realize. Businesses, which are on the ground, have come to realize this, and have crafted innovative ways to harness these opportunities.

In Africa, as in many other parts of the world, there is an economy beneath the formal economy. This other economy is a ghost economy, which is like a mist or a cloud - visible yet invisible. It stands out, yet it is difficult to grasp. Some people call it the second economy while others call it the underground, or parallel, economy.

A well-recognized name for this sector is System D. System D is a slang phrase pirated from French-speaking Africa and the Caribbean. The French have a word that they often use to describe particularly effective and motivated people. They call them *débrouillards*. To say a man (or woman) is a *débrouillard(e)* is to tell people how resourceful and ingenious he or she is.

The former French colonies have sculpted this word to their own social and economic reality. They say that inventive, self- starting, and entrepreneurial merchants who are doing business on their own, without registering or being regulated by the bureaucracy and, for the most part, without paying taxes, are part of "*l'economie de la débrouillardise*" - or, sweetened for street use, "*Systeme D.*" This essentially translates as the ingenuity economy, the economy of improvisation and self-reliance, or the do-it-yourself (DIY) economy. A number of well-known chefs have also appropriated the term to describe the skill and sheer joy necessary to improvise a gourmet meal using only the mismatched ingredients that happen to be at hand in a kitchen.[169]

In the book, *Stealth of the Nations*[170], author Robert Nieuwirth estimates the informal economy to be worth over $10 trillion globally. This would place the informal economy in the top three economies in the world by official records.

In Africa, the second economy is estimated to be worth hundreds of billions of dollars. What makes Africa's economy unique to that of many other countries is that in several African countries, their second economies are estimated to be larger than their formal economies. This may be what is keeping Africa afloat, agile, and strong during the global economic downturn, expected to last through 2016, according to Lauri Elliott, Chief Strategist for Afribiz.

In fact, building African economies to leverage the strengths of informal economies ,instead of swallowing them up, may keep Africa on the move for decades as change is so rapid in business today that hierarchical, high infrastructure environments cannot keep pace. However, informal economies can and their dynamics may be significant to re-inventing a new global economy structure, according to Elliott.

---

[169] Nieuwirth, R. (2011). *The Stealth of Nations: The Global Rise of Informal Economies.* Pantheon (Random House): New York, NY.
[170] Ibid.

Nigeria offers a good example of a massive second economy. Lagos is Nigeria's most populous city and its economic hub. Its population is estimated to be anywhere between 9 – 15 million residents.

Some local authorities estimate that 80% of the working people in Lagos are in the informal economy. Their activities are estimated to account for 70% of Nigeria's gross domestic product - or approximately $145 billion. Some economists question the truth of these figures along with the actual size of the informal economy in Nigeria and elsewhere. In recent times though, new interest in the informal economy has sparked further research into the sector, and one thing most researchers agree with is that the African informal economy is vast.

There are street markets all over the city of Lagos with hawkers selling drinks, clothing items, small appliances, toys, food items, educational materials, music and video DVDs, and many other items. These markets and traders are unlicensed, and operating below the "radar." They do not pay taxes, they are not registered on any formal database, and the statistical systems do not count them. In fact, national statistics sometimes qualify them as "unemployed." An average visitor would view the street sales as absolute confusion.

However, such a view would be wrong. There is a method behind the madness: there is vast capital involved; volumes are traded daily; many livelihoods are sustained. Though many of the people in this sector are not officially counted as employed, they could easily be said to live average middle class lives.

Behind these street sellers and hawkers, are one or more rows of players made up of distributors and/or importers. It's a multi-million industry at this level. Many of these are likely unregistered, unlicensed operators.

For any investor, being able to identify and understand this economy is absolutely necessary. A clear insight into the second economy in Africa, its size and the way it works, opens one's eyes into the true size of the consumer market, as well as the potential in trade in most African economies. The people at the ground level will point out that most formal studies do not accurately estimate these possibilities.

It Is Not the Criminal Underworld!

The informal economy sometimes borders on the fringes of criminality. It sometimes involves smuggling, illegal trade, and the breaking of several laws. However, we must be careful not to classify all informal trade as criminal.

Informal economies have developed as a citizens' response to government policies, or the lack thereof. Many governments have not responded fast enough to the economic needs of their nations. It is noteworthy that in recent times African governments have been constantly reforming, making it easier to start businesses and simplifying tax codes. However, it has taken decades to get things going (some governments are still far behind). People need to make a living, hence, many have had to function informally. Most players in this economy are ordinary people striving to make a living, employing amazing entrepreneurial skills to do so. Most are not involved in any criminal practices but rather working within the confines of the system in which they find themselves.

Neuwirth in writing about his experience with an informal market trader describes it well, "The word 'informal' didn't express (the trader's) worldview. To him, Astron (his firm) wasn't surreptitious or suspect or in any way informal: instead, he and his firm were engaging in an open, independent, admirable exercise in self-reliance."[171] Neuwirth states that:

> *The growth of System D (informal economy) presents a series of challenges to the norms of economics, business, and governance it has traditionally existed outside the framework of trade agreements, labor laws, copyright protections, product safety regulations, antipollution legislation, and a host of other political, social, and environmental policies. Yet there's plenty that's positive, too. In Africa, many cities (Lagos, Nigeria, is a good example) have been propelled into the modern era through System D, because legal businesses don't find enough profit in bringing cutting-edge products to the third world. China has, in part, become the world's manufacturing and trading center because it has been willing to engage System D trade.*

Neuwirth also points out that System D is synonymous with entrepreneurial-ism and employment, spreading technology at prices even the poor can afford, bringing commerce and opportunities to neighborhoods that are off the government grid, distributing products more equitable and cheaply than big companies can, running public services such as trash pick-up, recycling, transportation and even utilities.

In Africa, the informal economy has been at work for a long time. The term "informal economy" was first coined in Kenya in the 1970's. This sector offers vast investment opportunities that will help build capacity and grow profits.

Informal markets are popular for a number of reasons. First, they are perceived by local shoppers as the best source for a good deal. Second, they also offer new products much earlier than the more formal businesses.

---

[171] Ibid.

These products are usually imported through a meandering network of friends or relations overseas.

Third, the informal markets are populated by small business people and are thus relational in nature. They understand and respond to the immediate environment of their customers, they are fluid and flexible.

A successful business is one that finds innovative ways to plug into this economy. Businesses, which harness the potential of the informal economy, will also be positioned for further growth by plugging into a "virtuous cycle," e.g., as investment is made into the informal economy more jobs will be created, more people will move out of poverty, and the potential consumer market will be expanded. In the long run, as African economies grow and get more structured, there will be room to lift these informal operators into the formal economy and get them regulated.

Bridging the Informal with the Formal

It would be completely erroneous to think that the informal economy in Africa will totally disappear in the near future. Even the most developed economies still have a sizable informal economy. Africa's informal economy will be around for some time.

In some parts of Africa, governments view the informal economy as undermining the states access to revenue. They are seen as a hindrance to the modernization of local economies. However, the informal sectors have continued to grow.

In recent years, several African economies, such as Rwanda, Ghana, Morocco, and others, have been among the world's leading reformers, according to Doing Business reports by the International Finance Corporation (IFC). These nations are making it much easier for people to start and run a business. As the business climate improves, there will be a general tendency for many informal traders to migrate into the formal sector. In South Africa, for example, several tax amnesty programs have made it possible for informal operators to enter into the formal economy and access the relevant benefits.

The informal economy is already linked to the formal economy. But there is also additional potential to use technology and systems from the formal economy to support and empower the informal economy. The formal economy has several advantages: its impact is broad; it leads to more solid economic growth; it is the way to go in the long run. However, it cannot achieve its full potential without the informal sector. Businesses, which create ways of bridging the two, will be more likely to succeed.

The following three sections share illustrations of how important the informal economy is to business and the national economy.

How MTN Nigeria Leveraged the Second Economy

After about three years of studying the market, MTN decided to launch its operations in Nigeria. They were one of the first mobile operators licensed to operate in Nigeria and came from South Africa, which has a much more regulated and formal economy. MTN laid out a formal approach, designed for use in developed markets - it required dealers to be registered with the Corporate Affairs Commission, own a business name, and be licensed. The company also decided that it would sell its recharge cards in specific denominations and only through MTN branded stores. Customers would be sold monthly plans; hence, a proper tracking system was necessary.

This system failed from the start. MTN had to cut its losses and re-think its plans. They observed that in Nigeria, as in many other African countries, most potential customers were "off the grid," meaning they were without any formal identification.

Potential customers had money to pay for the product, but a monthly payment plan simply couldn't work because no one would be able to guarantee regular payment nor even the credit-worthiness of the client. They decided that a pre-paid option would probably work better.

This option had to be cheap and widely available. The new plan was based on sales through umbrella stands. Almost all of their products would be sold by street hawkers and vendors. Airtime would be available in the smallest possible denominations. Consumers would simply be able to buy airtime, load on their phones, and use. They would use what they paid for.

MTN put in a system where their recharge cards were sold to distributors, who in turn sold to sub-dealers. The sub-dealers then sold to the folks on the street - the umbrella stand owners, who in turn sold the cards to the informal, retail consumer market.

Anyone who wanted to make a call to another part of Nigeria, or elsewhere, could simply do so at any of these umbrella stands for a small per minute charge. Otherwise, he could buy recharge cards and load up his phone.

This system worked. Since 2007, MTN has been making revenues of about $ 2.4 billion yearly from Nigeria. It has 40% of the mobile phone market share in that country with over 30 million users.

The truth is that the street hawkers are not the most reliable sales people. Some have other jobs, and most work at their own pace. They are no strings attached, no way to formally trace them or control them. MTN realizes this and has designed their system to take all of these challenges into consideration. All transactions are cash based, and the system works.

Prepaid systems have come to be very popular in Africa and beyond. Even mobile phone operators in countries such as the U.S. are experiencing fast-growing, pre-paid consumer markets. In Africa, many other industries, such as insurance, electricity, water, waste disposal, and others have moved into pre-paid offerings. This has allowed them to be able to reach far more consumers.

Jua Kali: Kenya's Experience with the Second Economy

In Kenya, informal economic clusters are known as Jua Kali. They have produced flourishing economic clusters in cities and rural areas.

These clusters bring together producers, traders, labor and customers. Service providers, such as lenders, also bring their services to these clusters.

It is believed that some of these clusters have become extremely large. For instance, the Gikomba cluster in Nairobi, Kenya's commercial capital is one of the largest of such clusters in Africa and globally.

In the book, *Making Do: Innovation in Kenya's Informal Economy*[172], author Steve Daniels notes the core reason for their success consists of three elements: resourcefulness, relationships, and reason (or knowledge) of the entrepreneurs. Daniels goes on to say:

> *Resourceful engineers make treasure out of trash - from oil lamps made of soup cans to grass cutting machines made of scrap sheet metal - and at the end of their useful life, these items are fed back into the web of production by scrap pickers, closing the cycle. In the absence of formal institutions, relationships take the place of contracts. Yet, entrepreneurs manage to pool machines, labor, and savings without lawyers, cutting out the middleman.*

---

[172] Daniels, S. (2010). *Making Do: Innovation in Kenya's Informal Economy.* http://analoguedigital.com/makingdo/. (Accessed online January 13, 2012.)

An understanding of the local context is deeply embedded in informal business. Engineers continuously adapt production methods to available materials and product quality to customers' wallets - precisely the flexibility needed to thrive in that context, however frowned upon by regulators.

The True Size of the South African Workforce

The South African economy is Africa's most developed. It's more diversified, structured, and regulated than anywhere else on the continent. The South African Department of Statistics works better than all such similar departments in other parts of Africa.

In 2011, ADCORP, South Africa's biggest employment agency and leading authority on labor market trends, carried out a study to prove that whereas the unemployment rate in the official economy is a staggering 23.5%, the rate of people totally excluded from any form of economic activity, including the informal sector, is possibly as low as 7.9%.

Through this research, Adcorp also learned that many official statistical gathering methods are arcane and impractical, and fail to take into account what's really happening on the streets. These studies end up hurting the countries indirectly because they do not attract policies and approaches aimed at harnessing the entrepreneurial spirit that is abundantly available.

Some analysts, like Lauri Elliott of Afribiz, believe that these official methods, in several African countries, were deliberately skewed in the past in order to depict mass poverty and justify their demand for international aid. However, things are changing and African governments are realizing that trade is the way forward, inspiring the slogan trade not aid. Ghana has already re-adjusted its measures and recorded a dramatic increase in economic activity. Other countries like Kenya and Nigeria are looking into doing the same thing.

Africa's prosperity lies in creating wealth, jobs, and new entrepreneurs. Africa needs investment into its private sector for this to happen and for this kind of investment to be made, there has to be a true picture of the market.

The Size of the Informal Consumer Market

In the past, one of the most discouraging perceptions for potential investors into Africa was the perceived market size. Any business wants to ensure that there are consumers who can pay for their products. Many studies present the picture of a large chuck of the population living below $2.00 per day.

This kind of picture discourages the casual observer. This perception of Africa often causes investors, who do not perform due diligence, to assume that investing in Africa is not a viable option.

As a result, many potential investors and businesses have walked away from good opportunities and missed having a head start on what is possibly one of the last great investment opportunities in the world. However, the examples in the previous sections illustrate that the market is usually much larger than it seems on the surface. So, businesses and investors should reconsider their preconceived notions about Africa, if they haven't already.

In *Redefining Business in the New Africa*, I laid out several examples showing evidence that the consumer market in Africa there. But, the key question is, will you heed and take advantage of the under tapped consumer markets?

Developing a Framework to Tap Informal Markets

At this point, the businessperson begins to ask himself, "Can my product or service work in Africa?" In most cases the answer is yes. There is always a market out there, sometimes small or sometimes quite significant depending on the product.

Information technology has opened the eyes of the average African consumer to products and services globally. It is most likely that your type of product or service is already being consumed to some degree.

The average African consumer is young and a member of the fast growing middle class, which means that anyone who enters the market now is entering a growing market.

Having come to terms with this reality, where do you go from here? Here's a list of questions which will help you form a framework for launching your business in Africa:

- **Have I been on the ground in my target market?** - We advocate visits to your target market and on-the-ground research or observation of Africa as a key step to doing business on the continent. I once traveled to a small West African town with an American business person. On the first day, he was shocked at the lack of structure. To him it seemed that everything he would need to run his business was unavailable and he began thinking of making plans to ship everything to Africa. Over the next few days, to his surprise, he discovered that everything he needed to do business could be found in the very same town. Nothing beats the practical, on-the-ground, unbiased experience of visiting Africa. A closer study on the ground will reveal where the opportunities are and how to access them.

- **What sort of innovative solutions do I need to create?** – Obviously, there is a gap in the market and that's why you are there, to fill it. The structure is much different from what you are used to, but the need still exits. Some key questions are: 1) How do you make your product or service adaptable to local needs? 2) How do you do it in such a way that is it feasible and profitable? 3) How do you interface with the second economy? Consider the MTN example. The company had to develop an innovative way of offering a solution to its consumers. The prepaid solution was very ingenious and new to its market at that time.

- **Have I paid attention to the local suggestions and solutions?** - In many cases, Africans already have solutions to what may be perceived as barriers to trade, listening to their advice is crucial. Their solutions may just need simple tweaking, or some form of enhancement through improved technology, to be applied to your needs. This will save you lots of money and an extended learning curve.

- **Have I identified solid, local intermediaries to help me access the local economy?** - In more developed economies, the DIY concept is popular. In Africa, you are much better off if you work through trusted intermediaries. It is not as expensive as it sounds and in the long run you may save a lot of resources. You do not have to become informal yourself to reach the informal economy. In most cases, if you are a foreign business, you will find it difficult or impossible to slide in "under the radar." This is also not advisable. It's best you keep all your business transactions transparent. However, you can easily connect with the second economy through intermediaries e.g.; distributors, sub-distributors, representatives, and agents. These are established local companies who understand the workings of the system.

- **Is my pricing policy acceptable to the local consumers?** - The second economy thrives on lower pricing. It's an economy that functions with fewer overheads. This is one area where the Chinese businesses in Africa have gained an advantage over other foreign businesses. The fundamental thinking behind this is affordability. The median disposable income in Africa is sometimes low, there is little bank finance available, and consumers have to buy with cash. This drives them to be price sensitive. If your product or service targets the mass market, you need to be able to price from a local perspective and ensure that the average person can easily buy your product. This mindset demands that your product or service is primarily developed from a price perspective. For example, many mobile phone companies in Africa experienced a surge in their sales when they reduced the minimum value of recharge cards from $10 to $1. This made it more affordable in the short term, and hence increased subscription.

- **Do I have a grasp of the short term-long term mindset?** - This sounds like a contradiction, but it is not. In Africa, you need to be in business for the long term. It takes time to settle, understand the dynamics, face the challenges (many of them unexpected), and achieve true profit. That's one side of the deal. On the other hand, your consumers will rarely make long term considerations when purchasing. The informal economy means unreliable trade structures. There are hardly any "contractual" sales strategies and you cannot bank on a "captive market." Your customers will tend to engage in once-off transactions. However, according to Brian Herlihy, CEO of SEACOM, Africa is proving to be a model for transaction-based business models. Also, the market conditions are historically unstable which has led the consumer to make short term considerations. This may not always be the best way to function, however, as a business you need to respond to the immediate needs of your market and then possibly gradually influence the mindset of your consumers. In summary, establish your business for the long term, but offer your products with an understanding of the short term. In the initial phases, you may very well need to wear the "short term hat" yourself.

- **Can I harness existing hubs, trade routes, and structures?** - The informal economy works though hubs within cities, nations, or regions. In the informal markets, these hubs and routes are defined. For instance in West Africa, Lagos and Accra are hubs. Traders from all over West Africa buy their electronic items from Lagos and export these by road to the other cities. On the other hand, traders buy items, such as clothing materials, beads, and food from markets like Accra and Dakar in Senegal. These are then transported to Lagos, where they are re-distributed to other parts of Nigeria. In East Africa, Nairobi is one of the major economic hubs. However on a lower level, there are less popular hubs within the nations. For example, traders will buy the same imported clothes from major importers in Lagos and transport these over to minor hubs within Nigeria, such as the city of Aba. Then, retailers from neighboring towns will buy from the city of Aba and, in turn, transport the items to shops within their towns. Most consumers will buy from the retailer nearby. There is always a particular way trade flows from the manufacturer through the distributors to sub-distributors to retailers and, eventually, to the consumer. Because of its informal markets, it may not be defined in any research material, buts it is there, clear and evident. There are also existing trade routes through particular routes to other cities. It is best to plan your business in such a way that you can harness the existing distribution structures within these hubs and routes especially in your early years.

- **Can I deploy a lean start-up?** - A huge informal economy means potential for unexpected twists and turns. The MTN example above is a good one. At the start, they lost money from deploying a system that was not friendly to the informal economy. The informal economy is not as efficient as it should be. Working with these types of systems adds to the overall cost of doing business, which can be quite high in Africa. Many unexpected expenses will show up from time to time. In the starting phases, you need to keep your business lean, until the income starts rolling in. You can learn something from the informal traders- low overheads, high turnovers, and high return on investment.

Conclusion

This chapter introduced you to elements of the informal markets in Africa and how to tap into them to aide your business venture on the continent. One key perspective to keep in mind that although informal markets can seem disorganized and chaotic, they often have their own fluid structures and organizations that make things work. Connecting and leveraging these structures is a great way to create a significant footprint in Africa.

11

Shaping Value to Enter African Markets
Lauri Elliott

In *Redefining Business in the New Africa*, I shared about leveraging trust networks to do business in Africa, offering a straight-forward framework. But, I also noted that trust is not enough. Leveraging any network in global business needs to incorporate value and trust, hence, the name "trust-value" networks.

In trust-value networks, the aim is to have high trust/high value networks. Networks with high trust and low value, or low trust and high value, are not healthy and have problems growing in an organic fashion. In today's world of rapid change, only networks and organizations that can move fluidly and dynamically will remain strong.

This chapter focuses on the process of developing the right value proposition in Africa, including a discussion of how cooperatives and entrepreneurial ecosystems can help you build the right value proposition for African markets. First, an economy is driven by the delivery of something of value to end consumers – things that they cannot do or produce for themselves, or prefer not to. When a consumer finds something of value that he or she wants or needs, the person transacts an exchange to acquire that value. The currency of the exchange can vary from money to information to resources to other tangible assets. In the end, however, a value exchange has occurred.

Second, it's important to know that value is defined by what the consumer perceives, not you as the provider of that value. In general, we can say that the higher the value the more people will pay for it. However, in strained economies and emerging markets, you need to factor in how much people are willing and able to pay. People may think what you provide is of high value, but they may also think the price is too high to acquire it or they cannot afford it.

Third, businesses are responsible for adding value to consumers, but that should translate to revenue and profit for the businesses. The other part of the equation is that businesses need to educate consumers on the value they bring. You can have a great product, but if consumers don't know about it, don't understand it, and/or don't know the value it brings them you cannot tap into the potential of the market.

There are three waves of expressing value to others – all benefits, favorable points of difference compared to your competitors, or key differentiators that provide the greatest value to the customer.[173] The first wave, all benefits, focuses on translating all features of a product or service to language that expresses the benefits to the customer. The key question answered is, "Why should the customer purchase your offering?"

The second wave, favorable points of difference, focuses on identifying all favorable points of differences between your offerings and that of your competitors. It builds on what you have done in the first wave. The key question answered is, "Why should the customer purchase your offering instead of a competitor's?"

The third wave, key differentiators, focuses on identifying the one or two points of difference that provide the customer the greatest value and on which your competitors cannot match or exceed you. It builds on what you have done in the first and second wave. The key question answered is,

---

[173] Anderson, J. C., Kumar, N., & Narus, J. A. (2007). *Value Merchants: Demonstrating and Documenting Superior Value in Business Markets.* Harvard Business School Press: Cambridge, MA.

"What are the most worthwhile, distinct, and unique aspects of your offering that customers should keep in mind?"

If you haven't noted already, this is a process. You must first understand and be able to communicate all benefits of your offering, then you must understand and be able to communicate the differences in favor of you against your competitors. Then finally, you can hone or refine your pitch to a few key differentiators that make you stand out amongst all the competitors. All of this is based on dynamics, e.g. customer characteristics, of the market in which you want to enter. For example, customer characteristics differ in Africa compared to Europe or North America. So, the importance of being able to adapt the expression of your value to different customer segments or markets is important.

Through this process you are conceptualizing and formulating a value proposition. The basic definition of a value proposition is the total package of benefits a customer receives for paying you. However, as I have stressed before, you want to focus on unique competitive space (UCS), so you want to create a unique value proposition (UVP).

Note that you may have offerings that offer very similar benefits to those of your competitors; however, the way you package, or configure, them may create that UVP. In this case, you want to try to make it something that competitors cannot easily duplicate, at least in the short run. This is where leveraging your strengths help you create UVP that your competitors will find difficult to compete with.

The unique configurations of offerings you create, based on your strengths, can give you an edge over competitors. Networks in which your organization is a significant member is an example. In our case, we have developed good partnerships with networks that others have ignored or haven't served well. This is another point about creating UVP – also create your own unique market in the open space no one else is serving appropriately.

In Africa, there are more obvious open spaces in markets than in any other region in my opinion. There are enormous amounts of valuable assets that are underdeveloped in Africa – human capital, land, water, etc. Africa's problem is not poverty, but wealth potential that is lying fallow because it hasn't been developed.

One example of this is mangos, which grow wild in several African countries like Mozambique and Sierra Leone. Each season mangos fall to the ground and rot because they are not harvested and processed. In Sierra Leone, Juice Felix developed a processing plant to transform these mangoes into juice which is sold in the local markets because there is strong demand. The supply chain incorporates villages in which the wild mangos typically go to waste because they are not good to eat, but are suitable for juice. Juice Felix has added value to what was going to waste while bringing revenue to poor communities.

There is tremendous potential for small and large enterprises that can operate in the open space in Africa. Being able to do so is actually a competitive advantage itself.

Taking this approach will help you accelerate entrance into markets anywhere on the globe. It will also save you finances and resources to ramp up against competitors. If you top it off with strong partners, who can help deliver the market to you, you are way ahead.

Mapping the Value Proposition

Also, remember that not only do you need to develop the right value proposition you need to be able to communicate it in a way that potential markets will understand and buy into. Your unique value proposition is an expression of your business model. It is the heart of your business model, like the business model is the heart of your business plan.

You can focus on discovering UVP from two angles. The first frame asks, "What are the customer segments served and what does it take to serve them?" You could have all the elements to serve them or not in this scenario.

I prefer the second frame when looking at new or under tapped markets. The second frame asks, "What components do I have available to me, including my own strengths, like networks, skilled personnel, intellectual property? What customer segments will these possibly service? What patterns or configurations can I create to provide high value?" I would add that you should not only think about your own capacities, but those of others that you can tap into readily. The second frame gives you a sense of momentum instead of being stuck on what you might not have.

Discovering your UVP is really part of the business model creation process and like it can be an ongoing effort in this climate of rapid change. Key questions involved in developing a business model are:

- Who are your key partners that help you deliver value to your market and what do they bring to the table?
- What are the key activities involved in delivery of value to your market?
- What are the key resources needed to deliver value to your market?
- What are the customer relationships that are involved?
- What are the channels you use to deliver value to your market?
- To which customer segments can you deliver this value?

- What are the costs and revenues associated with delivering value to your market?
- What are the value propositions for the targeted customer segments?

To visualize your value proposition represented by your business model, Alexander Osterwalder and Yves Pigneur developed the following business model canvas template, which can be used along with the questions above. [174]

Key Partners	Key Activities	Value Propositions	Customer Relationships	Customer Segments
	Key Resources		Channels	
Cost Structure			Revenue Structure	

---

[174] Osterwalder, A. & Pigneur, Y. (2010). *Business Model Generation: A Handbook for Visionaries, Game Changers, and Challengers.* John Wiley & Sons: Hoboken, NJ.

Extending Value to Other Stakeholders

Businesses tend to think of value they bring to customers and shareholders; however, in our connected world we need consider all key stakeholders. It can seem a daunting task, but we should do no harm with the goal of doing good for all. Business models today need to be inclusive and consider everyone impacted. While it is impossible to manage all scenarios, you can at least learn to include significant stakeholders from different levels of society, which according to the C4[175] stakeholder model are:

- **Corporate** – These are all the stakeholders that work within the boundaries of your business, including employees and contractors. You typically have more control and influence over their activities on behalf of your company. Their work directly impacts your ability to perform and your reputation. Your business should also be accountable to them as you are to shareholders.

- **Channels** – These will be strategic partnerships, such as alliances and joint ventures. It can include suppliers, distributors, agents, technology partners, etc. You have less control over this group, but still typically have significant influence when relationships are healthy.

- **Customers** – Customers are a unique class as they will tend to have more influence over you than the other way around. How your corporate and channel stakeholders help deliver value to them will, however, influence their satisfaction and loyalty.

- **Community** – Community can be the neighborhood in which you provide products or services, or opportunity. It can also be representative of local, regional, national, and international

---

[175] C4 Stakeholder Model developed by Lauri Elliott.

communities. Social issues of inclusive business models and environmental preservation are examples of growing global concerns that businesses cannot ignore.

It's important for firms to develop value propositions to a certain degree for all significant stakeholders. The following are good starting questions for this process:

- Who are our significant stakeholders?
- What value do we provide each significant stakeholder?
- Are we doing anything that would lower the value any significant stakeholder places on what we provide?
- How do our significant stakeholders relate to one another and interact?
- How can we engage each significant stakeholder positively?

In the African context, the entire ecosystem of your stakeholders must be addressed. For example, if you are doing anything with land, like mining or agriculture in rural areas, you have to be cognizant that although the government may have given you permission to commercially develop the land there are often communities living on those lands. If you want to maintain good relations for the long-term, it is better to work with the community as well to make sure that their needs are being addressed. Don't just assume the government is doing it.

Finding Value that You Can Leverage

The concept of networks of value (separate from the trust-value nexus) is built on the collaborative environment. Today, collaboration goes on within organizations and between organizations. In some instances, competitors also collaborate, which is often called co-opetition. However, in my experience collaboration doesn't necessarily bring better results. The collaboration process needs to be facilitated so that more value is created and leveraged. One great way to do that is to plug into existing networks or ecosystems with which you have complementary value. In this section, I will introduce you to two – cooperatives and entrepreneurial ecosystems.

Cooperatives

A cooperative is defined as "an autonomous association of persons united voluntarily to meet their common economic, social, and cultural needs and aspirations through a jointly owned and democratically controlled enterprise," according to the International Co-operative Alliance, they are "based on the values of self-help, self-responsibility, democracy, equality, equity, and solidarity."

While cooperatives are generally formed when a group of people in the same industry unite with the intention of creating better business opportunities for everyone, there are actually a few countries in Africa that have cooperatives that are run through the government, like they are private companies. Mozambique, Ethiopia, and Malawi are three of the countries that are home to successful cooperatives. The majority of them involve rural farmers, and in some cases miners, combining their resources to get their products out to a larger consumer market. Taking things a step further, Ethiopia has a commodities exchange where crops, which are harvested by their cooperatives, are bought and sold on the international market through the Ethiopia Commodities Exchange (ECX).

So, how can SMEs get in business with a cooperative in Africa? Paul Guenette, Senior Vice President of ACDI/VOCA, recommends that you first know what products you want to target and find a cooperative that is on the verge of success - one that could be put over the top with your involvement. "The more sophisticated among the cooperatives are out there doing marketing. The opportunities for SMEs and entrepreneurs are at the mid-level, where they're not already riotously successful. I think that at the mid-level, SMEs and entrepreneurs are more likely to find a good deal because you will find cooperatives that are looking for a partner for commercializing their product." Essentially, it's a win-win scenario for everyone involved.

Guenette recommends that when searching for the right cooperative to partner with you should be looking at capacity, reliability, volumes and quality of the products that a cooperative can make available, and conditions associated with seasonality. Find out if there's a period of time when they can supply their products, but then have a lengthy down time. "And you want to look at the validity of the cooperative, as well as the capacity of the executives managing it," Guenette adds.

There is an inherent risk in doing business anywhere, but developing regions have their own set of risks. Fortunately, there are mechanisms in place, in the form of NGOs, which are willing to bear some of that risk for you, in the hopes of seeing cooperatives succeed. According to Guenette, "Entrepreneurs are apt to find international organizations, such as ACDI/VOCA, who are out there strengthening producer groups. We'd like nothing more than to have private business opportunities for those cooperatives."

Entrepreneurs should check with their embassy in a particular country to see who is working with cooperatives as a starting point. There might be public-private partnerships in which they can become involved. Entrepreneurs might find some allies on the ground that are in the business of strengthening local cooperatives - their transparency, accounting, management, strategic planning, marketing, technical skills, and the ability to deliver those technical skills to their members.

In this scenario, entrepreneurs form a three-partner business deal in which the cooperative and entrepreneur do business and the international NGO supports that endeavor. This can help lower the risk of the business opportunity.

Another factor to consider is whether a cooperative is certified. There are a variety of certification programs, including ISO-certification and fair trade. It shows a demonstrated level of capacity, as well as a serious dedication to quality and detail, on the part of the cooperative. "We've got rural coffee cooperatives in Rwanda that are organic and fair-trade certified and really sharp,…the fact that they are certified, and are re-certified each year by an international body, gives a nice signal to an incoming investor to their degree of seriousness and capacity," notes Guenette. It's also a good shortcut to getting into the market quickly.

Guenette believes that cooperatives are not only beneficial for everyone involved, but a great way for world economies to rebound from their recent hardships. "…We're at a turning point in the world's development where there's this huge body of rural producers who are at risk of being disenfranchised and left behind as (economies) move forward and globalize. The irony is that cooperatives and producer groups are a solution that makes business sense. So, it's a nice concept and mechanism to have when you're looking at what's otherwise a really daunting global situation. To find such an obvious business solution is a great thing."

Entrepreneurial and Business Ecosystems

There are numerous entrepreneurial and business ecosystems affiliated with Africa directly or indirectly, formally or informally – on the continent and around the world. The first type of entrepreneurial/business system is that created through academic affiliation.

Many foreign universities have established business and/or entrepreneurial campuses and programs on the continent. Some examples include Babson College, Regent University, and Carnegie Mellon in Rwanda, as well as the University of North Carolina Chapel Hill in South Africa. Academic institutions also have global, or regional, entrepreneurial competition in which African entrepreneurs will compete. A good example is MIT's Global Startup Workshop. It's easy to check with business schools at universities to see if they have campuses, or programs, in Africa.

There are open platforms, like VC4Africa, which provide a place for entrepreneurs and investors to connect and interact. The Kauffman Foundation is in the process of mapping the entrepreneurial ecosystem of Africa across 50 countries in a project called E-Pulse, which will follow with a platform to connect with these ecosystems.

There are also organizations that focus on the development of entrepreneurs which, like the capacity building for cooperatives, is a vital part of the equation in finding entrepreneurs that will add value to your network. Some examples are Endeavor, Kauffman Foundation, Ashoka, and Enablis. The South African Chamber of Commerce in America (SACCA) developed a report[176] on the Missing Middle Initiative, which lists several organizations and agencies that support SMEs and entrepreneurs.

---

[176] South African Chamber of Commerce in America. (2010). *The Missing Middle Initiative: Highlighting the Problem, Accelerating the Solution.* http://www.sacca.biz/backend/media/2272010113630PM/MissingMiddleInitiative WEFJan.10.pdf. (Accessed online on January 15, 2012).

A particular sub-set of entrepreneurial networks are venture acceleration networks. In the report, *Nurturing Innovation: Venture Acceleration Networks*[177], they are described as consisting of, "experienced, skilled, and well-connected individuals who provide hands-on support to entrepreneurs. They help propel viable business ideas to the marketplace by accelerating the regeneration of ideas and connecting entrepreneurs to the market." Many of the organizations mentioned previously, e.g. Enablis and Endeavor, are forms of venture acceleration networks.

It is advantageous for businesses and investors to be involved in these networks in Africa. First, like organizations that support cooperatives, venture acceleration networks help entrepreneurs develop capacity and validate the viability of ventures. So, in a sense, businesses and investors are presented with "bankable" venture opportunities.

Second, these networks can actually help firms embed themselves in the heart of the industry in Africa, as being present in Silicon Valley helps firms to do this in the global tech sector. Instead of trying to find a door into the industry, you become a part of the industry more readily than traditional market entry models that take a long time to develop. You support the ecosystem and you receive benefits from the ecosystem. This is a win-win situation.

---

[177] World Bank. (2011). *Nurturing Innovation: Venture Acceleration Networks.* http://siteresources.worldbank.org/FINANCIALSECTOR/Resources/VentureAccel erationNetworks1.pdf. (Accessed online on January 8, 2012.)

Conclusion

Africa is a complex environment which is difficult to navigate, as are many other emerging market environments. There are a myriad of pathways to enter African markets. Each business and investor will need to discover their own unique path.

However, alliances, joint ventures, and other forms of partnerships are key to success in African markets overall and increasingly in global business. The basis for forming these partnerships needs to be a balance of value and trust, hence, the term "trust-value" network.

The value portion of this equation must be mutually beneficial. For businesses and investors entering African markets, they must know, be able to communicate, and demonstrate the value they bring for customers, partners, and other key stakeholders.

At the same time, it is important also to know networks that have value you can leverage to create a successful footprint in Africa. The use of existing networks that are not as obvious for market entry strategy can make a significant difference in how you are able to grow on the continent.

Cooperatives and entrepreneurial networks are just a few examples. If you can approach Africa with an out-of-the-box mindset, you will find networks with under tapped value in obvious and not so obvious places.

12

Conclusion:
Accelerating Opportunities and Business in Africa
Lauri Elliott

For all that we've shared in *Redefining Business in the New Africa* and this book, it doesn't mean much if it cannot be executed. Africa is a vast continent with numerous opportunities of which multinationals have always taken advantage. The problem is that middle market, small businesses, and start-ups (whether foreign or local) are still greatly underrepresented and challenged on the continent. If these segments of business do not accelerate in the next decade, Africa will again fall behind and small businesses around the world will lose access to tremendous opportunities. There are a lot of solutions, some better than others, but still insignificant progress.

As we looked at the landscape in Africa, we wondered what could be done differently and have developed a few prototypes – city cluster and Afribiz Accelerator™ - that seem to hit the mark and incorporate a lot of the learnings we shared in these books to accelerate and scale business execution in these segments. I will close out by introducing them to you.

City Cluster

In order to catalyze economic, trade, business, investment, and capital flows between African countries, as well as the continent and other countries, The Africa Consortium, Conceptualee, and Afribiz establish "city" clusters,

271

which leverage the synergy of businesses across sectors, as well as supporting institutions in government, academic, and social sectors.

A cluster is a group of loosely connected entities working together as a single entity to share and leverage resources, networks, knowledge, etc. The concept of clusters is very familiar in business settings, e.g., Silicon Valley tech cluster. We have adapted the framework for cities to incorporate businesses across sectors, as well as supporting institutions in the government, social, and academic sectors. The cluster is made up of 70-300 entities from the city. Each city has a unique DNA that makes it competitive and we use the strength of this to connect to and execute opportunities in Africa.

The cluster is kept active through two Synergy Action Forums run each year, approximately six months a part. These one- or two-day events use large scale intervention techniques to synergize entities to priorities chosen by the members and put them to work to get results on these priorities.

The Charlotte Africa Initiative (CAI) is the cluster started in Charlotte, North Carolina. It is spearheaded by the Africana Studies Department at University of North Carolina at Charlotte, Conceptualee, Inc., and The Africa Consortium (base of operation).

To date, we have been able to start collaboration with another cluster in Charlotte, the Charlotte Energy Cluster. This cluster consists of over 200 companies in the energy sector, representing perhaps the largest energy cluster in the U.S. We will use the synergistic power of this cluster to help make greater impact on the energy gap in Africa will creating economic opportunities for U.S. and African firms that work together in partnership. Other strategic alliances and collaborations to date include the International House of Charlotte (houses the Africa Council which brings together the African Diasporas in the Charlotte region), Pan African Chamber of Commerce and Industry (officially recognized by the African

Union as the collective voice for business in Africa), North Carolina A&T University International Trade Division (focuses on agribusiness value chains, from production to market access), and Blacks in Government Africa Partnership Secretariat (BIG represents the three million African American government workers, who can bring technical capacity, Diaspora integration, and investment to Africa).

CAI's current projects include:

- Trade finance program for African SMEs who buy American products
- Agricultural farms in DR Congo
- Network of entrepreneurial ecosystems in various African countries called Afribiz Accelerators™

In a partnership with Millabaltica of Spain, Conceptualee will establish the Madrid Africa Cluster in 2012. And in partnership with Lex Noir and Nixon Peabody Africa Practice, mini-clusters will be established in over 10 U.S. cities in 2013. Afribiz Accelerators™ are being launched in Congo Brazzaville, DR Congo, and South Sudan in 2012.

Afribiz Accelerator™

There is a significant need to help the entrepreneur and SME segments in Africa grow as these strata are the economic engines of any country and create the most jobs. Within this, an acceleration of the growth of youth and women enterprises is a priority.

We propose to do this through a for-profit, social enterprise model (Afribiz Accelerator™), which focuses on integrating entrepreneurship/leadership training for youth, economic opportunity development for youth, social/business network leverage, an incubator/venture accelerator, SME/entrepreneur venture capital fund, and development of an SME/entrepreneur support industry. The Afribiz

Accelerator™ is being cascaded across several countries (DR Congo, Botswana, Congo Brazzaville, Swaziland, Niger, Sudan, and South Sudan to start) through young African entrepreneurs that were a part of the 2012 Young African Leaders Initiative sponsored by the U.S. State Department, who decided to create a greater impact on the continent by joining forces.

While the model itself may be innovative, it is rooted in several separate models that have proved effective but are combined in a new way. The following sections will highlight the key components mentioned previously.

Entrepreneurial/Leadership Training
As indicated by the African Economic Outlook 2012, African countries, training centers, and schools have not done a good job overall of preparing a youth workforce to enter the job market. The same can be said for entrepreneurship /leadership skills. So, the first component is to embed the culture and skills of entrepreneurship into secondary, vocational, and tertiary institutions into key African countries, as well as offer these skills to youth who do not have access to these institutions. This is the "social" underpinning for this model, so whether it generates revenue or not itself the Afribiz Accelerator™ is committed to supporting this component.

The pedagogy for the entrepreneurship training is experiential/project-based versus classroom style and focuses on collaborative, or cooperative, entrepreneurship in which youth band together to take advantage of a business opportunity. Business, societal, and citizen leadership are embedded as part of the culture.

The initial stage of the entrepreneurial training is organized into a "boot camp" model which helps to quickly acclimate youth to both a business and entrepreneurial environment. For those familiar with corporate boot camps used in the ICT sector to quickly get new employees up to par at a company, the model is similar and was piloted in South Africa in 2008.

Economic Opportunity Development

From the boot camp, youth can be funneled into economic opportunities that lead to employment or development of entrepreneurial enterprises. One example is using youth as market researchers for business, government, and NGO clients, helping them to become infopreneurs. The Council of Scientific and Industrial Research (CSIR) in South Africa has an existing project in this area that can be adapted to suit other African countries. The key to successful outcomes for providing economic opportunities for the youth is that the Afribiz Accelerator™ will serve as an intermediary between youth and organizations, providing jobs or opportunities for youth enterprises. In essence, the Afribiz Accelerator™ will serve as project manager, lead facilitator, or primary contractor to ensure quality and service to clients or employers while making sure the youth receive the support and development opportunities they need. This will provide one of several streams of revenue for the Afribiz Accelerator™.

To execute the entrepreneurial/leadership training and economic opportunity development component, the international and local project office will develop and support a cadre of local economic opportunity facilitators who will be responsible for conducting the entrepreneurial training, developing economic opportunities for youth, serving in the liaison and facilitator role to execute economic opportunities, and developing and mentoring new economic opportunity facilitators.

Social/Business Networks and Partnerships

Both informal and formal social networks are known to facilitate business. However, in most instances there is little lasting benefit to a significant number of people as individual interests ebb and flow. As with the previous components, the Afribiz Accelerator™ will serve as a facilitator, connecting disparate networks and fostering partnerships between institutions locally, on the continent, and internationally.

A prototype for this has been launched in Charlotte, North Carolina in the United States called the Charlotte Africa Initiative (CAI). CAI provides a platform that catalyzes economic, trade, investment, capital, and business flows, as well as academic, social, and government linkages between the Charlotte region and Africa. It does this by synergizing business, social, and government organizations as a city cluster (adapted from the concept of industrial cluster) to leverage their knowledge, resources, networks, and access to capital. CAI is spearheaded by the University of North Carolina at Charlotte Africana Studies Department, Conceptualee, Inc., and The Africa Consortium in Charlotte. The model will be adapted for the local context of each African country and will be implemented through the Afribiz Accelerator™. CAI serves as a local hub, which will help foster and maintain the relationships with the Afribiz Accelerator™ that are located in Charlotte, as well strategic relationships in the U.S, and other countries.

Incubator/Venture Accelerator

The Afribiz Accelerator™ will provide a combination of incubator and venture accelerator services. There are many different models for this. The incubator will focus on providing basic services like ICT, space, mentoring, networking, etc., as well as strategic services like partnership development for SMEs and entrepreneurs that decide to become members. The venture accelerator is a more intense intervention to assist start-ups with getting off the ground. These are growing quite rapidly in the ICT sector. Both aspects will be open to existing entrepreneurs or SMEs, as appropriate, so that the

Afribiz Accelerator™ becomes embedded in the entrepreneurial and SME ecosystem in the African country in which it is established to serve as a hub of activity.

This component will also serve as the core source of revenue for the Afribiz Accelerator™. Like Limbe Labs in Cameroon, the Afribiz Accelerator™ will generate revenue from a variety of streams like service fees, training, and consulting, as well as equity investments into enterprises who are members, or participants.

The entrepreneurial training and economic opportunity development components of the Afribiz Accelerator™ are solely focused on developing youth and women as entrepreneurs and will serve to feed this audience into the incubator and venture accelerator programs.

The incubator/venture accelerator will focus on three primary sectors – agriculture, ICT, and small-scale manufacturing or processing – as these can leverage existing structures and resources in the country, help diversify the economy, and/or provide empowerment to a wide population. The incubator portion will also provide its services to any sector within its capacity as cross-pollination is also important. The venture accelerator will not only look at these primary sectors, but also be opportunity driven so that if there are gaps in the market that can be served through the development of key enterprises, the right partners exist, and the environment is favorable a focus area will be developed.

The model for the incubator/venture accelerator will make extensive use of existing models and resources that have shown success like InfoDev incubators, ICT incubators spread across Africa, and Raizcorp in South Africa.

SME/Entrepreneur Support Industry Development

In the majority of Sub-Saharan African countries, the SME support industry is non-existent or nascent. In other countries, there are significant gaps that need to be filled. In either scenario, the Afribiz Accelerator™ can be used to catalyze this industry due to the cluster model, (e.g., CAI) being used for networks and partnerships.

Standard Bank's new SME banking and GroFin's growth finance are good examples of how organizations have taken a holistic view to SME development and found profitable business models. However, this is not sufficient. There needs to be a bringing together of these organizations to form a more robust industry, which will greatly help to accelerate entrepreneur and SME development. This is the space where the Afribiz Accelerator™ can provide unique value.

Another element to this component is information exchanges. The Afribiz Accelerator™ will provide a channel to bring information and intelligence to SMEs and entrepreneurs in the African country, as well as share information and intelligence about business, investment, and opportunities in African country with the world. Afribiz and Africa the Good News are making their platforms and channels available to this effort.

SME/Entrepreneur Venture Capital Fund

While there are a growing number of funds dedicated to SMEs and entrepreneurs in Africa, there are not enough. The network of Afribiz Accelerators™ will develop a Pan African fund and will also be working with other entities to bring access to funding through the SME/entrepreneur support industry. Start-ups and SMEs that are members, or participating, in the incubator and venture accelerator programs will be eligible for the fund.

Capital will be raised through a variety of channels, including a percentage of the profit from the Afribiz Accelerator™, crowdfunding, and matching funds from development and private sector organizations.

Key Approaches to Success

Each component of the Afribiz Accelerator™ has its benefits. However, the only way to accelerate the development of the SME and entrepreneur sector is to use a systematic, integrated approach like the whole of the Afribiz Accelerator™. In addition, there are elements that need to be embedded which are not obvious:

- Creating a mentoring culture between youth, new entrepreneurs, SMEs, and corporates. As the Afribiz Accelerator™ helps entrepreneurs reach key milestones, the entrepreneurs will be looked at to mentor others through similar milestones.
- Instead of using ad-hoc interventions, create focus, energy, and drive for the SME and entrepreneur sector in an African country by having the Afribiz Accelerator™ serve in the role of a "network weaving/synaptic" facilitator.
- Becoming a microcosm not only of business and the economy in the country in which the Afribiz Accelerator™ exists, but also in Africa and the world through linkages and partnerships across borders.
- Develop a respect of culture between the generations and genders.
- Embed social leadership and responsibility into the ethos of the business environment.

Sustainability and Replication

The Afribiz Accelerator™, as a for-profit social enterprise, is focused on sustainability across the triple bottom line – people, planet, and profits. The previous sections illustrated sustainability in terms of people and profits, but did not address the planet, or the environment directly. The Afribiz Accelerator™ will incorporate "green" solutions and promote the development of green ventures as capacity is available.

The Afribiz Accelerator™ can stand on its own, but its impact will not be broad unless it reaches a broad geographic area. It is the intent to establish other Afribiz Accelerators™ in each province, or states, in a country in which a national hub is established. These accelerators will be linked together in a federated ecosystem along with those in other countries. They will increase strength through working as one entity, but each one remaining independent and relevant to the local context of each country. They will also be linked into other entrepreneurial ecosystems across the continent and around the world.

Lauri Elliott

Lauri's primary role and gifting is as a strategist. She has over 25 years of business experience, specializing in global business, innovation, technology, and new ventures and start-ups. She serves entrepreneurs, small, micro, and medium-size enterprises (SMMEs), and individual investors.

As the Director of Afribiz™ Media, a Division of Conceptualee, Inc., Lauri has developed a solid reputation as a new media leader. She is the primary host of Afribiz.fm™, a regular online radio show about doing business and investing in Africa. She also writes frequently for publications such as *Brainstorm* magazine, an ITWeb publication, in South Africa.

In addition, Lauri is the author of *Export to Explode Cash Flow and Profits: Creating New Streams of Business in Asia, Africa, and the Americas* and *Going Global on a Dime: The Entrepreneur's Handbook to Tapping the Global Marketplace.*

Lauri sits on the board of advisers for the Center for Global Entrepreneurship and Enterprise Management (CGEEM) at Morgan State University, which focuses on equipping U.S. SMEs to enter international business. In this capacity, she is leading the development of the Emerging Market Information Team (EMIT), designed to provide information and intelligence particularly useful to SMEs. For her work on behalf of SMEs, she received recognition from the U.S. Congress for connecting U.S. businesses to business in Africa.

In addition to encouraging SMEs in the U.S., Lauri is also committed to the development of SMEs in emerging markets. While in South Africa from 2005 to 2008, she fostered local economic development systems driven by youth enterprises.

To reach Lauri, visit http://www.lauri-elliott.com.

Hartmut Sieper

Hartmut is a banker, business consultant, and investment specialist. Hartmut is convinced that the time has come for Africa to arise in many aspects, including business and finance. In anticipating this trend, he has founded the company Trans Africa Invest to attract businesses, companies, and investors from German-speaking countries to African markets. He is working closely together with local partners in 15 African countries. He is the sole investment adviser of a Luxembourg-based, Pan-African mutual fund which is investing in listed African securities.

He has written several books about investing. His latest books are *Investing in Africa – The Wealth of the Black Continent and Cape of Good Business – Strategies for Long-Term Success in South Africa* (both are written in German), as well as *Tapping the Wealth of African Stocks*. In the German media, he is considered as one of the leading Africa experts in Germany.

Hartmut is married and lives in northern Bavaria, Germany. Hartmut can be reached at http://www.trans-africa-invest.com.

Nissi Ekpott

Nissi is an entrepreneur, business developer, and catalyst for African restoration. Raised in Nigeria, he started his first business – a dry cleaning service - at the age of 15. Over the years, he gained experience through conventional education, and several hands-on experiences.

Nissi consults for small and big businesses in Africa, touching business and leadership development and providing services, including business tours and training programs for public and private sector officials.

Nissi coordinates BizConnect Afrika, a place businesses connect, as well as share ideas, opportunities, and resources. He also serves as a business journalist for Afribiz.net, a media brand of Conceptualee, Inc. (U.S.) and other websites and magazines in South Africa.

He lives in Johannesburg, South Africa with his wife and two beautiful daughters. To reach Nissi, visit http://www.neuafrika.com.

Other Contributors

Nwakego Eyisi

http://www.nwakegoeyisi.com

Nwakego Linda Eyisi is co-founder of Encompass Analytic of Nigeria, a research and business intelligence firm serving clients like MTN of Nigeria. She is a trained and experienced economist, who specialized in the pharmaceutical industry for many years.

Nwakego serves as a featured Afribiz columnist and occasional radio host for Afribiz.fm. She covers key economic forums for Afribiz, including G20, African Union, regional economic community, and trade bloc events.

Sam Mokorosi

Sam is a nation builder at heart, with a passion for economic development across the African continent. He holds an economics honors degree from Rhodes University in Grahamstown, South Africa. He has practiced in the finance field for over 10 years, including experience as a bond analyst for Standard Bank. Sam is based in Johannesburg, South Africa where he lives with his wife and six children.

BizConnect Afrika

www.bizconnectafrika.biz

*You want to get into Africa and do business,
but you do not know anyone in Africa.*

- How do you find credible networks and connect to real business people?
- How do you find "on the ground" information?
- How do you test your ideas and share ideas and resources?
- How do you gain a relational entry point into the continent?

BizConnect Afrika is a business network established to share ideas, opportunities, and resources between its members. BizConnect Afrika is designed to encourage the building of relationships and community through business. It is a virtual/face-to-face business network that bridges and connects businesses beyond borders.

BizConnect Afrika members realize that even though business is good, business deals are temporal while relationships are eternal. Hence, relationship and community building is necessary for true success.

Visit the BizConnect Afrika website at *www.bizconnectafrika.biz*. Register online and become part of a business community with a focus on Africa.

Trans Africa Invest

www.trans-africa-invest.com

You want to invest in Africa, but you do not know how.

- How do you find investment projects in specific sectors and countries where you can invest?
- How do you find reliable investment managers with strong local expertise in Africa, who are following business practices that are described in this book?
- How do you reduce investment risk?

Trans Africa Invest is a Germany-based investment and consultancy firm that introduces investors, companies, and technologies from developed countries into African growth markets.

Through private equity (PE) funds, which are launching in 2011, investors can choose viable projects in various African countries and different economic sectors in which to invest. An international team of investment professionals, both from Africa and the developed world, will manage the PE funds and support the portfolio companies in doing their businesses, thereby adding value to the portfolios. The PE funds will be domiciled in a well-known financial center, i.e. Mauritius. In 2011, we are specifically looking for:

- Viable projects in Africa (business plan is required)
- Investors that want to have exposure in Africa in a broad range of attractive projects in various countries

- Financial intermediaries in U.S. and selected European countries that will connect domestic investors with African investment projects, either by participating in our private equity funds or by creating joint ventures

Afribiz

www.afribiz.info

*You want to learn more about business in Africa,
but you don't know where to go.*

*Afribiz.info is the leading, and premier, independent portal about
doing business and investing in Africa.*

Afribiz provides free and premium resources, intelligence, information, tools, insights, and strategies to help you navigate business and investment in Africa. If you want to know something about business in Africa, Afribiz is the best place to start.

Afribiz.info is our portal bringing together resources about African business from around the world into one place. No need to find resources one by one. We help you accelerate your research and strategy efforts.

Afribiz.net is the site for our premium, mostly original content provided as text, audio, and video that can be interacted with across computing and mobile platforms.

Afribiz.fm (www.blogtalkradio.com/afribiz) is our publicly broadcast audio content. Hear from experts and entrepreneurs how they make things happen in business in Africa. This is no ordinary program. You hear and learn what you can do to make things happen for you.

We also develop publications, e.g., books, magazines, and guides, conduct webinars and teleconferences (live and on-demand), host face-to-face events, and provide facilitation and consulting to help you navigate business in Africa successfully.

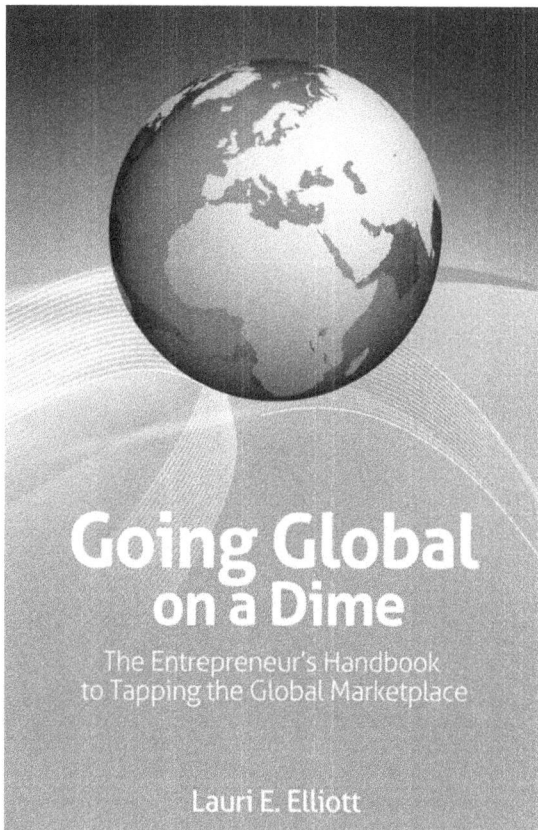

www.goingglobalonadime.com

Going Global on a Dime answers the "how" of going global from both a strategic and practical approach, focusing on new and existing firms considering or just starting the going global process. It re-wires the framework for going global so firms can navigate the course dynamically while minimizing costs, managing and maximizing cash flow and return on investment, streamlining processes, and keeping the "small" firm ready to take advantage of profitable opportunities.

a **Leverage Point Strategy**™book

INVESTING

Tapping the Wealth of African Stocks

Building a Valuable Stock Portfolio

Hartmut Sieper

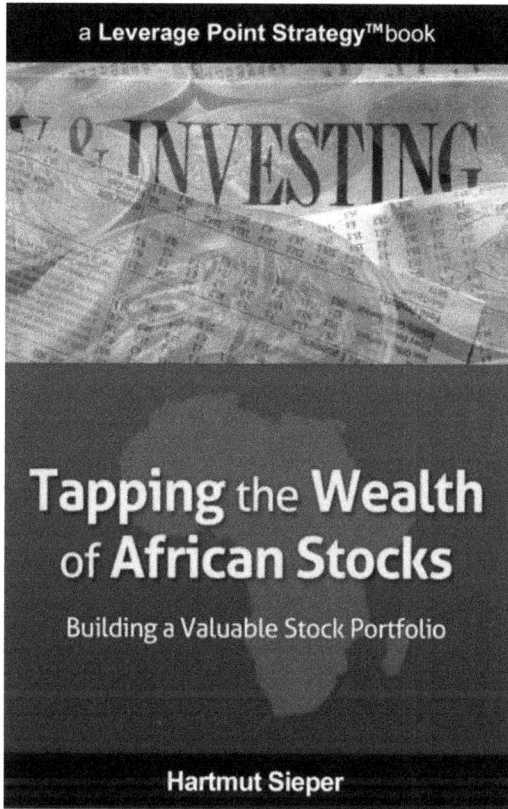

www.tapping-wealth-of-african-stocks.com

Warren Buffet says, "The critical investment factor is determining the intrinsic value of a business and paying a fair or bargain price." Where can investors go to find these businesses today?

Africa is one place. "African stocks continue to be undervalued, providing greater value for investors interested in long-term investments," says Hartmut Sieper, the author. *Tapping the Wealth of African Stocks* helps individual investors understand how to access African stock markets.

a Leverage Point Strategy™ book

Export
to
EXPLODE
Cash Flow and Profits

Creating New Streams of Business in
Asia, Africa, and the Americas
with Little Investment

Lauri E. Elliott

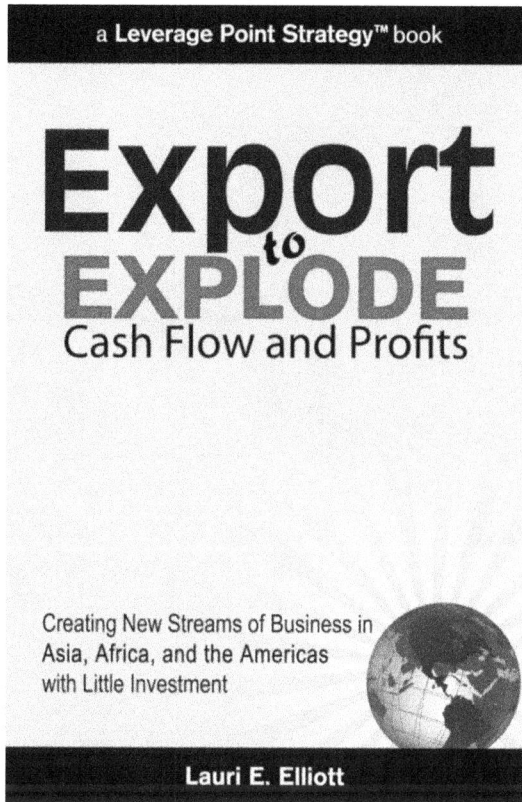

www.export-to-explode-cash-flow.com

Exporting is one of the strategies for conducting international business or trade. With the *squeeze* on businesses during the global economic recovery, there is no better time to explore new avenues to generate revenues and profits. *Export to Explode Cash Flow and Profits* specifically shares 12 different leverage points, e.g., demand-driven exporting, multinational ecosystems, and cities and economic hubs that you can use to help formulate strategies for exporting to the emerging markets in Asia, Africa, and the Americas.

www.ingramcontent.com/pod-product-compliance
Lightning Source LLC
Chambersburg PA
CBHW060327200326
41519CB00011BA/1863